I0749057

REPORT

ON THE

AGRICULTURE AND GEOLOGY

OF

MISSISSIPPI.

EMBRACING A SKETCH OF THE

SOCIAL AND NATURAL HISTORY OF THE STATE.

BY

B. L. C. WAILES,

GEOLOGIST OF MISSISSIPPI;

MEMBER OF THE AMERICAN ASSOCIATION FOR THE PROMOTION OF SCIENCE;
CORRESPONDING MEMBER OF THE NATIONAL INSTITUTE,
AND OF THE BOSTON SOCIETY OF NATURAL HISTORY, ETC. ETC.

PUBLISHED BY ORDER OF THE LEGISLATURE.

E. BARKSDALE, STATE PRINTER.
1854.

PREFACE.

The following pages contain the substance of a Report made to the Legislature of the State of Mississippi, with such alterations and modifications as the writer was authorized and instructed to make, and which became necessary to bring the publication within the means appropriated for that purpose.

This occasioned a partial abridgment, and rendered the omission of the larger portion of the plates, designed to illustrate it, unavoidable.

These changes in the scope and proportions of the work, obviously detract, in some degree, from its perspicuity and completeness, and must found some claim to indulgence for its defects.

The circumstances which devolved the preparation of this work upon the author, and the disadvantages under which it was executed, are explained in the Introduction; and these also, the indulgent reader will doubtless admit, should screen from a too rigid criticism the performance of one wholly unpractised in the art and mystery of book-making.

To some extent local in character, and addressed mainly to the agriculturists of the country, a class to whom a popular style and an avoidance of abstruse speculations are most acceptable, it is not expected that the work will greatly interest the proficient in science.

The naturalist, nevertheless, may not be wholly disappointed in the perusal of these pages, and perchance may glean some information as to the geographical distribution of the Fauna and Flora of our country, their local habits, and characteristics, and extend his knowledge by an acquaintance with our palæontology.

For these he will be indebted, in part, to those gentlemen who have kindly lent me their aid in some of these departments. The name of Agassiz stamps with authenticity the catalogue of southwestern fishes that has been given. Prof. Baird, of the Smithsonian Institution, verifies the list of our reptiles; and Mr. Conrad has found in our collections the means of establishing forty new species of Eocene fossils—no inconsiderable contribution to mineral Conchology.

The casual reader may find something to interest him in the early history of our State, as well as in the progress of our agriculture, and in the cultivation and preparation of our important staple, which, beyond the cotton-growing States, has been little understood.

It is, however, to the favor and indulgence of my own fellow-citizens, for whose information and benefit it was chiefly prepared, that I commend the work.

Satisfied with their approval, my gratification will be

complete, should my labors contribute in any degree to their knowledge or prosperity.

Of the mechanical execution of the work, it is scarcely necessary to speak. The neat typography of Collins needs no commendation; and the chromo-lithographs of Rosenthal exhibit in a most creditable manner the progress of this art in our country, and give examples of a style of illustration for works of this character, which has not yet been surpassed.

CONTENTS.

APPENDIX.

ILLUSTRATIONS.

INTRODUCTION.

The Agricultural and Geological Survey of the State originated in an act of the Legislature, approved the 5th of March, 1850, to take effect on the first of June following, entitled "an Act further to endow the University of Mississippi;" and its execution was committed to that Institution.

Dr. John Millington was appointed, by the Trustees, principal Professor of Geology and Agriculture, in connection with the professorship of Chemistry then held by him in the University.

No assistant was obtained until the latter part of 1851, and the gentleman then appointed relinquished the situation shortly after; having merely commenced a reconnoissance of the State, of which no report was made.

The situation was tendered to the present incumbent on the 14th of January, 1852. Since that time he has been occupied in the performance of the duties committed to him, which were somewhat augmented by an amendatory act of the Legislature, passed after his appointment, by which a room in the State House was set apart and placed under his charge, for the better preservation of the collections in Natural History, which, as the State Geologist, he was required to make.

In the prosecution of this work, a considerable portion of the State has been traversed, with a view of gaining such general knowledge of its character as would best guide and direct the subsequent, more detailed, and minute examination to be made.

More than seven thousand three hundred miles have been travelled, collections amounting to several thousand specimens have been made, and the character, peculiarities, and productions of the different sections visited, have been observed and noted.

It was doubtless with a general knowledge of the geological features of the State that the Survey was authorized by the Legislature.

Consisting chiefly of the more recent formations, the absence of the primitive and metalliferous rocks, in place, gave no reason to expect the existence of those ores and minerals which belong properly to an earlier period, and which constitute the chief resources of less favored and fertile districts than ours. The discovery of mines of copper, lead, or of the more precious metals, or, even of the true coal-fields, was obviously not to be expected. It was, therefore, mainly in reference to its influence and bearing upon the agricultural prosperity of the State, that it was undertaken.

The effects produced in New Jersey, Virginia, and several other States, in the restoration of exhausted lands to their primitive fertility, by the application of the marls or mineral manures which similar surveys have brought into notice, exerted the chief influence in setting on foot an enterprise for developing our own resources of this character, which were suspected, with good reason, to exist in the great tertiary field that overspreads the State; and the examination which has so far been made, establishes the fact, that our stores of calcareous fertilizers are as abundant, as varied in character, and excellent in quality, as any other State can boast.

To ascertain and point out the chief deposits of these marls, and to determine their relative value and chemical constituents, becomes now an object of much importance. Exact analyses of the different varieties, characterizing them by the prevailing fossils, when such exist, so as at once to be identified by the planter, should be made; numerous experiments in their application should be encouraged; and the effects upon the growth of our different agricultural productions should be diligently observed, and accurately detailed.

The attention of planters has been pointed to these fertilizers on all suitable occasions, and in a few instances experiments on a limited scale have been commenced, the result of which cannot of course yet be given. Specimens have also been collected, with their associated and characteristic fossils, and have been deposited for general inspection, in the State Cabinet at the Capitol, and in the Cabinet of the University at Oxford.

Analyses of many varieties of our marls and soils should have been given in this Report. Few of these, however, have been procured, owing, in part, to a defect in the law authorizing the Survey, and to the illness and subsequent resignation of Dr. Millington, the principal Professor of Geology and Chemistry, in the State University.

The latter event occurring at a period so nearly approaching to that at which a report of the progress of the Survey was required, devolved unexpectedly upon the assistant that duty, which, under the existing circumstances, must otherwise have been unperformed.

Interrupted by a severe and protracted indisposition,

and surrounded by a pestilence, the source of perpetual and distracting anxiety, the writer feels that the duty which has been so untowardly postponed, and in the end so hurriedly executed, has been very imperfectly discharged, and trusts that these considerations will be regarded as constituting some claim to indulgence, for the many imperfections which may be charged against this Report.

Whilst captious and ill-natured criticism is ever to be deprecated, a fair and proper correction of error is as much to be desired; and in an essay of this character, in which the object is to impart useful knowledge, is rather to be invited.

Errors have doubtless occurred in treating of the multifarious topics which are embraced in this Report; and to the end that the greatest accuracy may be attained, the writer will be gratified to have them pointed out, in order that they may be corrected and avoided in future.

Of the plan of this Report, it will be seen that, with the sanction of approved precedents, it has been considered that a short preliminary sketch of the discovery and early history of the country, not hitherto separately written, would not be out of place.

In compiling and *abridging* this from other writers, it has been a somewhat difficult task to *condense* it within the required limits, except at the expense of much of the interest that would attach to a more detailed account.

To the works of Martin, Stoddard, and Gayarre, and to the Journal of Ellicott, the United States Commissioner for receiving possession of the country, I am indebted for many of the facts which have been given, and I have not unfrequently adopted the language in which they were originally detailed. To these highly respectable and authentic sources of information with respect to our early history, it gives me pleasure to acknowledge my indebtedness.

From the manuscript correspondence of the late Mr. William Dunbar "of the Forest," I have also been enabled to glean some interesting facts, and to the representatives of his family I have to express my thanks for the opportunity afforded me of consulting it.

The Spanish archives preserved in the State, have also, to a limited extent, been consulted, and, had time permitted, might have been more profitably explored. I have to regret, notwithstanding, that this sketch is not more complete; the more so, as there is reason to believe that some authentic and interesting documents are preserved in the State, not as yet made public, which, if accessible, would no doubt serve to fill up some of the chasms and otherwise explain and illustrate our early history. These I should have been pleased to avail myself of.

As a subject of interest to the landed proprietors of the State, the chapter on Land Titles was considered as germain to the subject, and entitled to the short space which it occupies.

An attempt has been made to give a view of the early agriculture of the country, derived mainly from the accounts received from many of our older inhabitants, with whom I have conferred, aided by my own recollections. In the details given of the different agricultural productions, the mode of cultivation, and the machinery for preparing these, I have been similarly aided.

In all that has been said in this connection, universal concurrence is not expected.

On matters in which there is such diversity both in

theory and practice, as in the course of cultivation and choice of implements especially, this is not to be attained. If it be maintained that any of these details are erroneous, I can only say that any such will be most willingly corrected, when it can be done on *better authority* than that on which any specific fact or statement has been given.

The tables of agricultural and other statistics have been prepared from the best sources, and will form matter for convenient and useful reference.

At this stage of the Survey, and in the first, and as it may be termed preliminary report, the notice of the Geology and other departments of natural history, will necessarily present a mere outline, and cannot assume that form and shape which will properly be given them in a final report. Such an arrangement has been adopted, however, as far as these subjects are embraced, as will, it is believed, give a reasonably comprehensive and *familiar* view of those departments of the Report.

Of the Fauna and Flora of the State, in the notice that has been taken of them, my own observations have been directed by the best available authorities; and in the former department, among others the works of DeKay, and of Audubon, and Bachman, among the most recent published, and by inference, the most complete and correct, have been consulted. The aid of distinguished naturalists, also, has been liberally afforded; and I have to acknowledge my indebtedness, and express my thanks, to Professors Agassiz and Baird, and to Mr. Conrad, for their contributions to this department of the Report. The catalogues furnished by them, although not so complete or perfect as they will hereafter be made, have the stamp of authenticity and accuracy to recommend them. I should be remiss, were I to omit to acknowledge the obligations I am also under to Dr. Leidy and Mr. Cassin, of the Academy of Natural Sciences, of Philadelphia.

As to the illustrations which accompany this Report, the limited means appropriated to the Survey, and the dearth of artistic skill available in this quarter, have made me dependent upon the early, imperfect, and self-taught attainment of drawing; and which, having been almost wholly unpractised for nearly thirty years, makes an apology necessary for their rude and unsatisfactory execution.

In making the collections required, the cases in the State Cabinet attest that a reasonable progress has been made with the means appropriated to this object, and upwards of a thousand duplicates have been deposited in the University at Oxford, for its cabinet.

When this collection is further advanced towards completion, on the plan I have proposed, it will form, to some extent, a museum of economic geology and agriculture, in which, not only specimens of natural history, the soils, marls, and minerals, may be preserved; but also improved and rare agricultural productions and implements may be exhibited with profit and instruction to the planter, at the same time that the collection will form one of much interest to the scientific visitor, to say nothing of the means of instruction and gratification it will afford to the young and the curious of all classes.

In my travels through the State, on this not very generally understood or properly appreciated mission, it was to be expected that occasionally little either of information or assistance would be afforded. Such, however, has rarely been the case; and the degree of interest which has often been manifested in my pursuits has been very gratifying, and augurs favorably for the future and more minute prosecution of this investigation.

To those gentlemen whose hospitality and assistance have been kindly and liberally extended to me, on my various excursions in different quarters, I can only offer my sincere thanks, and express the hope that they may derive some gratification, if not profit, from the final issue of the Survey.

WASHINGTON, MISS.

The River Mississipi
Yassous
River
EORGIA
CHAUCTAWS
IN AMITY WITH THE FRENCH
Pascagoula
River
Mobile
River
Nautches
lately
destroyed by the
French
Rosalie
Lalleman River
Part of
Albamous
PART O
Naniaba
Mobiliens
Statues
Laux Cochons
Tunica's
SIANA
Tansas
Taouachas
Apalaches
Carrieres
Flor
Branche Espagnole
Fort St Louis
Rau Chien
Mobile
Bay
Chataux
Bay
Minet
Belle Fountain
Pascaboula
R. au Poisson
La Laque
R del Amirante
Mile R
R. de Iberville
R. au Perle
Petite boye S. Louis
Billoxy
NEW
ORLEANS
Lac
Maurepas
Manchac
Colapissa
Lac
Ponch
artrain
Pleou
Breton
Petits Chenaux
Gd Chenaux
I. au Chat
I. aux Vaiseau
I. at Chevreuil
I. Ronde
La Corne
I. Dauphin
Mouth of the Mobile
Pensacola
I. St Rose
Les Coquillas
Oumas
Point aux Isles
Isles
de la
Chandeleur
La Fourche
Mississippi
Detour a le Anglois
Laux des Sitimachas
Sitimachas
I. au Breton
A MAP
OF THE
COUNTRY COMPRISED IN THE S
MISSISSIP
as known in the year

I. HISTORICAL OUTLINE.

In presenting a view of the agriculture of the State, and tracing its condition and progress from the first occupancy of our territory by a civilized race, a brief sketch of the discovery and settlement of the country seems appropriate and necessary. Were a precedent required to sanction the very abridged historical outline here introduced, a distinguished one may be found in the able and elaborate memoir that forms the introduction to the Reports on the Natural History of New York, embracing a much wider scope than is here proposed, and comprehending the political history and social progress of the State.

To keep this sketch within the prescribed limits, and to exclude all matter not intimately connected with the subject, it will be restricted to occurrences strictly within the present boundaries of the State, except so far as may be necessary to preserve the natural sequence of events. It will embrace little more, therefore, than a chronological outline, which, if desirable, may, as far as necessary, be enlarged in the final report of the Survey.

The State of Mississippi lies between the thirty-first and thirty-fifth parallels of north latitude, with the addition of that portion lying between the first-mentioned

2

parallel and the Gulf of Mexico and Lake Borgne and east of Pearl River. On the west it is bounded by the Mississippi and Pearl Rivers, and on the east by a line dividing it from the State of Alabama, which is drawn from the mouth of Bear Creek on the Tennessee River to the northwestern corner of Washington County, Alabama, and thence south to a point on Grand Bay on the Gulf of Mexico, about seventeen miles due west from the Bay of Mobile. The State also embraces the islands in the Gulf within six leagues of the northern shore, the principal of which are Horn, Ship, and Cat Islands.

The width of the State along the northern boundary is one hundred and twenty miles; on the sea-shore seventy-eight miles; and along the 31° of north latitude one hundred and eighty-six miles. The greatest length from north to south is three hundred and thirty miles. It embraces an area of 55,500 square miles or 35,520,000 acres.

EXPEDITION AND DISCOVERY BY DE SOTO.

About the close of the year 1540, Fernando de Soto, in his adventurous and romantic expedition, commenced the preceding year at the Bay of Espiritu Santo, and designed for the conquest of Florida, penetrated to the country of the Chickasaws in the northeastern part of the State.

With his shattered and disabled forces, the remnant of the most gallant and imposing expedition, for the magnificence of its equipage and the rank and opulence of those engaged in it, that ever set foot in the New world, he sought rest and repose during the winter in the Chicaza towns, after nearly two years of continual contest and warfare with the Indian tribes that he had encountered. Here he continued, notwithstanding his disasters and the persevering and galling attacks of the Indians, until the 1st of April, 1541. The position of this winter encampment is conjectured to have been near the northeastern part of Pontitoc County, where, it is said, remains of ancient fortifications are still to be seen, and relics of European origin probably pertaining to this expedition have also been found. Thus, far in the interior, distant from the sea-shore, and remote from the Mississippi, was the territory of the State first entered upon by Europeans.

It is needless to trace his subsequent wanderings if it were practicable, even with approximate accuracy, to do so. There is little doubt, however, that De Soto traversed the country comprising the county now bearing his name, and in May of the same year discovered the Mississippi River, called by the natives "Cicuaga," at a point near the extreme northwestern corner of the State.*

After crossing the Mississippi at or near the Chickasaw Bluffs, and consuming another year in fruitless and wasting excursions far to the west, he returned to the Mississippi, where his career was terminated at the village of Guachoya, "which was situated on two contiguous hills a bow-shot from the Mississippi," probably the site of the present town of Hellena in Arkansas,† and his

* According to Marbois, the northern Indians, bordering on Canada, called the Mississippi the "Namesi-si-pou," or River of Fishes.

† This is the only point on the western side where the highland or "*hills*" jut in upon the Mississippi below the Ohio. Some writers assign the mouth of the Arkansas, and others that of Red River, as the place of De Soto's death; and the town of "Guachoa" is laid down on an English map published in 1764 at the latter place. Neither of these points, however, answers to the description given of the

remains were committed to the great river which he was the first to discover.

Still a year later, his followers, now led by Louis de Muscoso, failing to reach Mexico by land, returned to the same village on the Mississippi, on which the small remnant of the expedition, reduced to about three hundred and fifty survivors, little more than one-fourth of the number of which it was first composed, embarked on the 2d of July, 1543, for a final departure from the country, pursued and sorely harassed by the Indians, and arrived at the sea-shore after a voyage of twenty days.

From this period, for an interval of nearly one hundred and thirty-eight years, the native tribes were left in undisturbed possession of the country; and it was not until February, 1681, when La Salle, accompanied by the Chevalier de Tonti, descended the Mississippi from Canada, that the country was revisited by European adventurers. In April of this year, La Salle, having reached the ocean, on his return touched at the settlement of the Natchez, from which the hostile bearing of that people hastened his departure.

Failing in his subsequent expedition, fitted out in France with a view to the establishment of a colony, to reach the mouth of the Mississippi by sea, having passed to the west of it, La Salle perished miserably in Texas by the hands of his despairing and mutinous followers; and another interval of eighteen years elapsed before the country was again visited by Europeans.

site; nor can we suppose that the fugitive remnant of the expedition, flying from a pursuing enemy, could have consumed twenty days in the descent from Red River to the mouth of the Mississippi. The authority of the map is not to be relied upon, since, among other inaccuracies, it places New Orleans above the Lafourche.

AS A COLONY OF FRANCE, 1699—1763.

In February, 1699, an expedition led by Iberville arrived upon the coast, and occupied Ship Island. Iberville had offered to prosecute the plan of La Salle to colonize Louisiana, and under the patronage of Count de Pontchartrain, the French minister of marine, was put in command of an expedition fitted out at La Rochelle, consisting of two frigates and two smaller vessels, to be employed in this service. After exploring the shores and inlets in that quarter, it was resolved to establish the proposed colony on the main land in the vicinity, and accordingly a landing was effected on the eastern extremity of the Bay of Baluxi. A fort of four bastions, with twelve pieces of cannon, was commenced on the first of May following, the colonists brought over by the expedition numbering about two hundred, including women and children, were settled around the fort, and the first European settlement was established in Mississippi.

Iberville, leaving his brothers in charge of the settlement, the elder, Sauvolle, as governor, and the younger, Bienville, as his lieutenant, set sail on his return to France for the purpose of reinforcing the infant colony he had founded, and procuring for it the necessary supplies.

In July, soon after the departure of Iberville, the colony was visited by two missionaries, Montegay and Davion, who had wandered from Canada, and had been residing among the Indian tribes. Father Davion, who had been in turn among the Yazoos and Tunicas, had established himself at an eminence on the east side of the Mississippi, where an indurated clay or imperfectly formed sand rock is seen; hence the place became known to the French as "La Roche à Davion," (Davion's Rock.) It is the point now known as Fort Adams, and the same called by the English, Loftus Heights.

Bienville, who engaged actively in exploring the passes and outlets of the Mississippi, encountered an English ship in the river, commanded by Captain Bar, one of two vessels sent out by Daniel Cox of New Jersey, to take possession of a grant of land of which he was then the proprietor, made by Charles the First of England, in 1630, to Sir Robert Heath. It comprised a tract of truly royal dimensions, embracing not only the present State of Mississippi, but included several other adjoining States. Captain Bar, doubting whether the stream he had entered was the Mississippi, was easily induced by Bienville to retrace his steps; and the great bend in the river, at which his progress was terminated, has ever since been known from this circumstance as the "English Turn."

In December, Iberville returned from France with two large armed ships. *He brought out Leseur, a Geologist, who was sent by the French government to examine a greenish earth or ochre which had been noticed on the banks of the Mississippi.** Furnished with a detachment of twenty men, Leseur proceeded up to the River St. Peter's, which he ascended a considerable distance. A greenish ochre was found covering the ground near a copper-mine, thirteen thousand pounds of which were gathered, brought to Baluxi and shipped to France; but no further notice appears to have been taken of it.

In 1700, the Chevalier de Tonti, hearing of the establishment of the French colony, descended the river in a

* This geological surveying expedition, fitted out within the limits of our State, was probably the earliest undertaken on our continent.

pirogue, accompanied by seven men, to ascertain the truth of the report. This was the third voyage of this energetic and enterprising man down the Mississippi, first in company with La Salle, when he explored the river to its mouth, and again for the purpose of meeting his old associate and friend, who, he was apprised, was attempting to enter the Mississippi by sea, in which he was grievously disappointed. De Tonti had distinguished himself in the European wars, and had lost a hand, which he had had supplied by an artificial substitute of iron, of which at times he was wont to make a formidable use, and which procured for him the sobriquet of the "Iron Hand." He met Iberville and Bienville at Bayou Goula, and they accompanied him on his return up the river as far as Natchez. There they met with St. Come, a missionary from Canada, who had fixed his residence among this people.

The Natchez, greatly advanced beyond the other Indian tribes in civilization, had been reduced from a once powerful nation, and now numbered only about twelve hundred warriors. The Great Sun, as their king was termed, welcomed the French at the head of a large retinue, borne in state on the shoulders of some of his attendants. They were worshippers of the sun, and maintained a perpetual fire in their temples.

One of these, during the visit of the French, was set on fire by lightning, when the frenzied and superstitious women, at the call of the vociferating and demoniac priests, cast their infant children into the flames to appease their irritated divinity.

The country of the Natchez greatly interested Iberville, who, considering it the most eligible position for the principal establishment of the province, selected a commanding situation on the river for a town, for which he proposed the name of Rosalie, in honor of the Countess of Pontchartrain.

Sauvolle died in July, 1701, after the departure of Iberville, and was succeeded by Bienville as governor.

The colonists suffered greatly from the want of provisions; and in the fall, disease following in the track of famine, many died, the number of survivors being reduced to one hundred and fifty. The return of Iberville from France, late in December, afforded a timely relief.

Besides the supplies, he brought with him also a reinforcement of troops.

Under instructions from the king, Bienville moved his head-quarters to the western bank of Mobile River, leaving a detachment of twenty men in charge of the fort at Baluxi.

A fort, with barracks and stores, was also erected on Dauphin Island, which possessed a better port and more convenient landing than Ship Island afforded.

The seat of government of the Province being transferred beyond the present limits of the State, and there remaining within it but the small settlement at Baluxi, it will suffice to state, in reference to the progress of the colony for many years, that it was characterized by an entire neglect of agricultural pursuits, and that it was subjected to great hardships from famine and disease, the occasional supplies derived from France, St. Domingo, and Vera Cruz, being so inadequate as to render it necessary occasionally to quarter the troops upon the adjacent Indian tribes to gain a precarious subsistence by hunting and fishing.

In the mean time, Iberville had died, and the French government, disappointed in the slow progress of the colony, the limited extent of its trade, and the utter failure in the discovery of minerals to which its expectations had mainly been directed, was induced, in September, 1712, to make a grant of the colony and its exclusive commerce, with extensive privileges, to Anthony Crozat, an eminent merchant.

Bienville, being appointed to the command of the establishments on the Mississippi, learning that the Natchez had plundered and killed some Frenchmen, led a detachment of troops against them, in 1716, and, having decoyed some of their chiefs into his camp, compelled the restoration of the plundered goods and the punishment of the offenders; after which he accompanied the Natchez to their village, and with their assent commenced a fort on the spot Iberville had before chosen.

It was called Rosalie, and in June a small garrison was established in it under the command of an officer named Pailloux.

The earthen mound or embankment which tradition points out as the site of this fort, is still to be seen crowning the bluff of the river, immediately below and in the suburbs of the city of Natchez.

When the country came under the dominion of Great Britain, it was called Fort Panmure, after a barony of that name in Scotland, a name it retained during the subsequent rule of the Spaniards, being so designated in all the grants of land made by that government.

Three of Crozat's ships arrived in March, 1717, with three companies of infantry and fifty new colonists. Bienville was superseded as governor; and although the order of knighthood was conferred upon him in reward for his services, yet the arrival of L'Epinay, his successor, occasioned him much mortification, which the decoration of the cross of St. Louis, and the Royal patent conceding him the title to Horn Island, could not wholly allay; his popularity with the colonists, and the jealousy of his partisans towards the new chief, occasioned a schism in the colony very unfavorable to its progress.

Failing to establish a commerce with the Spaniards in Mexico, and disappointed in all his expectations, Crozat, in August, 1717, surrendered his grant to the king.

During his administration, a period of about five years, neither the commerce nor agriculture of the country was increased, and the whole population of every description, including the troops, did not exceed seven hundred persons.

Marbois, however, attributes to him more statesmanship than was possessed by the ministers, and adds that his plans were wisely conceived, and as far as depended upon him he sent to the colony only robust and industrious people, and families recommended by their morals, who were the only settlers that succeeded.

In September, 1717, a charter was granted to a new corporation, styled the "Western Company," which originated with the celebrated Scotch adventurer and financier Law, a *protégé* of the Regent Duke of Orleans. It was also known as the "Mississippi Scheme."

The lands, coasts, harbors, and islands of the colony were granted to this company for a term of twenty-five years from the 1st of January, 1718, with the exclusive commerce, in which all other French subjects were prohibited from engaging.

The company was authorized to nominate the governor and other officers, to grant lands, to levy troops, make treaties, and wage war with the Indians, and generally to exercise the most unlimited and extraordinary powers.

On its part, the company engaged to introduce, during

the term of its privilege, six thousand whites and three thousand negroes.

Of this powerful and privileged company, John Law was appointed Director-General.

One of the first acts of the company, in February, 1718, was to recall L'Epinay, and to reinstate Bienville as governor—a measure which gave great satisfaction to the troops, and to the inhabitants generally.

The failure of the plans of Crozat induced the company to turn its attention to the introduction of agriculture, as promising better results than the fruitless searching for mines, or prosecuting a commerce so trivial as that derived from the traffic with the Indian tribes.

As the most effectual mode of encouraging agricultural enterprise, it was deemed expedient to make considerable concessions of land to wealthy and powerful personages: among these were grants of large extent, on the Yazoo River, to a company consisting of Le Blanc, Count de Belleville, Leblond, and others; and on St. Catharine's Creek, near Fort Rosalie, to Hubert, and a company of merchants of St. Maloes. The Bay of St. Louis was granted to Madame de Mezieres, and Pascagoula Bay to Madame de Chaumont.

The condition of all such grants was, the introduction of a certain number of emigrants upon them within a stated time.

The experiment seems not to have been wholly successful; a few destitute peasants were first sent out to improve these lands, many of whom were prematurely swept away by the diseases attending the improvement of a new country and a change of climate.

Experience also showed that, although these large grants facilitated the transportation of settlers, little was obtained from the labor of men brought over from a distant clime to cultivate lands, the proprietors of which remained behind.

It was a fatal error that the plantations had not been established nearer together for mutual protection. As Marbois remarks, the colonists feeling free from restraint settled wherever fancy or hope conducted them, indifferent even to the sanction of a grant to secure their possessions; they scattered themselves among the natives, and taking the Indian women for wives, were cordially received, and by right incorporated into the tribe.

In June, 1718, De la Housaye and Scouvion, with their followers, eighty-two in number, settled upon the Yazoo. Of the emigrants of 1720, three hundred were destined for Natchez, and three hundred and ninety for the Yazoo.

Three hundred colonists arrived in 1721, for the lands of Madame de Chaumont, at Pascagoula.

In 1719, Bigart had been sent with a small detachment to the Yazoo River, where he built Fort St. Peter's. War having broken out between France and Spain the same year, the attention of the colonists was mainly directed to attacks upon the Spanish possessions. Pensacola was taken without resistance, but was surrendered again in August to a force sent from Havana to retake it. Three ships of the line arriving on the 1st of September, the place was again taken by the French with the Spanish shipping and eighteen hundred prisoners.

In the summer and fall of 1720, Beaumanoir brought over sixty settlers to the grant on the St. Catharine's. In May, 1720, after a brief existence of little more than two years, the Royal Bank established by Law, and with which the company was intimately connected, failed; and in December, Law was compelled to fly from France, attended by a universal malediction, an object of popular abhorrence.

A change in the seat of government being again determined upon by the directors of the company's concerns, in opposition to the views of Bienville and Hubert, the Bay of Baluxi was chosen for that purpose; a detachment of troops was sent to the western shore of the bay to erect houses and barracks, and the place thenceforth became known as New Baluxi.

The privileges and powers of the Mississippi Company had been greatly enlarged by the acquisition of the possessions and effects of the China and India Companies, which were dissolved; and from that time it assumed the style and became known as the Company of the Indies.

Although a peremptory order had been given for the removal to Baluxi, both Bienville and Hubert were opposed to it; the former thought New Orleans was the most eligible site, and the latter went to France to induce the directors of the company to decide in favor of Natchez, near which, on the St. Catharine's, he had an immense grant with a large plantation and considerable improvements. He was unsuccessful in his mission, and died a few days after his arrival. Finally, after considerable delay and opposition in the summer of 1722, the order of council was executed, and Bienville and his staff removed to Baluxi.

Large additions to the colony had been made the previous year, chiefly of Germans, and negroes from the coast of Africa. On the 4th of June, 1722, a company's ship, commanded by the Chevalier d'Arensbourg, brought over two hundred and fifty Germans.

With this vessel came the confirmation of the utter failure of Law and his schemes, and the consequent ruin and distress which had ensued in France. This intelligence was received with great dismay, and an apprehension was felt that the affairs of the colony, if not wholly neglected, would be prosecuted with less vigor; an apprehension soon realized to some extent in the failure of supplies. To provide against impending famine, the troops were distributed in small detachments on Pearl River and Pascagoula, among the Indian tribes, to procure subsistence by hunting and fishing.

Exasperated by hunger and distress, some of these mutinied, and attempted to reach the English settlements in Carolina. The Indians were sent in pursuit, and all of them were captured or slain. The arrival of a ship in September afforded some relief, and it was learned that the Regent, after the failure and flight of Law, had placed the affairs of the company under the direction of three Commissioners.

In December of this year, Father Charlevoix descended the Mississippi River from Canada; he visited the fort on the Yazoo, and spent his Christmas in Natchez. At that time, according to his account, the company had a warehouse, in charge of Seur Le Noir, at the latter place; the appearance of the country he describes as very agreeable, extensive meadows and handsome clumps of trees presenting themselves on every side, after surmounting the hill at the landing-place. Fort Rosalie is spoken of by him as a *kind of redoubt* inclosed with a single palisade.

The great village of the Natchez was situated near the St. Catharine, a few miles from the river, and about midway between the two French grants which formed a triangle with the fort, being distant from the latter and each other about one league; the St. Maloes grant being the lowermost on the creek, which discharged itself into the Mississippi about three leagues below. He describes this plantation as being "*screened on all the back parts by a magnificent cypress forest.*"

The village of the Natchez he represents as reduced to a very few cabins; the more populous towns of the tribe being at some distance, in order to be more out of the reach of the Great Chief, or Sun, who had a right to take from his subjects anything they possessed.

The *Tioux*, allies of the Natchez, had a village in the neighborhood.

Charlevoix regarded the country about Natchez the finest and most fertile in all Louisiana.

In January, 1723, Laharpe, on his way to the Arkansas, touched at Natchez, and found Fort Rosalie in a state of ruinous decay. Maneval, who commanded it, having only eighteen soldiers. Ascending the Yazoo River at the distance of nine miles from the mouth, he reached the settlement called Fort St. Peter, commanded by De Grave. According to his statement, there was not more than thirty acres of arable land surrounding the fort, which was hemmed in by stony hills. The site of this fort was at the place now known as Hayne's Bluff, where the limestone is seen cropping out of the base of the hills. A group of mounds, one of them of considerable size, and about thirty feet high, is situated near the spot.

At that period, the Mississippi still flowed through what is now known as Old River; the cut-off, or present channel of the river, according to Charlevoix, having been recently formed, was not passable for boats, except at a high stage of water.

In May, the copper coinage provided for the colony arrived at Baluxi. It was ordered to be used in payment of the troops, and was made a lawful tender in the company's stores. Specimens of this coin have been found at St. Peter's, and at several other points in the

State, formerly occupied by the French. An earthen vessel of Indian fabric containing several pieces of it was dug, some years since, from an Indian mound near the mouth of Pearl River.

One of these coins, found on the reputed site of the governor's quarters in New Baluxi, is preserved in the State cabinet; and a similar one, from the mound, in the cabinet of the State university. These coins bear date in 1721 and 1722. They bear on the face the cipher of Louis, the French monarch, surmounted by a crown, and surrounded by the legend, "Sit nomen domini benedictum." Across the reverse is inscribed: "Colonies Françoises," with the date below.*

The seat of government was again removed beyond the present limits of the State, and Bienville, in accomplishment of his long-cherished desire, fixed his headquarters at New Orleans.

In September, a destructive tornado desolated the Province, prostrating many houses in New Orleans, and extending to Baluxi and Natchez; the crops were destroyed, and the inhabitants were menaced with impending dearth. An unexpected crop of rice, however, springing from the seed scattered by the hurricane, promised some relief.

The Indian tribes were becoming more open in their hostilities.

In 1723, a predatory band of Chickasaws killed a sergeant belonging to the garrison at St. Peter's, and his wife. The Natchez also became involved in an affray with a sergeant at Fort Rosalie, in which an Indian was killed; the Indians retaliated, and in considerable force attacked the settlement, but were repulsed with

* See Plate.

the loss of several of their number. Guenôt, the director of the grant on St. Catharine, was fired upon and wounded; some negroes were shot; two planters were taken and their heads cut off, and a number of cattle and horses were stolen. When Dustine, an officer of the garrison, arrived at New Orleans, bringing this intelligence, two suns of the Natchez were on a visit to Bienville. No punishment was inflicted upon the offending Indians; but these chiefs were dismissed with presents, under a pledge to put a stop to these outrages.

In consideration of the spiritual wants of the province, a number of Jesuits, and monks of other orders, as well as nuns, were introduced into the colony, and liberally provided for by the company, and curates were also provided for the missions.

For several years, great distress was felt in the colony, growing out of the failure of Law's Scheme, and the attempts of the French government to regulate the currency, and to palliate the consequent embarrassment by the alteration of the value of money.

The colony, notwithstanding, had made rapid strides since it passed under the charge of the company. The military force had increased to eight hundred men. Twenty-five hundred redemptioners, and eighteen hundred Africans had been introduced, and agriculture had engaged to a greater extent the attention of European capitalists.

In 1724, Bienville was called to France to answer to charges preferred against him. Notwithstanding his able defence, he was removed, and Perrier was appointed in his stead on the 9th of August, 1726.

Of the Indian tribes occupying the country at the period of its settlement by the French, the Choctaws, Chickasaws, and the Natchez were the most numerous.

3

There were many others, however, though too feeble and insignificant to merit more than a passing notice.

Among these were the Baluxis and Pascagoulas to the south. The Yazoos, Ionicas, Coroas, Offagoulas, Otasees, Chachoumas, Outayhis, and the Tapouches were distributed along the Yazoo and its tributaries.

Of the larger tribes, the Choctaws were by far the most numerous and powerful. They owned fifty important villages, and could assemble twenty thousand warriors. They were first attached to the French, who managed, by their diplomacy and presents, to retain, throughout, a large majority of them in their interest.

The Chickasaws are described as a turbulent, warlike, and ferocious race; from their intercourse and trade with the English of Carolina, they espoused their interest, and were readily engaged in hostilities towards the French, and were consequently embroiled in continual warfare with the Choctaws.

The Natchez, by far the most enlightened and furthest removed from barbarism, were rapidly declining from the condition of a numerous and once powerful tribe. The institution of human sacrifices engrafted into their theology was the most efficient cause of their rapid course towards extinction. They were pacific in their disposition; but the French, by their harshness and encroachments upon their rights, forfeited their friendship and provoked their deadly hostility.

It was the policy of Bienville, and most of the other governors, for the security of the colony from the united hostilities of the Indians, against which it could not have existed, to encourage the feuds among themselves.

The Choctaws, the most powerful of these, were conciliated, and aided in repelling the attacks of their chief enemy, the Chickasaws, until, in turn, they became their persevering and victorious assailants. This was done chiefly by keeping the traffic with them in their own hands, to the exclusion of the English traders of the Carolinas, and by supplying them with goods suited to their wants.

Perrier, as the successor of Bienville, proved more harsh and less politic in his intercourse with his Indian neighbors; and when, from the failure of the necessary remittances from France, it became impossible to supply all the wants of their red allies, and to make them the customary presents, a considerable faction of the Choctaws became disaffected, and united with the Chickasaws in a scheme of general and concerted hostility with a view to the total destruction of the French colony in all its settlements; and although this design was suspected, and for the time disconcerted and postponed, the day was approaching when the French colonists were to receive a severe and ruinous blow.

The commandant at Natchez under Perrier, an officer named Chepar, was a man of intemperate habits, and of overweening vanity and self-importance. Professing an utter contempt for the Natchez, his conduct towards them was severe and exacting.

On a beautiful and elevated plain on the western margin of Second Creek, about ten miles from Fort Rosalie, was situated the "Whiteapple Village." A group of mounds, two of them of considerable elevation and extent, yet clothed with stately elms and evergreen oaks, which have spread their umbrageous shades over them for centuries, and which the good taste of the past and present proprietors have religiously preserved, still marks the spot. The land embracing this favorite village of the Natchez was coveted by Chepar.

Alleging the orders of Perrier, the surrender of it was

rudely demanded, with a threat to seize it by force if not voluntarily yielded before a stated period, which was not remote.

The Natchez could not bring themselves to submit to this new act of aggression. But their remonstrances were unheard, nor was the offer of other lands as an equivalent embraced. They were constrained, therefore, to feign a reluctant acquiescence in the demand.

The suns and chieftains of the different villages held a secret council, and, resolving against submission, determined themselves to become the principals, instead of auxiliaries in the conspiracy against the French. Accordingly, they set to work to secure the co-operation of other tribes hostile to the French, and to destroy the whole settlement.

The necessary messengers were dispatched, each provided with a bundle of sticks of equal numbers, one of which was to be withdrawn daily, to insure a concert of action between the allies, the attack to be made on the day that the last stick was removed.

This conspiracy was designed to be kept a profound secret among the chiefs, and especially from the women, some of whom were known to be too well affected to their French neighbors. That some secret and momentous measure was on foot was soon divined by one of the most shrewd and observant of the female suns, who, severely upbraiding her son in private for his want of confidence in her, artfully drew from him the details of the plot, which she lost no time in imparting to an officer of the garrison; but her warning was unheeded.

Chepar, deluded into false security by the address of the chiefs, with whom he was even engaged in drunken revels on the very eve of his destruction, would listen to no caution, or credit any intimation of the intended assault. Not satisfied with this, the female sun, having in consideration of her rank access to the fane in which the bundle of sticks for her village was kept, secretly withdrew one or two of them at a time, trusting thus, by precipitating the attack by the Natchez before the arrival of the confederates, to afford the French a further chance of escape.

Deceived by this artifice, and tempted also by the arrival of some boats laden with merchandise just landed from New Orleans, on the morning of the 29th of November, 1729, before the arrival of the day first appointed, a simultaneous attack upon the garrison, town, and different plantations was made, a shot fired upon the boats, by a party who had secretly descended the hill for that purpose, being the concerted signal. So well was the attack planned that, in less than three hours, upwards of two hundred Frenchmen were massacred, two only, a carpenter and tailor, being spared. Ninety-two women and one hundred and fifty-five children, and all the negroes, were captured.

The usual atrocities practised by savages ensued; the fort, houses, and boats were pillaged; and the liquor obtained furnished the means of a long-continued scene of carousal and debauchery.

A few only escaped, and succeeded in reaching New Orleans, bearing the first intelligence of this sad disaster.

The first of these who arrived was Richard, followed shortly after by Couillard, and a few others.

Among the principal persons who fell were the Kollys, father and son, who had just arrived to take possession of the grant of Hubert on the St. Catharine's, which they had purchased. One house only, that of Laloire, the principal agent of the company at the post, made any defence. This was made good through the day with the loss of six out of eight men, by whom it was defended. The two survivors escaped under cover of the night.

Laloire himself, who chanced to be on horseback when the attack commenced, defended himself bravely, and killed four Indians before he fell; these, with eight others killed from his house, twelve in all, constituted the entire loss of the Natchez.

As to Chepar, he was held in such contempt and abhorrence, that death by the hands of a warrior was deemed too honorable for him, and at the conclusion of the massacre he was dragged from the garden to which he had fled, and beat to death with clubs by the most degraded of the Natchez race.

The destruction of the fort at Natchez being complete, and the habitations of the French reduced to ashes, some of the Yazoo tribe who were present at the massacre, accompanied by a party of Natchez, proceeded to the settlement on the Yazoo. The fort was garrisoned by only twenty men, and the commander, Du Codier, having already perished at Natchez, where he chanced to be on a visit at the time of the massacre, was easily surprised, and the soldiers and the few families settled near it were put to death.

Thus the French settlement on the Yazoo was entirely destroyed about the 1st of January, 1730.

It has been charged that the Choctaws were to have aided in this massacre, and to have made a simultaneous attack upon New Orleans; and that, in consequence of the derangement of all their plans, and their disappointment in not sharing the plunder, by the premature attack made by the Natchez, they determined to avenge themselves by the destruction of that people.

How far other and better motives may have operated

with some of the principal chiefs and their followers, they co-operated afterwards with the French, not only against the Natchez, but subsequently, in the war that ensued with the Chickasaws, with general fidelity and efficiency.

No sooner had they learned that the Natchez threatened to put to death the women and children that had been captured, than they assembled a considerable force, headed by Leseur, a Frenchman, and attacked the Natchez on the 27th of January, whilst revelling on the banks of the St. Catharine, killed many of them, rescued the carpenter and tailor, and upwards of fifty French women and children, recovering at the same time about one hundred of the negroes. In this attack fell the chief who had instigated the Natchez massacre.

Perrier, the governor, who was assembling a force at Tunica to march against the Natchez, was less prompt in his movements.

The Choctaws had marched a great distance by land, and were compelled to wait for many days for the arrival of the French, with whom they were to co-operate; and it was not until the fourteenth that Loubois, the French commander, after fruitless parleyings, had posted his artillery, and made his arrangements for an attack upon the forts in which the Natchez had entrenched themselves. The guns of the French were mounted on the mound on which stood the great temple, and commanded the forts of the Indians; they were, however, only four pounders, hardly fit for service, and so badly managed that they made little impression. The Indians opposed three pieces, which were still more clumsily handled. More than ten days were consumed in this siege.

On the 15th, intimidated by the more active preparations made by the French, but more by the threats of Alibamo Mengo, one of the most formidable of the Choctaw chiefs, the Natchez were brought to terms; and on the 27th, delivered to the hands of the Choctaws all the women and children, and most of the negroes in their possession.

On the night of the 18th, eluding the vigilance of the besiegers, or, as some assert, *with the connivance of the French!* they made their escape, crossed the Mississippi, and took refuge among the Washitas.

Thus, with the escape of the Natchez, ended this expedition, so little creditable to the French arms, in which the rescue of the captured women and children, and whatever else of success attended it, were owing mainly to their Choctaw confederates.

The women and children thus rescued were sent down the river to New Orleans, and most of them were eventually settled on concessions of land made to them at Point Coupie. The country being thus abandoned, the French commenced the erection of a brick fort, the command of which, with a garrison of one hundred men, was given to the Baron de Cresnay.

Another expedition was set on foot, at the head of which Perrier placed himself, and in January, 1731, having discovered the place of retreat, and the fortified camp of the Natchez, near the junction of the Washita and Tensas, eventually succeeded in capturing forty-five men and four hundred and fifty women and children; the others escaped.

The prisoners captured by Perrier, including two suns and a princess, were taken to New Orleans, transported to San Domingo, and sold into slavery.*

* In January, 1731, application having been made to M. de Maurepas to relieve the company of the expense incurred on account of

Although driven from their country, and destroyed as a separate nation, the Natchez were not exterminated. Those who escaped from Perrier were headed by the Chief of the Flour, who led such of his tribe as he could collect against St. Deyns at the Post of Natchitoches, whom he attacked with a force of about two hundred warriors; but he was repulsed.

Pursuing his advantage, St. Denys, at the head of his small force, a few Spaniards and an inconsiderable number of Natchitoches Indians, sallied out, forced the entrenched camp of the Natchez, killed ninety-two of them, including all of their chiefs, and put the rest to flight. Thus St. Denys, with a very inconsiderable force, inflicted upon the Natchez the most fatal blow they had yet received.

The survivors of this fated race were now scattered among the Washitas and other small tribes; but most of them sought an asylum among the Chickasaws, with whom they incorporated themselves. They continued for several years, in conjunction with the latter tribe, to attack and harass the French on all favorable occasions, and still numbered two hundred warriors.

When informed of these disasters, the company of the Indies decided that it was impracticable to sustain any longer so profitless and expensive a colony, and the directors proposed to surrender to the king the charter, the obligations of which it was thought would involve it in ruin. After much negotiation, the retrocession was accepted, the French government resumed the administration of the colony, and on the 15th of November,

these Indian families at Cape Francois, he replied that he was not aware of any other course to adopt than to order their sale or to send them back to Louisiana. They were thereupon ordered to be sold.—*Marbois.*

1731, issued the necessary ordinances for winding up the affairs of the company, which, after a struggle of fourteen years, had failed to fulfil its sanguine but visionary expectations.

The hostile disposition of the Indians, which had been so disastrous, and which seemed to be extending to all the tribes, was attributed in a great degree to the harshness of Perrier; and the return of Bienville was urged under the belief that his mildness and humanity would conciliate the Indians, with many of whom he had ever been a favorite, and possessed great influence. Accordingly, under the new organization of the colony, Bienville was reappointed governor in 1734, and on his arrival, which was hailed with much joy by the colonists, Perrier returned to France.

From this period until near the close of the French rule, the country embraced in the limits of the State was little more than the theatre of Indian hostilities and warfare.

The Natchez and the Yazoos, who had taken refuge among the Chickasaws, resumed their predatory war upon the remote settlements of the colony, in which the Chickasaws frequently united with them, and intercepted or obstructed all communication by the way of the Mississippi. Bienville, therefore, sent an officer to the Chickasaws to demand that the Natchez should be given up. This being refused, he commenced the preparation of an expedition against them. Leblanc, one of his officers, was sent with orders to the Chevalier d'Artaguette, who was in command at Fort Chartres in the Illinois, to repair to the country of the Chickasaws, with all the French and Indians he could collect, to co-operate with the troops to be sent from New Orleans by way of Mobile and the Tombigbee River about the 10th of May.

The party of Leblanc, although attacked by the enemy near the Yazoo River, reached its destination. Another officer was sent among the Choctaws, and by the aid of liberal presents engaged the chiefs to unite their warriors with the force Bienville proposed to lead from New Orleans.

The Chevalier d'Artaguette had distinguished himself in the war with the Natchez, and had subsequently been placed in command of the Fort at Natchez. In obedience to his orders, with such forces as he could assemble, he repaired to the place of rendezvous on the 9th of May, the day previous to that on which he was directed to arrive. He encamped in sight of the enemy until the 20th, when he was no longer able to restrain his auxiliaries, who determined to fight or withdraw.

Thus situated, he embraced the first alternative, and with an impetuous charge drove the enemy from the fort before which he was encamped, and the village it protected; the second fort was carried with equal gallantry; and he was in full pursuit of the foe, retreating to their third and last entrenchment when, unfortunately, he fell under repeated wounds. His Indian confederates now basely deserted him, and fled in all directions. Forty-eight soldiers, all he could bring with him, and Father Senac, his chaplain, stood bravely by in defence of their prostrate leader; but they were too few to resist the overwhelming force by which they were assailed. Overpowered by numbers, many of them were captured and led prisoners, with their wounded chief, to the fort.

And where was Bienville and his army in the mean time? Having sent before a strong detachment to erect a fort on the Tombigbee, two hundred and fifty miles above Mobile, as a depot for his provisions and ammunition, with the regular troops at his disposal, two companies of militia and nearly fifty negroes officered by free blacks, a force amounting altogether to nearly six hundred men, he embarked on the Bayou St. John with thirty boats on the 4th of March, and did not arrive at the fort on the Tombigbee until the 20th of April. On the 4th of May he reached his landing-place within twenty-seven miles only of the nearest Chickasaw village; here the last detachment of his Choctaw auxiliaries joined him, amounting in the whole now to twelve hundred warriors. Here they loitered, erecting houses and stores, within a day's march of the enemy, for more than twenty days.*

At last their march commenced, and on the following day, the 26th of May, 1736, at noon, the army arrived before an entrenched village protected by a strongly constructed fort.

The British flag was flying, and several Englishmen were observed in the fort, which was surrounded by thick palisades pierced with loopholes for firing through; and within, the Indians were further protected by trenches, from which they could securely fire without exposing themselves to the shot of their assailants.

Bienville wished to avoid this village, and attack a neighboring one of the Natchez, against whom the expedition was chiefly designed; but the Choctaws, supposing this town would yield the most plunder and

* This landing-place and depot of Bienville was doubtless at the point now known as Cotton-gin Port. Since the settlement of the country by the present inhabitants, two small field-pieces and a box of bullets have been here recovered from the river, into which they were probably thrown on the retreat of the French army.

afford some provisions, of which they began to be in need, overruled the designs of the commander.

Against this stronghold the force of Bienville was therefore led, powerless to inflict damage on an enemy thus protected, whilst the assailants were exposed and galled by an incessant shower of balls, which, however, was sustained for several hours, when, several of the best officers being killed or disabled, a retreat was ordered, after a loss of thirty-two killed and sixty-one wounded.

The French did not renew the attack. The following day the Choctaws had some desultory skirmishing with the enemy, and on the 29th the army commenced its retreat for the landing-place, where it arrived on the third day with the wounded. After distributing the remainder of his goods to his Choctaw allies, Bienville re-embarked his troops, floated down the river, and returned to New Orleans; thus terminating a most disastrous expedition, reflecting the deepest disgrace upon the French arms, the prowess of which was lowered immeasurably in the estimation of the savage foe.

In the mean time, the gallant but unfortunate D'Artaguette, suffering with his wounds, had been kept a prisoner, with his captured companions, under the belief that their ransom would secure favorable terms from Bienville, of whose imposing force, on its approach, they were in great dread. When it was known that he had been repulsed, and had ingloriously withdrawn, these gallant men were brought out into the plain, and D'Artaguette, Father Senac, and fifteen others were burned alive. A sergeant of D'Artaguette's party succeeded in obtaining his liberty, reached New Orleans on the 1st of July, and made known the fate of his gallant commander.

The foregoing account of this unfortunate expedition

is derived mainly from *Martin's Louisiana*. Gayerre gives a somewhat different version. According to his account, the force of D'Artaguette was much greater than represented; and his attack, although sufficiently gallant, was less successful. He had also been apprised by a messenger of the delay of Bienville, and the cause.

The battle of Ackia was so called from the town of that name, on which the attack was made. It was situated, among several other villages, in a beautiful prairie of about six miles in extent, probably near the site of De Soto's encampment of 1541.*

The attack on this point was, as has been stated, made contrary to the judgment and wishes of Bienville, to accommodate the views of his Choctaw confederates, who, however, during the fight, kept at a very safe distance, wasting their ammunition and expending all their valor in the most savage yells, adding to the horrors of the fray.

The French officers were also deserted by the larger portion of their men, whom it was impossible to force into battle.

Feats of daring heroism were performed by the officers and a few of the men, many of the former being killed or wounded. Among the slain were the Chevalier d'Contre Cœur, Captain De Lusser, and D'Jusan. Of the

* The Chickasaws appear to have been much harassed at an early period by the Northern Indians, and for common defence were settled in contiguous villages at the place known now as Old Town, in Pontotoc County. It was not until after the British sent McIntosh among them as agent, that they were induced to leave their towns and form separate settlements. To effect this dispersion, considered essential to the welfare of the nation, the agent established himself at a place near Tocshish, in the same county, represented in the early maps of the country as McIntoshville.

wounded, were the Chevalier d'Noyan, the nephew of Bienville, who led the attack, D'Hautrive, Grondel, and others. It is due to the reputation of Bienville to say that he alleged, in defence of his retreat, that he had reason to apprehend the desertion of the Choctaws, and could place no reliance upon the cowardly vagabonds who had been sent him as soldiers, very few of whom were five feet in height, and many of them under that stature.

A second expedition against the unsubdued Chickasaws was recommended to the French government by Bienville, to proceed up the Mississippi, instead of by the more direct and truly less objectionable route up the Tombigbee, formerly pursued, to be undertaken when the proper force, and an armament suited to the object, could be furnished.

The plan was approved, and, after considerable delay, Bienville was supplied with artillery, arms, ammunition, and provisions, and seven hundred men. With these was M. de Noailles d'Aime, with bombardiers, cannoniers, and miners, to be used in this second expedition *if deemed of absolute utility.*

D'Noailles was especially recommended "as having the necessary talents and experience to command," an intimation that implied a doubt very mortifying to Bienville of his own fitness for such service.

The greater part of the year 1739 was occupied with preparations for this expedition.

In the mean time, the Choctaws had become somewhat disaffected, and many of them had espoused the English interest. This produced a civil war among them, in which the French party were predominant, and continued to harass the Chickasaws; and the English traders were plundered and put to flight.

D'Noyan, who was sent into the nation, succeeded in engaging thirty-two out of forty-two villages in the French cause, and parties of warriors were formed to unite in the great expedition now on foot.

In August, 1739, D'Noyan, with the advance guard of the army, arrived near the site of the present city of Memphis, the place of rendezvous appointed; the troops from Illinois and Canada, including a company of cadets under Celeron, soon after joined him, and whilst awaiting the arrival of the main body of the army, erected a fort called Assumption.

Bienville, leaving New Orleans on the 12th of September, claims much credit for the celerity of his movements in arriving with his army in only two months.

Much precious time had already been lost; the troops fresh from Europe, and from the more northern districts, exposed for months during the most sickly season to the miasma of the river bottom, became fatally diseased, and a large number of them perished.

Bienville's force, when reviewed after his arrival on the 12th of November, amounted to twelve hundred white men, and two thousand four hundred Indians. Yet, with this imposing force, under the pretence of seeking a practicable road to the Chickasaw towns, the army remained here inactive in a state of indecision until February, 1740, when, their provisions becoming nearly exhausted, a council of war, composed of the principal officers of the expedition, decided that, under all the *untoward circumstances*, it would be *hazarding the reputation of the king's arms* to march against the enemy.

The most remarkable feature of this affair was that, after the principal part of the army had moved off down the Mississippi, Celeron led his company of cadets, together with about one hundred Frenchmen and four or five hundred Indians, against the Chickasaw towns, and those Indians, alarmed at the vast preparations the French had made, and believing Celeron's party was only the advance guard of the French army, presented themselves before him, and sued for peace in the humblest terms, promising to deliver up the Natchez in their possession, and to exterminate the rest of that doomed race. Celeron, accepting the terms, dispatched some of the chiefs after Bienville, who was overtaken on the Mississippi, and concluded a peace with them on the proposed conditions, not including the Choctaws, however, in this pacific arrangement, that nation being left free to prosecute their hostilities at pleasure.

The Chickasaws, according to the stipulation of the treaty, delivered a few of the Natchez to Celeron, who transferred them to New Orleans, and after demolishing Fort Assumption, returned to Canada, being the only officer who had distinguished himself or gained any reputation in this pompous and abortive expedition.

The miserable remnant of the Natchez, finding no longer any security among their late friends, retired finally among the Cherokees in Georgia, with whom they found a secure asylum, and in time became merged in that nation.

In 1741, the Marquis of Vaudreuil was appointed governor of Louisiana, and Bienville, who had asked to be recalled, left the province for France, never more to return, much esteemed and regretted by the colonists. For more than forty years he had been connected with the colony, remaining in it continually, except during the administration of Perrier, and most of that time as the chief in command. He was perhaps more devoted to its interests, and did more to advance them than any other individual; but he was peculiarly unfortunate in his expeditions against the Chickasaws, for his failure in which the attempted defence in his dispatches to the French government did not satisfactorily account nor wholly excuse.

Of the condition and progress of that part of the colony, embraced within the limits of our State, for more than twenty succeeding years, the accounts of historians are meagre and unsatisfactory in the extreme.

We have therefore little to chronicle during that long period; yet the archives of the French government would doubtless, if carefully explored, afford some materials for filling up this broad hiatus in our history.

Of the colony *generally*, it is recorded that, during this period, its commerce, relieved from the restraint of exclusive privilege, began to thrive; its agriculture was more prosperous; indigo was cultivated to a considerable extent, and with much success; the rice and tobacco produced afforded easy means of remittance to Europe, whilst lumber found a market in the West Indies. In what degree our portion of the province contributed to this trade, is not said.

The Chickasaws had for some years been less troublesome, but making an irruption again upon some of the back settlements, the Marquis of Vaudreuil, in 1752, led an army of seven hundred men, and a large number of Indians, into their country by the route pursued by Bienville in his first expedition against that nation.

Finding the Chickasaw towns strongly fortified, and defended by block-houses, in the construction of which they were aided and instructed by the English among them, he lost little time in fruitless sieges, but contented himself with overrunning their country, destroying their crops, and wasting their supplies. The expedition, although not very satisfactory or successful, probably inflicted as much injury as a more direct attack would have done.

The Choctaws continued their hostilities against the Chickasaws during many years with constantly increasing success, and the latter seemed in danger of sharing, in the end, the fate of the exterminated Natchez.

Sorely beset, they sued for peace to the French, but were left to the mercy of their vindictive and persevering foe.

The Marquis of Vaudreuil having been appointed governor of Canada, on the 9th of February, 1753, Kerlerec, a distinguished officer of the French navy, who had displayed much courage and ability, and received several wounds, was installed governor of Louisiana. He adopted a liberal policy towards the Indians, whom he endeavored to conciliate by dealing more justly by them, and providing larger and better supplies of goods for the Indian trade. He undertook also to ransom several prisoners who had long been detained among the Indians.

Indulging less in pomp and splendor than his predecessor, he was less popular; and however faithful and energetic he might have been, or judicious and well intentioned in the reforms he proposed, his administration was unfavorably compared with that of Vaudreuil by the disaffected and factious.

Although menaced by the English, exposed to Indian incursions, and distracted by internal broils, to the aggravation of which the different orders of priesthood contributed, the French government not only failed to afford the necessary aid to meet the emergencies of the times, but also withdrew a large portion of the military force from the colony. It is no matter of surprise, therefore, if Kerlerec proved unequal to the crisis which the colony was rapidly approaching.

France and England having engaged in a war, the final issue was the fall of Canada, and with it the loss of all the possessions of France in North America.

By the treaty of Paris of the 16th of February, 1763, all that part of the colony, embraced in the State of Mississippi was ceded to Great Britain, terminating the French rule over that district, which had lasted sixty-four years.

It becomes interesting to inquire, at this juncture of the affairs of the colony, as to the then situation of the once promising settlements made near Natchez, and on the Yazoo, which we have seen were from time to time so largely and liberally reinforced with emigrants and laborers, about the period when the colony was placed under charge of the Mississippi Company.

What had become of the extensive plantations and the hundreds of emigrants and slaves that had been settled upon them? Conjecture alone must answer the inquiry, for our historians have failed to enlighten us. With all the disadvantages of climate and exposure, these people could not probably have so speedily perished by the ordinary course of nature, and the massacre cannot account for all, certainly not for a tithe of those settled on the Yazoo.

Many of them doubtless wandered off among the Choctaws, became traders and hunters, adopting their mode of life and intermarrying with them, founding families, perhaps, as the Laflours, Jusans, and others, whose descendants yet remain; the residue probably withdrew to the newly-founded city of New Orleans, and contributed to its population; the negroes perhaps being transferred to the plantations nearer the city.

But in the long period of thirty years after the Natchez were driven from the country, were not those favorite and desirable settlements reoccupied? We must infer not, or to a very limited extent. We glean that, after the massacre, the erection of a fort at Natchez was *commenced* by Perrier and garrisoned; but it appears also that the troops from all such interior posts were drawn off wholly or in part to be employed in the Chickasaw wars. That no new settlements had been made in that quarter, may be inferred from the fact that the most recent attacks by the disaffected Choctaws and other hostile Indians were made as low down as the settlements of Point Coupee, at the German coast, and even on the lakes near New Orleans.

In a census of the colony, taken in 1745, it appears that there were only eight white males and fifteen negroes at Natchez. Baluxi and Pascagoula are not mentioned at all in the returns, although it is difficult to suppose that these, the earliest and once most populous settlements, had been wholly broken up.

In 1751, when Governor Vaudreuil had received an accession to the military force of the colony, fifty soldiers were stationed at Natchez.

AS A BRITISH PROVINCE; 1763—1779.

Great Britain had acquired, at the same time that the French possessions east of the Mississippi had been ceded to her, the possessions of Spain in Florida also.

The knowledge of the extent and geographical features of the country, by the English at least, was then exceedingly imperfect, as may be seen by a reference to the early map of the country published by Eman Bowen, an English geographer in 1764. A portion of this map, embracing the present territory of the State, is annexed to this report.

Many changes in the channel of the Mississippi have taken place since that period, but the greatly exaggerated width of the river, and the numerous islands with which it is studded, could not even at that time have had any foundation in truth; the former extending over much of the swamp lands periodically overflowed. The position of New Orleans is singularly inaccurate, being placed above the Lafourche; the more correct position would have been one near that occupied on this plan by the Oumas village.

Pearl, the principal river, having its entire extent in our State, is scarcely noticed upon the map, whilst its true sources are connected with the Pascagoula.

Of these joint acquisitions two provinces were formed, called East and West Florida; the latter extending to and embracing all the territory of our now State south of the 31st degree of north latitude. The seat of government was established at Pensacola, and in 1764, George Johnston, a captain in the royal navy, was appointed governor.

By the treaty between Great Britain and France, the inhabitants within the ceded district were secured in the free exercise of the Catholic religion, and eighteen months were allowed them to dispose of their property to British subjects and to retire from the country. Complaints were subsequently made, however, that some of the British officers had required the French inhabitants to take the oath of allegiance within three months to be secured in their property.

In February, a number of officers, with three hundred and twenty soldiers, commanded by Major Loftus, with a number of women and children, embarked at New Orleans in ten large batteaux and two pirogues, to ascend the Mississippi to take possession of the newly-acquired establishments of the British in Illinois. On the 19th of March, the boats reached Fort Adams, or as then called, *La roche à Davion*, when the pirogues, which were in advance, were fired upon by a small party of Indians, not exceeding thirty in number, belonging to the Tunicas, Yazoos, and some other small tribes who were concealed on the bank. Six men were killed and seven wounded. Suspecting the treachery of the French, and supposing that a large Indian force was lying in wait for them, without firing a gun, the boats dropped down the river and returned to New Orleans. The place became known thereafter as Loftus Heights.

The subsequent charge made by Major Loftus, who returned to head-quarters at Pensacola, that this attack was made by the instigation of the acting governor, D'Abbadie, was exposed as a black and atrocious calumny. On the contrary, the governor had used his utmost endeavors to induce the Indians to remain quiet, having caused them to be harangued in behalf of the English, and ordered the French commandants of the posts on the river to afford aid and protection to Loftus and his party; an interpreter had been furnished, and in fact everything in the power of the French had been done for the security of the expedition.

The Indians of many of the villages in amity with the French were exceedingly averse to a change of rulers, and many of the Choctaws, Tensas, and Alibamons, from their aversion to the English, crossed over to the west of the Mississippi, and settled on lands given them by the French.

It being represented to the British monarch that there

were considerable settlements on the left bank of the Mississippi above the thirty-first degree of north latitude, by the commission of Governor Johnston, dated the 10th of June, 1764, the northern boundary of the province of West Florida was extended so as to embrace them, the line being drawn due east from the mouth of the Yazoo River.

During the summer of 1764, a large detachment of British troops occupied Fort Rosalie at Natchez, which was thenceforth known as Fort Panmure.

In 1765, a number of families, chiefly from the Roanoke River in North Carolina, came to West Florida and settled above Baton Rouge; some of these families subsequently removed to the neighborhood of Natchez.

In December, 1766, a small stockade fort was built at the Bayou Manchac, the extreme southwestern point of the British possessions, which was named Fort Bute. This post being on the line of the Spanish dominions, and convenient to New Orleans, became a place of illicit trade, which was carried on with the inhabitants of Louisiana on a considerable scale, as it was also at Natchez. This trade, profitable as it was to the English, was so convenient and advantageous to the colonists of Louisiana, that it was indulged in with little restraint on the part of the Spanish authorities. Supplies of goods were accumulated at those posts, and in "floating warehouses" which traded along the coast, and, with the connivance of the public officers, even supplied the French boats trading to Illinois and up Red River and the Arkansas.

The proclamation of the 7th of October, 1763, by the king of Great Britain, seems to have been the first official act of the British government in reference to its newly-acquired possessions on the Mississippi. By that proclamation it was that the province of West Florida was established with the thirty-first degree of north latitude for its northern boundary.

Grants of land were authorized to be made to the inhabitants of the province, or those who might resort thereto, in quantities suited to their means of cultivation, and under such moderate *quitrents, services, and acknowledgments as had* been prescribed in other colonies.

To testify the royal sense and approbation of the conduct of the officers and soldiers of the army, the governor was also empowered to make to such reduced officers and privates as had served in North America in the late war, and who should actually reside there and apply for the same, grants of land in quantity proportioned to their rank. Field-officers to be entitled to 5,000 acres, captains to 3,000, subalterns to 2,000, non-commissioned officers to 200, and privates to 50 acres. Officers of the navy, who had served at the reduction of Louisburg and Quebec, were entitled to similar grants. All persons were interdicted from acquiring land by purchase or grant from the Indians.

In January, 1768, the first grants of which we have any record were made under the authority of the king's proclamation. They were executed by Monfort Browne, lieutenant-governor of the province of West Florida at Pensacola, among the first being two grants of 3,000 and 2,000 acres respectively to Daniel Clarke, a reduced captain of the Pennsylvania troops. These grants were situated on the St. Catharine, about three miles south of Fort Panmure, and embraced lands that had been in part cleared and improved under the French government. Similar grants were made to others, by Lieutenant-Governor Browne, in the following year. Grants dated in January, and to the 19th of March, 1770, were signed by Elias Durnford, as lieutenant-governor.

On the 2d of March of this year, the limits of West Florida having been extended to the Yazoo, as has before been stated, Peter Chester was commissioned the successor of Elliott, as governor of West Florida.

No subsequent grants are known to have been made during this, or the following year.

In 1772, and each of the succeeding years to the 3d of September, 1779, numerous patents, many of them for tracts of large dimensions, were granted by Governor Chester.

Philip Livingston was Secretary of the province in the years 1772, 1773, 1776, 1777 and 1778. Alexander Macullough held that office in 1774 and 1775; and Elihu Hall Bay, afterwards a distinguished Judge of the State of South Carolina, and himself the grantee of several large tracts, as well as the proprietor by purchase of many others, was the Secretary in 1779, and at the close of the British rule in the province.

In 1768, Daniel Clarke was the Clerk of the Council under Lieutenant-Governor Browne, and Francis Poussett held that office in 1769 and 1770. Charles Durnford was the Surveyor-General, and E. Rush Wegg, under whose revision the patents all passed, was the Attorney-General of the province.

These grants, and the deeds of conveyance by which they passed to other hands, are exceedingly prolix, and abound with the technicalities and minute legal phraseology of the age. The following extract from the former is worth preserving, as a curious illustration of the estimation in which some of the ceded rights and privileges were then held, which are at this day common and disregarded. The patents ran as follows:—

"WEST FLORIDA, *ss.*

"GEORGE THE THIRD, by the Grace of God of Great Britain, France and Ireland, King, Defender of the Faith, and so forth.

"To all to whom these presents shall come greeting. Know Ye that we, of our special grace, certain knowledge, and mere motion, have given and granted and by these presents, for our heirs and successors do give and grant unto, &c. &c., his heirs and assigns, all that tract or parcel of land, &c. &c., together with all the woods and underwoods, timber and timber trees, lakes, *ponds and fishings*, waters, watercourses, profits, commodities, &c. &c., together with the privilege of *hunting, hawking, and fowling*, &c. &c., reserving, &c. &c. With a quit-rent of one penny sterling per acre, to be paid at the feast of St. Michael's in every year."

Then follow the conditions of clearing three acres out of every fifty, of seating and seeding, draining marshes and quarrying rocks, &c., proof of which is to be made under a penalty of forfeiture within a stated period.

The following are among the principal grants made in the Natchez District: The Earl of Egglenton, 20,000 acres near Natchez; Captain Amos Ogden, 25,000 acres on the Homochitto; Thaddeus Lyman, 20,000 on both sides of the Bayou Pierre, between Port Gibson and Grand Gulf; the Earl of Harcourt, 10,000 acres; Admiral Bentinck, 10,000 acres; the heirs of Thomas Comyn, 10,000 acres; Elihu Hall Bay, several tracts, 16,000 acres; Admiral Sir George Bridges Rodney, 5,000 acres; Sir William Dalling, 5,000 acres; Philip Barbour, Governor of Virginia, 2,000 acres on the Mississippi near Grand Gulf; Admiral Sir Richard Onslow, 1,000 acres, and Colonel Anthony Hutchins, several large tracts embracing the White Apple Village of the Natchez on Second Creek.

Two of these grants, known as Ogden's Mandamus and Lyman's Mandamus, were of a different character from the others, emanating directly from the king.

To Captain Amos Ogden, a retired officer of the Province of New Jersey, the king, at the Court of St. James, on the 13th of May, 1767, issued his order to the governor of his majesty's province of West Florida, to cause 25,000 acres of land to be surveyed in one "contiguous" tract, in such part of said province as the said Ogden or his attorney shall choose, and to pass a grant therefor to the said Ogden under the seal of the province.

On the 14th of April, 1772, Captain Ogden sold 19,000 acres of this grant for the sum of nine hundred pounds *proclamation money* of New Jersey, to two brothers, Samuel and Richard Swayze. This grant was located on the Homochitto River, about fifteen miles from Natchez, and the purchasers, with their families and connections, removed to it and formed what is known to this day as the Jersey settlement.

Major-General Phineas Lyman, of Connecticut, had served with distinction against the French in Canada, and subsequently led a large detachment of provincial troops to co-operate with Lord Amherst against the West Indies, and after the fall of Havana was placed in command of that place. Standing in high favor with the British government, and contemplating after the close of the war the establishment of a company of military adventurers chiefly composed of the officers and soldiers who had served with him for the purpose of making a settlement on lands in the west, he repaired to England in 1763, to solicit the grant of a body of land for that object. Before his arrival, a change had taken place in the English ministry, and his friends were out of power; he remained, however, nearly ten years in fruitless attendance upon a court which seemed to have forgotten his services until he had become old and dispirited, and was fast sinking into a state of imbecility resulting from chagrin and disappointment. Finally, he obtained a similar mandate as that of Ogden to the governor of West Florida, for a grant of 20,000 acres. Returning to Connecticut, and finding that many of his old associates had died or removed, and most of the others disinclined from advancing age to encounter the hardships incident to new settlements, after a short delay, he proceeded with his eldest son Thaddeus, and a few friends, to Mississippi to locate his lands. Before this was completed he died, and the patent was granted on the 2d of February, 1775, to his son Thaddeus on condition of his conveying portions of it to his brothers Thompson and Oliver Lyman, and his sisters Elizabeth and Experience, which was done. Four thousand acres of his portion of the tract were also sold in different parcels to some of the officers of the government at Pensacola, Livingston, Macullogh, and Bay.

It has been seen that the British government was profuse in its grants of land in the Natchez District, and it becomes interesting to know its actual condition and the progress that had been made in its settlement. We have the testimony of some of the early settlers, who survived to an advanced age, and whose statements have been preserved, that, in 1776, twelve years after the English first occupied the fort at Natchez, the town then consisted of only ten log cabins and two frame houses, all situated under the bluff. The site of Fort Rosalie was overgrown with forest trees, some of them more than two feet in diameter; several old iron guns were lying about, supposed to have been left by the French. About seventy-eight families, dispersed in different settlements, constituted the whole population of the district, few of which, according to these statements, had emigrated to the country previous to the year 1772. There were four small mercantile establishments in the town; these were owned by Blomart, James Willing, Barber, and the firm of Hanchet & Newman. Blomart was a reduced British officer, Willing became afterwards unfavorably conspicuous, and Hanchet was one of the followers or associates of Lyman.

In 1777, the British held a treaty with the Indians at Mobile, when the limits of the Natchez District were defined; and in 1779 the eastern boundary line was surveyed and marked; between this line and the Mississippi, the Indians relinquished all their claims. The line commenced on the thirty-first degree of north latitude, about fifty miles east of the Mississippi, running rather west of north and approaching the river by a not very direct line, until it reached the Yazoo River, passing only about six miles east of the present city of Vicksburg. A large portion of the district bordering on the Mississippi and the principal streams was covered by British grants, which were now being rapidly settled by the emigrants resorting to the country.

The war of the Revolution had broken out; but it was not to be expected that so remote and inconsiderable a settlement as this, absorbed with the cares and struggling with the privations and difficulties incident to newly-settled countries, would take any active part in the contest, or that the peaceful and absorbing avocations of its inhabitants would be interrupted or disturbed by hostile incursions. Circumstances, however, prevented the neutrality that otherwise would have been observed, and led the inhabitants to resent wrongs wantonly inflicted upon them in the name of a cause towards which there is no reason to doubt many of them were well affected.

In the city of New Orleans, some merchants from Philadelphia, New York, and Boston, had established themselves, who were warmly interested in the cause of independence. The most prominent of these was Oliver Pollock, who possessed much influence, and enjoyed the favor of the Spanish governor Galvez. These men succeeded in accumulating considerable supplies of arms and ammunition for the American troops, probably with the aid, and certainly with the knowledge, of Galvez. To procure these military stores, Colonels Gibson and Linn were dispatched from Fort Pitt in 1766, and succeeded in transporting them safely up the Mississippi, to be used in defence of the American forts on the Ohio.

In the following year, Captain Willing, of Philadelphia, and lately one of the few merchants at Natchez, was dispatched by the Continental Congress to New Orleans, on a similar mission. He visited the English settlements on the Mississippi, and enjoyed the hospitality of his former neighbors and acquaintances; but they could not be induced to take a part in the war; the sparseness of the population, the remoteness from the other colonies, and the consequent difficulty of receiving aid or assistance from them in their need, influenced their conduct, and inclined them to neutrality.

In January, 1778, Willing again visited New Orleans with a party of about fifty men. Pollock now acted openly as the agent of the Americans, with the countenance of Governor Galvez, who, at different times, contributed seventy thousand dollars out of the royal treasury, by which means the frontier inhabitants of Virginia and Pennsylvania were furnished with arms and ammunition for the defence of their forts.

Willing now engaged in a marauding excursion against the planters on the Mississippi. At Manchac, he captured a small vessel, which was lying there at anchor, and proceeded as far as Natchez, laying waste plantations, destroying stock, burning houses, and carrying off all the slaves he could seize; the inhabitants being too few and scattered to make any effectual resistance. Among those plundered in this manner were Colonel Anthony Hutchins, Isaac Johnson, and Alexander McIntosh. This wanton and unwarrantable attack upon the inoffensive inhabitants, standing in no hostile attitude, the liberality and hospitality of many of whom Willing had enjoyed the year previous, and now requited by burning their houses and plundering their effects, was regarded as an enormity justified by no laws of war, and uncalled for by his commission. Well affected as the people of Louisiana were to the cause of the United States, they viewed with indignation this wanton and unprovoked attack upon a helpless and unoffending community.

Returning to New Orleans with his booty, a party of new recruits, under the command of Willing's lieutenant, returned up the river to prosecute further depredations against the other plantations which had so far escaped. Intelligence of the approach of this party being conveyed to the inhabitants, many of them put their effects out of its reach; among these, Mr. William Dunbar, and others acting under his advice, removed their slaves across the Mississippi into the Spanish possessions. A party of Natchez settlers was also raised, and headed by Hutchins, Blomart, McIntosh and Percy, assembled at the White Cliffs, or Ellis Landing, where the boats of the approaching party were decoyed into shore. A skirmish ensued, in which the lieutenant and five or six of his men were killed.

Shortly after the foregoing occurrences, Governor Chester sent Colonel Magellan to raise four companies of militia, and with orders to fit up Fort Panmure. The command of these troops was given to Lyman, Blomart and McIntosh, who were soon ordered to Baton Rouge in consequence of the prospect of a war with Spain, and a Captain Foster, with a hundred men, was left in command of Natchez.

The British rule in the province was, however, now on the eve of a very sudden and unlooked-for termination. In May, 1779, war was declared by Spain against Great Britain. Don Bernardo de Galvez, who had hitherto been acting temporarily, received with the intelligence of this rupture the king's commission as governor; and a royal order of the 8th of July having authorized the subjects of the king in the Indies to take part in the war, Galvez proposed an immediate attack upon the English possessions in the neighborhood. A council of war, however, rejected the proposition, being inclined to postpone the enterprise until a reinforcement of troops could be obtained from Havana. Galvez, impatient of inactivity, set about collecting a body of men of sufficient force to justify him in taking the responsibility of acting in opposition to the will of his advisers. There were, at this time, many persons in New Orleans from the United States, who offered their services; these, with the volunteer militia, and the regular troops at the disposal of the governor, amounted to a force of fourteen hundred men. After a forced march, which considerably reduced his force by disease, he reached Fort Bute on Bayou

5

Manchac, which was taken by assault on the 7th of September, in less than sixty days from the date of the royal order authorizing the king's subjects in America to take part in the war. Without loss of time the army was marched to Baton Rouge. Colonel Dickson, in command of the British garrison at that place, had a force of about five hundred men, including militia; he was well supplied with ammunition and provisions, but his men were sickly, and the fort was out of repair. Galvez immediately invested the fort, mounted some heavy ordnance, and a cannonade of little more than two hours compelled a surrender.

On the 21st of September, 1779, Colonel Dickson agreed to a capitulation, which included also Fort Panmure at Natchez, and another small post on the Amite River.

This expedition, so promptly conceived and successfully executed, reflected much honor upon Galvez, and afforded an example of energy and ability that had not for a long period before been exhibited by the rulers of the colony. Don Carlos de Grand Pré was left in command of Baton Rouge, with two officers under him in command of Fort Panmure and Fort Bute. Thus closed the British rule in the province of West Florida, which had existed, dating from the Treaty of Paris, about sixteen years.

AS A PROVINCE OF SPAIN; 1779—1798.

By the capitulation of Colonel Dickson, commanding the British garrison at Baton Rouge, on the 21st of September, 1779, the Natchez District, including Fort Panmure, and two small posts on the Amite and Thompson's Creek, passed under the dominion of Spain, and the British rule that had existed for sixteen years was terminated.

Spain now, two hundred and thirty-nine years after the discovery and exploration by De Soto, was for the first time possessed of the country.

Galvez, leaving Colonel De Grand Pré in command at Baton Rouge, with two officers under him at Fort Bute and Fort Panmure, returned to New Orleans.

In the mean time, four years before the close of the war of Independence, Congress, informed of the rupture between Spain and Great Britain, entered into negotiation with the former, claiming this territory as part of the United States, and insisting upon the right to the free navigation of the Mississippi.

This claim was resisted by Spain, by whom it was contended that no part of the territory was included within the limits of any of the States, but that as a part of Florida, it was a possession of the British crown, and as such might be legitimately subdued by the Spanish arms, and held as a permanent acquisition. This conquest by Spain was therefore made under a virtual protest by the United States.

The population of the Natchez District was at this time composed in a great part of the English; reduced officers and soldiers of the British army, and their associates, together with numbers who had emigrated from the American States. None of these were well affected towards the Spaniards, and the sudden change of rulers and of institutions was very repugnant to their feelings. They complained that they had been sacrificed, and the country surrendered, by the capitulation of Baton Rouge, without giving them an opportunity of resistance.

Uninformed of these changes, Congress, in the same

year, commissioned James Robinson, a friend and companion of Willing, who with thirty or forty followers came to Natchez, to carry out the enterprise first undertaken by Willing with the view of securing the allegiance of the inhabitants to the United States. Finding the country in the possession of the Spaniards, the expedition was broken up and dispersed, and the leader soon afterwards died. In July, 1781, Don Carlos de Grand Pré, Lieutenant-Colonel of the Regiment of Louisiana, came to Natchez as the civil and military commandant of the District.

Galvez, in the meantime, had reduced Mobile, and was besieging Pensacola, when, with a confidence in the invincibility of the British arms which the result did not justify, some of the leading inhabitants of the district, among whom Thaddeus Lyman, son of General Phineas Lyman (who has before been spoken of in connection with his extensive grant of land under mandamus of the king), and his associates were prominent, offered to produce a diversion in favor of the British cause by taking Fort Panmure, and re-establishing the British authority.

The persons who took the lead in this enterprise, according to the late Calvin Smith, and given as the recollections of his boyhood, during which he witnessed the scenes of rebellion and resistance to the Spanish authorities, were Colonel Anthony Hutchins, Captain D. Blomart, a late British officer, Jacob Winfrey, Christian Bingaman, the two Alstons, and Turner Mulkey, a Baptist preacher. An application was made to Governor Chester at Pensacola for aid. Distrusting his ability of maintaining Pensacola against the assailants, the governor hesitated to encourage the revolt, fearing that the Natchez inhabitants might be precipitated into an unsuccessful and ruinous struggle. Such supplies as he could spare, however, he sent, and Mann, the messenger from Natchez, was directed to set out upon his return; but to stop in the Choctaw nation with Fulsom, a white man who had married an Indian wife and become a chief, and there to await further instructions.

Feeling assured that, in the event of defeat, *they* at least would be secure from Spanish retribution by a timely retreat among the Choctaws, Mann, by representing to Fulsom the prospect of gain from the plunder of the Spanish fort, and of some boats expected to arrive from Illinois, engaged his co-operation, and, disregarding the prudential instructions of the governor, resolved to precipitate the attack. Assembling some twenty white men and as many Indians, Mann and Fulsom proceeded to Natchez, where the inhabitants engaged in the plan of revolt, and, being apprised of their approach, sanctioned, as they supposed, by Governor Chester, and whose support they might consequently calculate upon, flew to arms. Assembling at the house of John Row, afterwards the residence of the late Job Routh, the British flag was raised *on the* 22*d April,* 1782, in full view of the fort.

Seeing these preparations for an attack, an officer was sent by the commandant of the fort to the insurgents to represent to them the folly and danger of the rebellion, to counsel them to deliver up their leaders, and to promise the royal clemency should they disperse. These overtures were not listened to, the disaffection of the inhabitants was too decided and general to think of relinquishing their designs. There was no sympathy between the people of the two nations; speaking different languages, and cherishing so many social and national antipathies. Restive under the government of their foreign rulers, and feeling a false confidence in their superior force, and *having little else to employ them*, the people ran to arms in a spirit of reckless frolic and bravado, without duly considering their true situation, and the great evils to which they were exposing themselves.

An old damaged field-piece, ploughed up at the French Meadows on the St. Catharine's, probably left there by the French at the period of the Natchez massacre, and two swivels, captured from a boat ascending the Mississippi, which was waylaid below Natchez, at a point where the strength of the current compelled the crew to land, were mounted near Row's house to the southeast of the fort, where the assailants were protected by a deep ravine.

From this point the attack was carried on against the fort, Blomart being in command, aided by Captain Winfrey and Lieutenant Smith. A small house, behind which some of the besiegers had sheltered themselves, was demolished by the guns of the fort, and a shot from the assailants passed through the commandant's house in the fort, and a corporal in the garrison was killed, the only life lost, it is said, during the attack.

The fort was strong, the ramparts eight or ten feet thick, of solid earth, and protected by a stockade of thick cypress timber. The guns of the assailants were too light, and at too great a distance to do much damage, and the siege was continued for more than a week with more noise than effect, when an emissary or spy of the insurgents found means to introduce himself into the fort, and represented to the commandant that the fort was undermined and would be blown up in a few days. A number of persons having been seen as if engaged in some proceeding in a deep ravine which ran near the works, gave some coloring to this report, and other circumstances tended to persuade the garrison and the commandant that it was not unfounded. A parley ensued, when a capitulation was agreed upon. The fort was surrendered to the British party, and, after delivering up their arms, and taking an oath not to serve again against the British during the war, the prisoners were sent under escort to Loftus Heights, and suffered to proceed to Baton Rouge.

The fort was strong, and said to be well provided with provisions and ammunition, and capable of sustaining a long siege. The commandant excused the surrender, however, affirming that his men were worn down and exhausted by several days of fatigue and watching, and that his supplies were nearly exhausted. The apprehension of the explosion of the mine is generally regarded as the cause of surrender. Even to this day, the tradition is preserved among the Choctaws, who yet enjoy the ruse practised upon the commandant.

The escort with the captured garrison had scarcely reached Loftus Heights (now Fort Adams), when a considerable Spanish force, accompanied by a large body of Indians, was seen ascending the river.

The party met with at Loftus Heights proved to be a detachment of French militia from Opelousas, with a body of Indians, making a force of about three hundred; they landed and surprised a detachment of twenty men stationed at Captain Winfrey's house, fourteen of whom were killed. The inhabitants were forced to retire into forts, of which there were two between the French Meadows and Natchez; but being greatly harassed, aroused themselves to resistance, and the Spanish party were forced to retire, and take a position at the White Cliffs on the Mississippi. About the middle of June, the Natchez inhabitants had assembled a force of about two hundred men to attack them, when they were filled with consternation by the arrival of an express from Pensacola, bringing intelligence of the fall of that place. Finding that the British flag could no longer protect them, and that they were struggling as unsupported insurgents against the monarchy of Spain, the attack was relinquished, and Mulligan, the leader of the Opelousas party, was suffered to occupy Fort Panmure. With the fate of the victims of O'Reiley staring them in the face, many sought safety by flight. Among these were Lyman and many of his associates from Connecticut, who determined to make their escape to Savannah. The caravan was a large one, including women and children, and being compelled to take a very circuitous route to avoid the hostile Indians, they suffered incredible hardships, of which an interesting detail has been given in the travels of President Dwight, of Yale College.

Although the greater part of the inhabitants were involved in the rebellion, there were some memorable exceptions. Among these was Alexander McIntosh, who prudently kept aloof, and had consequently acquired the displeasure of his neighbors. They were now, however, glad to avail themselves of his services, and he was sent to New Orleans to negotiate an amnesty, and to sue for forgiveness of the offenders, many of whom were screened through his influence and exertions.

In the mean time, Mulligan's pledges of protection were ineffectual; for thirty days plundering parties roamed through the country, seizing the property and destroying the houses of the inhabitants, until Colonel De Grand Pré arrived with a battalion of troops, and took regular possession of the country.

The leaders of the insurrection who had not fled were

arrested, sent to New Orleans, and imprisoned. Among these was Blomart, styled in the proceedings had against his estate, the "Chief of the Rebels." It is believed he was subsequently sent to Spain for trial. Winfrey, George Alston, Smith and others were also sent to New Orleans in confinement. Bingaman was spared through the intercession of McIntosh; and Colonel Anthony Hutchins, subsequently discovered to have taken a part in the insurrection, was compelled to make his escape to Georgia, which he effected with some difficulty, whence he went to England and remained some years.

By the exertion of some unknown influence, Piernass, when Governor-General of Louisiana, suffered his property, with the exception of twelve negroes sent to New Orleans, to remain in the possession of Mrs. Hutchins. Subsequently, his extensive British grants were confirmed to his children, and in the end Colonel Hutchins was permitted himself to return to the country. He acquired considerable influence, and on some occasions was quite useful about the period of the surrender of the country to the United States.

One of the Alstons had escaped among a tribe of Indians called the "Chits," an abbreviation of the Chitimaches, it is supposed, carrying with him the principal part of his negro property. On the death of his wife, which occurred shortly after, the Spanish commandant at Natchez appointed Mr. McIntosh the guardian of her children, leaving the remaining property in his charge for their support, and annulling some fraudulent sales by which he had disposed of a portion of the property to keep it out of the reach of the Spanish authorities.

All sales executed at the time the rebels were in possession of the fort at Natchez were declared invalid. In the confiscation of the estates of Parker Carradine and

John Smith, sent to New Orleans as "rebels," and imprisoned, the rights of their wives to a separate property in their estates were recognized, and such property was left in their possession. The families of all the fugitives, it seems, were regarded with indulgence, and the part of the property held by them at least was assigned for their support.

The large British grant to Lyman of twenty thousand acres was confiscated, but upon application to Grand Pré, the sale of one-half of the tract was arrested, and it was granted to Salome, the daughter of Thaddeus Lyman, left destitute in the country with her grandfather Waterman Crane.

Butler, who derives his information chiefly from the oral account given him by the late Calvin Smith, states that many of the insurgents joined with Colbert, a Scotchman who was living with an Indian family among the Chickasaws, and established themselves at the Chickasaw Bluffs, now Memphis, and became quite formidable, stopping and plundering the passing boats at pleasure. To prevent the other refugees among the Indians from joining these predatory parties on the river, they were invited by proclamation to return to their homes in peace.

In September, 1782, Don Estevan Miro, Governor-General of Louisiana, *ad interim*, was at Natchez in the capacity of civil and military commandant. He was succeeded in the latter office in the following November by Don Pedro Piernass.

The war of the Revolution was now terminated, and by the preliminary articles of peace between Great Britain, France and Spain, of the 20th of January, 1783, the King of Great Britain acknowledged the independence of the United States, and recognized as their southern boundary the *thirty-first degree of north latitude.* The definitive treaty between Great Britain and the United States was signed at Paris on the 3d of September following.

Great Britain having, in the latter, warranted the province of *West Florida* to Spain, the claims of Spain and the United States were not easily recognized, as the King of Spain claimed to the line drawn east from the Yazoo River, as the north boundary of that province, it having been so extended by Great Britain in the commission of Governor Johnston of the 10th of June, 1764, and had remained unchanged to the date of the treaty. "The United States contended that *they* had the right of going as far as the thirty-first degree, and Spain could not urge her warranty from Great Britain against the United States, who had a *previous title* from her warrantor."*

Piernass having withdrawn to New Orleans in June, 1783, Francisco Collett, a captain in the garrison, became civil and military commandant *ad interim.* On the 3d of August, he was superseded by Don Philip Trevino, Lieutenant-Colonel of the Regiment of Louisiana.

That the Natchez District would soon cóme under the government of the United States, as embraced within her limits as established by the treaty recognizing her independence, was now the confident expectation and desire of many of the inhabitants, and the influence which a free and stable government would exert on the prosperity of the country was thus early foreseen. Mr. William Dunbar writes to his friend in June, 1783. "I am sorry to say that our plantation (near Baton Rouge) falls considerably *without* the American line, *in conse-*

* Judge Martin.

quence of which it may not be worth a *pinch of snuff* as a salable commodity. * * As Natchez is considerably above latitude thirty-one degrees, we believe here it must soon become a settlement of great consequence, although we have not learned the intentions of Congress respecting it. Mrs. Pollock gives out that her husband (Oliver Pollock, a merchant of New Orleans), is coming out as governor," &c. Again, on the 15th of August following, he adds: "The definitive treaty of peace has not yet reached us; the officers of government, also, declare themselves in the dark, having received no orders from their court consequential to the peace."

Such was the confidence of Mr. Dunbar, that this change was to be the immediate and natural consequence of the treaty, that he meditated an early removal above the thirty-first degree of latitude, a design which was not long after carried into effect. Many others, influenced by similar considerations, removed to the district.

In August, 1783, Don Philip Trevino assumed the duties of civil and military commandant of the district, and Spain continued to maintain her possession.

After the eighteen months had expired which, by the treaty, were allowed for the British subjects to dispose of their property, the Spanish government by proclamation *twice* prolonged the period two years or more, and it was not until after the second term that the lands were considered as reverted to the crown, and were granted out to petitioners.* The lands of the leaders of the rebellion were declared forfeited, and sold.

It was not until the 20th of April, 1784, four or five months after the date of our treaty establishing the southern boundary at lat. 31°, that Governor Estevan Miro

* Mr. Dunbar.

issued the first order of survey for lands in the district. From this period until the 1st of September, 1795, numerous orders of survey and patents were executed, the people becoming gradually reconciled to the Spanish government, and finding it more liberal and tolerant than they had been led to believe.

Emigration increased rapidly the facility with which lands were obtained by the actual settler, and their great productiveness attracted many to the country. "The prudent and circumspect had nothing to fear from the government; it depended upon themselves to render a residence in the country agreeable." As to the laws and their execution, it was said: "British property here is in the utmost security; an Englishman may come here and recover his debts, and obtain as much justice as in Westminster Hall."* The execution of the laws, it is true, was summary, but in the main just. The fraudulent who attempted to make way with their effects, or to abscond to avoid their creditors, were promptly dealt with. The property of such was seized, appraised by their neighbors appointed for the purpose, was sold after proper notice, and the proceeds were distributed, *pro rata*, on the spot to their creditors.

Most of the matters involved in dispute, such as the settlement of accounts or other claims, were adjudicated and settled on a petition to the commandant by arbitrators appointed by him; and the Spanish archives show that the men of the highest standing and greatest probity in the country were most usually employed in the settlement of these disputes.

On more than one occasion, the government interposed to protect the debtors from their too importunate foreign

* Mr. Dunbar.

creditors, by procuring further indulgence at times when the embarrassments of the inhabitants had become general, and the consequence of some transient cause; but in these cases an inventory of the property of the debtor was furnished on oath, and it was regarded as pledged for the debts. It had the effect of a judgment, and the property was subject to sale on failure to meet the debt at the stipulated time.

In October, 1785, Don Francis Bouligny came as commandant to Natchez; he was succeeded, in the March following (1786), by Don Carlos de Grand Pré, who returned again to resume that office which he henceforth filled until 1792, six years.

By the census taken in 1785, it was found that the population had greatly increased, that of the District of Natchez amounting to fifteen hundred and fifty persons. A garrison of sixty soldiers was maintained at Fort Panmure, at an annual expense to the Spanish crown of six thousand five hundred dollars.

This year a number of agents of the Jamaica merchants came to collect the debts due them. Governor Miro found it necessary to interpose for the protection of the debtors, and he allowed a resort to the last extremity only against those who acted fraudulently or with bad faith. He also extended the time allowed for British subjects to remain in the country and dispose of their property. This indulgence was approved by the King of Spain, who further directed that such persons should be permitted to remain permanently in the province upon taking the customary oath of allegiance and fidelity.

To render the priests more acceptable to the people, Irish clergymen were procured who spoke the English language, in order to induce the inhabitants and families to embrace the Catholic faith.

In June, 1786, Galvez was succeeded by Don Estevan Miro as Governor of Louisiana and West Florida.

Although the treaty of 1786 provided expressly that the navigation of the Mississippi should forever remain free and open to the subjects of Great Britain and the citizens of the United States, yet, with the exclusive policy characteristic of the Spanish nation, the claim of the United States to its enjoyment was resisted, and the boats of the western people, who ventured to descend the Mississippi, were arrested by the first officer who met with them, and, together with the cargo, were confiscated in every case. This state of things, so exasperating to the people of Kentucky, and of that quarter to whom the Mississippi afforded the only outlet for their surplus productions, continued until the Governor of Louisiana began to apprehend that the western people, already highly inflamed by the denial of this reasonable and, to them, essential right, might be excited, forcibly, to open a way for their trade. Under these circumstances, General Wilkinson conceived the idea of a regular trade to New Orleans, and with this view descended the Mississippi with a venture of tobacco, flour, bacon, &c. He stopped at Natchez, and the boat was suffered to proceed down the stream to New Orleans, the commandant of the former place forbearing to seize it under the belief that Governor Miro would be induced to make an exception in the case in which a distinguished general officer of the United States was interested. When the boat arrived in New Orleans, in advance of its owners, steps were taken for its seizure, and a guard sent on board by the revenue officers.

A merchant of some influence, and a friend of Wilkinson, called upon the governor, and intimated that the proposed step might be attended with unpleasant consequences, enlarged upon the exasperation of the people of Kentucky in consequence of the seizure of the property of those who attempted the navigation of the river, and hinted that the general possessed great popularity and influence among those who were capable of inflaming the whole of the western inhabitants; that, probably, the sending the boat to New Orleans, that it might be seized, was a scheme of the government of the United States to produce such an excitement as to induce the people to choose Wilkinson as a leader, and to overrun and desolate the country.

Alarmed by these representations, the governor directed the guard to be withdrawn, and the boat was delivered to Wilkinson's friend to sell the cargo without paying duty. In his first interview with Governor Miro after his arrival, Wilkinson artfully encouraged the delusion which had influenced his action.

The apprehensions of Miro being thus thoroughly awakened, he thought he could not do better than to secure the influence of Wilkinson in restraining his turbulent and dangerous countrymen from making an attack upon Louisiana.

Such, it is said, was the origin of the contract between Wilkinson and the Spanish government, and which secured him a monopoly of introducing the productions of the western country into New Orleans; a privilege which, however beneficial to both parties, and, perhaps, advantageous to the country at large, wrought much injury to the agricultural interest of the Natchez District.

The cultivation of tobacco had been found to succeed in the districts, and, to encourage it, the King of Spain became the purchaser of all that was delivered and passed inspection at his warehouses in New Orleans, at an established and liberal price.

The production of tobacco under this arrangement was found so lucrative that it was engaged in extensively, and for a few years the prosperity of the country was rapidly advancing. This, however, could not withstand the blighting and injurious effects of the competition with the Kentucky tobacco introduced under Wilkinson's contract, when the patronage of the king was withdrawn.

The cultivation of tobacco consequently gave way to that of indigo, which, however disagreeable and offensive, was much more profitable. To this succeeded cotton, which, up to the present day, promises to maintain its stand against all competition.

In 1788, another census was taken, and the population of the Natchez District was found to amount to 2,679 persons, an increase of 1,129 in about three years.

In 1789, General Wilkinson visited New Orleans for the second time, and was informed by Governor Miro that he was instructed to admit the immigration of settlers from the western country.

Accordingly, several tracts of land were granted to such settlers as presented themselves; these established themselves chiefly in the Natchez District and Feliciana. Many, however, under the pretence of settling permanently in the country, took advantage of the permission to make several trips and to introduce their goods and produce duty free, and in this manner a market was gradually opened for the produce of the Ohio.

On the 1st of January, 1792, the Baron de Carondelet was appointed Governor of Louisiana, and the following July we find Don Manuel Gayoso de Lemos, governor at Natchez.

At this time, the possessions of Spain on the Mississippi were seriously menaced in different quarters, of which the governor was early informed by the Spanish minister to the United States.

Genet, the Minister of the French Republic, conceived the project of reacquiring for his country the possessions she had lost in Louisiana by an expedition to be fitted out in the United States; and to this end commissions were issued by him to some of the citizens of the United States disposed to embark in the enterprise.

Danger was apprehended also of British invasion from Canada.

The United States having failed by negotiation to get possession of that part of its territory comprising the Natchez District, or to secure the enjoyment of the free navigation of the Mississippi, the inhabitants of Kentucky, or the "Western Country," became impatient and restive. Their increasing productions demanded an outlet to a foreign market, which they were resolved on some terms to obtain. But, however united on this point, they differed in their projects for attaining it. Some meditated the dismemberment of the country, and the establishment of a government independent of the United States. Of these, some favored a connection with Spain and a submission to her laws; others were inclined to the French interest. And still another party, to which some of the English royalists of the Natchez District adhered, looked with a distant and vague hope to the re-establishment of the British rule.

To counteract these adverse projects, and to foment and encourage others calculated to strengthen and perpetuate the Spanish authority, engaged Governor Carondelet in a course of intrigue during his entire administration.

His first step, after putting the country under his jurisdiction in an improved state of defence, was to dispatch an emissary, an intelligent Englishman named Power, to Kentucky, to confer secretly with the most influential individuals who were disposed to a separation from the Atlantic States, and an alliance with Spain; to give assurances of the concurrence of the government of Louisiana, and to make a tender of arms, ammunition, and money.

The affairs of the province were further complicated by the demand made by Georgia, through her commissioner Colonel Thomas Green, for the surrender of that part of the province lying north of latitude 31°, as being within her chartered limits.

The demand was treated with derision, but this bold assumption of Colonel Green, a Spanish subject, who had but recently emigrated from Tennessee, rendered him an object of suspicion, and on the first plausible pretext he was placed in confinement.

The vigilance of the government of the United States rendered Genet's scheme abortive, and his agents in the south were arrested in consequence of measures taken by the legislature of South Carolina.

Power, on his return, having recommended that an officer of rank should be sent to the mouth of the Ohio, to meet with several influential individuals of Kentucky whom he had visited, and who still entertained the design of a separation of the western people from the Union, Don Manuel Gayoso de Lémos, then the commandant at Natchez, was accordingly dispatched by Baron de Carondelet, early in the summer of 1795, on this mission, but with the ostensible object of erecting a fort at the Chickasaw Bluffs.

Power, sent by Gayoso for the purpose, met with Sebastian at the Red Banks. Innis, Nicholas, and others expected, were prevented by various causes from being present. Sebastian, however, claiming authority to treat with Gayoso in their names, was conducted by Power to the latter, who was found engaged with his party in some trivial works on the right side of the Mississippi, opposite the mouth of the Ohio. Gayoso proposed that Sebastian should accompany him down the river to a conference with Governor Carondelet, and after a short delay they proceeded together, accompanied by Power as far as Natchez, where they stopped. In January, 1796, Gayoso, Sebastian, and Power, went to New Orleans, from whence the two latter sailed for Philadelphia.

With a knowledge of these circumstances, the motives for procrastination, and the impediments thrown in the way of the surrender of the country to the United States, in pursuance of the treaty of San Lorenzo, which was concluded the 27th of October, 1795, will be better understood.

By the latter treaty, the southern boundary of the United States, as given in their treaty of peace with Great Britain, was fully recognized, and the navigation of the Mississippi for its *whole breadth*, from its source to the gulf, was declared free to the subjects of the King of Spain and the citizens of the United States.

The Spanish officers in New Orleans, however, had embraced the belief that this treaty was entered into at a critical junction in the affairs in Europe, to secure the neutrality of the United States, and to counteract the projects of Great Britain, in which latter they believed it had failed, and that Spain, no longer interested in fulfilling its stipulations, would not carry it into effect.

Under this persuasion, Baron de Carondelet renewed his negotiations with the Kentucky malcontents. Power was again sent among them to keep alive the scheme of secession by the western people. He delivered the packets given him in charge by the Spanish governor for General Wilkinson, at Greenville. On his return, however, he reported an entire change in the dispositions and views of the people of Kentucky, who, he now found, were perfectly satisfied with the Federal government, since it had obtained for them, by the late treaty, the principal object to attain which only the separation from the Union had heretofore been thought of; and such a measure was now viewed with utter aversion.

Not yet satisfied of the futility of his machinations, Carondelet determined on still another and final effort to detach the western people from the Atlantic States. Power was again sent on this errand. Bribery was to be adroitly employed; assurances were to be given that, "if a hundred thousand dollars, properly distributed in Kentucky, could induce the people to resist, it should be furnished;" and money and arms, including twenty pieces of artillery, were freely offered. General Wilkinson, then the commander of the forces of the United States, was to be dazzled with the prospect of the brilliant and easy career opened upon him; the glory of being the liberator and founder of the Western States was to be presented to his view; at the least movement, he was to be told, the people would hail him as the general of the new republic, his reputation would raise him an army, and France and Spain would enable him to pay it. Power again met Sebastian at Louisville, when certain stipulations were considered, without which none could be expected to embark in the enterprise. The former then proceeded to meet General Wilkinson at Detroit, and the latter was to communicate the baron's propositions to Innis and Nicholas.

On learning the arrival of Power, Wilkinson caused

him to be arrested, and brought into the fort; gave him a cold reception; and treated the baron's project as chimerical and impossible to be executed. The people having obtained, by the treaty, all they wanted, had no need of connection or alliance with Spain. He was told that a full compliance with the treaty, and the delivery of the country under existing circumstances, was all that remained for the governor to do.

In September, 1797, Wilkinson, delivering his answer for the baron to Power, sent him out of the country under a military guard.

The treaty with Spain had stipulated that the commissioners of both nations should meet at Natchez, within six months after the ratification. Andrew Ellicott was appointed commissioner on the part of the United States, and Gayoso on that of Spain. Furnished with a military escort, Ellicott left Pittsburg on the 23d of October, 1796. For the accommodation of his party and stores, he was provided with four boats, including a barge with a comfortable cabin, in which General Wilkinson had just ascended the river. About the close of December, his progress was arrested at the mouth of the Ohio by ice, in which his boats were blocked up for some time.

Here Ellicott met with Philip Noland, a man who had acquired considerable celebrity for his enterprise and travels among the Indians in the Spanish territory, where he had been engaged in taking wild horses; he had with him two trading-boats, and was induced by Ellicott to accompany him down the river, and proved very useful.

On the 2d of February, the expedition arrived at New Madrid. Ellicott's party was saluted by a discharge of artillery from the Spanish garrison, and was hospitably entertained by the commandant and officers of the garrison. Here the commandant communicated to him a letter received from the Governor-General Baron de Carondelet, in the preceding November, directing him not to permit the party to descend the river until the posts were evacuated, which could not be done until the water rose. The commandant remarked that he felt much embarrassed by the order, but, as the objection on the score of low water no longer existed, he agreed, upon the representations of Ellicott as to the delays he had already experienced, not to oppose any obstacle to his proceeding.

On the 8th of February, the party arrived at the Chickasaw Bluff. The commandant received the commissioner with politeness, but appeared embarrassed by his arrival and surprised that he had been suffered to pass New Madrid.

At the Walnut Hills (now Vicksburg), which was reached on the 19th, considerable works were found to have been erected by the Spaniards. The post was considered a very important one, and capable of being made very strong. The boats were brought to by the firing of a piece of artillery; but the same politeness and hospitality received at the other posts were extended to Ellicott and his party. The commandant, however, *affected* an ignorance of its object and even of the existence of the treaty.

A short distance below the Walnut Hills, Ellicott was overtaken by an express sent after him in a light boat, with a letter which had just been received at the fort. The communication was from Governor Gayoso, informing Ellicott that he was not prepared to evacuate the posts immediately for want of vessels, but which were soon expected, and to request him to leave the troops (composing his escort) about the mouth of the Bayou Pierre. The object was stated to be to prevent any unforeseen misunderstanding between the Spanish troops and those of the United States.

Although the request was deemed indecorous and unreasonable, the escort was left at the Bayou Pierre, where they arrived in the afternoon of the 22d of February. At this place, a friend of the commissioner, Colonel Peter Bryan Bruin, an officer of the revolutionary army, and subsequently one of the judges of the Mississippi Territory, had resided for some years, and from him Ellicott derived much useful information respecting the principal inhabitants of the country, and their sentiments towards the United States, and the measures proper to be adopted to carry out the important trust committed to him. In order to be of further service, it was agreed that Colonel Bruin should repair to Natchez, which, to prevent suspicion, and not to be seen with Ellicott until after the interview of the latter with the governor, he did, in one of Noland's boats, and the day after their arrival was formally introduced by Gayoso to Ellicott as an entire stranger.

Immediately after arriving at the Natchez landing, on the evening of the 24th of February, 1797, the commissioner addressed a note to Governor Gayoso, apprising him of his arrival, and requesting him to state when it would be convenient to receive his credentials.

On the same day the reception of the note was acknowledged through Mr. Vidal, the Secretary of the governor; but, as he avoided fixing a time for the proposed interview, several verbal messages were exchanged before this point was arranged. It was finally agreed that a meeting should take place at the government house, on the afternoon of the 25th.

The credentials of the commissioner were then presented, and the governor being pressed to name a day on which their operations should commence, named the 19th of the following month.

Having, on the 27th, notified the Governor-General, the Baron de Carondelet, of his arrival, by letter directed to New Orleans, Ellicott on the same day fixed his encampment on the hill at the upper end of the town, about a quarter of a mile from the fort. This encampment was a short distance to the northeast of the present site of the mansion house. On the 29th, the American flag was hoisted, and about two hours after a message was received from the governor directing it to be taken down, a request that met with a positive refusal, and the flag "wore out upon the staff."

The suspicions which the occurrences at the different Spanish posts in coming down the river had inspired, that the delivery of the country was to be delayed if not refused, were now confirmed.

Before encamping, Ellicott was informed, through a confidential channel, that Carondelet had stated in private conversation, before the arrival of Ellicott, that the treaty would not be carried into effect. Gayoso had made a similar statement in a letter to a *confidential* friend. The delay on their part, it was said, would render the treaty a dead letter. It was also asserted that the country either was or would be ceded to France.

From prudential considerations, and not to excite suspicions injurious to those from whom it was derived, this information was kept a profound secret. All the evasions and subterfuges which, it will be seen, were subsequently adopted, as shown in the correspondence with Carondelet and Gayoso, although assigned to different causes, were designed to gain time whilst Power was endeavoring to carry out the schemes of the governor-general in Kentucky.

The first step taken by Ellicott, under these untoward circumstances, was to sound the disposition of the inhabitants, when it was found that a large majority of them were desirous of becoming citizens of the United States. Although many of them had removed from the British colonies before the conclusion of the peace with Great Britain, with the suspicion of having been on the *wrong side* on the question of independence, and that not a few of the influential class were Englishmen who had been connected with the army or held office under the government of West Florida, yet now, under altered circumstances, and with better views, there were very few who did not prefer the free government of the United States to the intolerant and arbitrary one of Spain.

The party of Ellicott encamped in Natchez, *exclusive* of the escort under Lieutenant McClary, left at Bayou Pierre, consisted of about *thirty* persons, generally armed with rifles, and expert in the use of them; and the commissary was directed to procure privately, as large a supply of ammunition as could be done among their friends.

The Indians, of whom considerable numbers were always loitering about the town, having been insolent and made threats against the American party, Ellicott seized upon the occasion to justify an application to Gayoso to withdraw his objections to his escort's joining him at Natchez.

In reply, Gayoso stated that the conduct attributed to the Indians was very unusual there; but that he had foreseen some such difficulty from the time that Ellicott manifested a desire of having his colors flying, "before all the transactions were terminated," (alluding to the evacuation of the Spanish garrison.) As to the escort, he had not the least objection to its being withdrawn from its actual position; being answerable for the tranquillity of the country, however, he felt sensibly hurt at the *necessity* of withholding his consent to its landing at Natchez, feeling positively confident that some disagreeable circumstances would happen by the conjunction proposed.

He expressed his regret that the arrival of Ellicott had been delayed until after war had ensued between Spain and Great Britain, which had so added to the cares and duties of the governor-general that he could not leave New Orleans long enough to attend to the running of the boundary line, and that that duty had now devolved upon him, Gayoso, but that as yet he was unprovided with everything requisite for the business. The geometer, and other officers to be employed, were already on their way from New Orleans to Clarkesville, a point near latitude 31°, where the operations were to be commenced, and that he would himself repair thither as soon as his equipage should arrive.

He suggested, therefore, that Ellicott should repair to Clarkesville or Loftus Cliffs, where his escort might join him without apprehension of any disagreeable collision.

By the refusal, contained in this letter, of permission to land the escort at Natchez, Ellicott found himself in a dilemma, having already sent an express to direct Lieutenant McClary to join him with his command, and his arrival was momentarily expected.

He replied, therefore, immediately to the letter of Gayoso, objecting to leaving Natchez, as that place was designated in the treaty for the meeting of the joint commission; but he added that, as the *conduct of the*

Indians had ceased to be objectionable, he was now the *less anxious* that his escort should be stationed at his *present encampment*, and proposed that it should be directed to come down to Bacon's Landing, a short distance below Natchez, from whence it could secure its requisite supplies.

To this the governor politely assented by a communication through his aid, Major Minor.

On the next day the escort arrived and took up its encampment at Bacon's Landing.

Major Stephen Minor, above mentioned, was a native of Pennsylvania; he first visited New Orleans in 1780, to procure military stores for the American posts on the Ohio and Monongahela. On his return, with a caravan of loaded mules, not far from the present post of Arkansas, his stores were plundered and his men all murdered; his own escape being due to a most fortuitous detention by sickness, a few hours behind his party.

He afterwards repaired to New Orleans, joined Galvez in his expedition against Mobile, where his remarkable skill with the rifle, and his acts of gallantry during the siege, attracted the notice, and secured the favor of the general, by whom his position in the Spanish army was advanced.

In 1783, he was sent to Natchez, where his rank seems to have been that of "Aid-Major" to the post. He remained at Natchez during the whole term of the Spanish jurisdiction, acting during the latter period as aid to Governor Gayoso, by whom, when appointed as Governor-General of Louisiana, he was left as acting commandant of the post of Natchez; and De Grand Pré, appointed to succeed Gayoso, not assuming the duties of the office, Major Minor continued to act until the country was evacuated.

Subsequently, he acted as commissioner on the boundary line in place of Gayoso.

He is said to have endeared himself to his countrymen, the American settlers, by his acts of friendliness and protection, and was applied to on all occasions, in cases of difficulty.

Many were the instances in which his influence with the governor prevailed, where the party menaced had, through too great a spirit of independence, or perhaps, turbulence, become involved in a collision with the Spanish authorities.

Lieutenant McClary had been but a few days at his new quarters, at Bacon's Landing, when complaint was made that he had caused to be arrested and detained against their will, several persons claimed to be deserters from the American army.

About the same time, the artillery taken from the fort to the landing for shipment, was taken back and remounted.

On the 23d of March, Ellicott, in a letter to Gayoso, cites this fact, mentions some insolent treatment which American citizens had recently met with at the Walnut Hills, and adverts to the delay in entering upon the running of the boundary line, as giving grounds for apprehension that the treaty would not be observed with good faith by the Spanish government, and asks from the governor an explanation. He further inquired if it was not true that every exertion was then making, to put the post at Walnut Hills in a complete state of defence.

The explanations of Gayoso were considered inconsistent and unsatisfactory.

It was now known that Lieutenant Pope, with a detachment of troops, was descending the river.

Averse to any reinforcement of the American troops, Gayoso dispatched his aid, Major Minor, to the Walnut Hills, with a request to Lieutenant Pope, to delay his arrival until he was prepared for the evacuation of the Spanish posts.

Ellicott declined uniting with the governor in this request, as desired, but at the same time wrote to the lieutenant, that the sooner he arrived at Natchez the better.

About this time, an individual arrived at Natchez with a confidential communication for Ellicott. He appears to have had some connection with the designs of William Blount, of Tennessee; but, learning from the commissioner that their estimation of the character of that individual did not accord, the communication was not made.

He remained at Natchez a few weeks, in close association with Colonel Anthony Hutchins and Mr. Rapalje, both of whom were in the British military establishment.

Ellicott admits that he was much embarrassed by the mysterious conduct of this individual, whose name he withholds, but intimates that he held some office in the United States, and was paid for his services, whatever they were, by the public.

On the 29th of March, 1797, Gayoso issued a proclamation, assigning as a motive, his apprehensions that the dangerous insinuations of busy and malignant persons might agitate and disturb the public tranquillity. The public were cautioned against being led by their "*innocent credulity*," into any measures which might frustrate all the advantages they would have a right to expect, if they continued, as heretofore, their strict attachment to his majesty. These advantages are stated to be the support of his majesty to the rights of the inhabitants in their real property, and protection from distress on account of their depending debts. Assurances were given that although the established Catholic religion only could be publicly allowed, yet none should be molested on account of their religious principles, or hindered in its private exercise. And finally, the inhabitants were admonished not to deviate from the principles of adhesion to the government, until the negotiations *now on foot* between the United States and Spain were concluded, and thereby the *real property of the inhabitants secured.*

This proclamation, although artfully conceived by the governor, and calculated to attach two large classes of the community to his interests (the landholders and the debtors), yet failed fully to quiet the minds of the people. The fact, now distinctly announced, that the evacuation of the country was indefinitely postponed, or at least during the pending negotiations, produced much irritation.

To counteract this effect, when the governor became aware of it, he caused Ellicott to be informed that he had received orders from the Baron de Carondelet to have the artillery and stores removed from the forts, which were to be given up to the American troops on their arrival.

Under this excitement, a number of respectable inhabitants called upon Ellicott, and presented an address, drawn up, it was said, by Narsworthy Hunter, afterwards the delegate to Congress. In style, this address was inflated, and it must be confessed the enumeration of grievances exaggerated. It ended by calling upon Ellicott, "in the name of every friend of *that emblem of peace and science* (the American flag?) which had been recently displayed to them, to stand forth with a confidence suitable to the dignity of his commission, and demand of the governor passports with leave for all such as would dispose of their property and avail themselves of a change of situation by withdrawing to the United States."

Extracts from this address were communicated by Ellicott to Governor Gayoso. In doing so, he took occasion to state that, since his arrival in the district, he had uniformly counselled the inhabitants to submission to the government now in force, until the jurisdiction of the United States should be extended over them, the period of which could not be distant, and which they were led to expect. But his excellency's proclamation, the remounting the guns in the fort, and sending his aid to the Walnut Hills to stop the descent of the American troops, had produced doubts as to the intended delivery of the country to the United States.

The governor denied that there was a word of truth in the address. No notice, he said, had been taken of the satisfaction which some had expressed of speedily becoming citizens of the United States; nor had any one been molested on that account. There had been no instance of opposition being made to any person to the selling their property and removing from the country; the *demand* for such permission was therefore unnecessary. The proclamation had been deemed necessary to quiet the people, and to explain the cause of delay; and he was now authorized to state that the general-in-chief found it necessary to consult his majesty on a point of difference between himself and General Wayne, the latter requiring the surrender of the posts as they stood, and the Baron de Carondelet claiming that they should be dismantled and razed.

The intentions of the Spanish government being now

clearly understood, it became a matter of interest to secure the country to the United States, and to protect those of the inhabitants who had avowed their attachment to it; some of whom had indiscreetly committed themselves by intemperate expressions towards their present rulers.

Offers were made to Ellicott of aid in expelling the Spanish garrison, and taking forcible possession of the country. Among these, Col. Green, who, in 1793, had acted as the commissioner in behalf of Georgia, and had manifested an imprudent zeal in favor of the immediate surrender of the country, made an offer to Ellicott of his services, with a hundred volunteers, to seize upon it. Indiscreetly permitting his designs to become known to the governor, his arrest was ordered; but he had the fortune to escape to Tennessee.

The most extraordinary proposition was that which Ellicott states was made to him by Col. Anthony Hutchins, which was no other than to seize the governor by surprise, and convey him a prisoner among the Chickasaws.

Ellicott, who seems to have been at all times suspicious of the motives of the colonel, was particularly so on this occasion, for reasons which he assigns. The proposition was one of so singular a nature as not to be entertained for a moment. It was of course rejected; but in a manner not to give offence, as Col. Hutchins possessed much popularity with one class of the inhabitants, and might, at the proper time, be useful to the cause of the United States.

It being deemed prudent to increase the strength of the military escort, the officer commanding it enlisted several recruits.

This was complained of by the governor as an infringement of the sovereignty of the Spanish monarch, and he requested that the men should be discharged.

This was evaded, however, and the governor was informed that those enlisted were persons who could not be considered subjects of his Catholic majesty.

Some of the soldiers at Bacon's Landing becoming sick, the escort was removed on to the high land, about a mile and a half from the river, and the same distance from Ellicott's quarters.

Intelligence being received of the arrival of Lieut. Pope at the Walnut Hills, Ellicott immediately dispatched an express to inform him of the probability of an early rupture between the United States and Spain, and to advise him to come to Natchez immediately, that the inhabitants, nine-tenths of whom were attached to the United States, might, in the event of a rupture, have a *rallying-point.*

Doubting the propriety of this step after it was taken, Ellicott saw that it would be better, at all events, to have the sanction of the governor; an interview was had with him; the peculiar situation of Lieutenant Pope was forcibly represented. It was shown that, being a military man on a separate command, ordered to a certain duty by his superior, he must perform it or make the attempt; he had no choice; come or attempt it he must; and it would be better that it should be done in peace than that hostilities should be provoked by meeting with opposition.

The governor, under this view of the case, gave a reluctant consent that he should proceed down the river without interruption. A second express, with the necessary orders, was dispatched, and being stimulated to activity by extra compensation, he arrived a very short time after the first express, and barely in time to prevent a collision between the Spanish garrison and the American detachment, the latter preparing to embark, and the former to resist it.

On the 24th of April, in the forenoon, Lieutenant Pope arrived at the Natchez landing, where he remained until next morning.

In the mean time, orders were given to the escort below the city, and at an early hour next morning, the two companies met at the north part of the town in excellent order, colors flying, attended with their music, and after the usual salutations marched a short distance in the rear of the commissioner's tent, and encamped on a commanding eminence, having both the fort and the government house in full view.

The junction of the two detachments was not foreseen or intended by Gayoso, who saw with extreme chagrin the whole parade, but too late to prevent it.

This measure, and the good appearance of the men, inspired great confidence in the citizens, who had now no doubt of being able to keep possession of the country.

On the 1st of May, Governor Gayoso made Ellicott an official communication, as he states, by order of the commander-general, the purport of which was, that he was advised that an attack was proposed against the Spanish possessions in Illinois by the British from Canada; that, as such an expedition could not proceed except by passing through the territories of the United States, an official communication had been made to the United States government, requiring that orders should be issued to have their territory respected, which no doubt was entertained would be acquiesced in; that the commander-general found himself in consequence, under the necessity of putting the fortifications at the Walnut Hills in a state of defence, to cover Lower Louisiana in case the British should succeed against Illinois, for which purpose a competent force would be sent to the Walnut Hills to repair and defend that post; that this formed an additional reason for suspending the evacuation of the posts, and running of the line; and as, in consequence, considerable delay must ensue, the proposal was made to the commissioner, either to remain at Natchez, go down to Lower Louisiana, or, as was thought preferable, to remove to Villa Gayoso, where there were sufficient buildings for the accommodation of the commissioner's party, including the trocps.

Villa Gayoso was situated about twenty miles north of Natchez, on the Mississippi Bluff; the site handsome and commanding. The place was quite new, and the buildings, which were comfortable, and of recent construction, consisted of a church, priest's house, officers' quarters, and barracks for soldiers.

As Lieutenants Pope and Ellicott did not agree in the reply proper to be made to this communication, and as the lieutenant considered that it should come from him, Ellicott merely addressed a short note to the governor, reiterating his intention, previously expressed, of remaining at Natchez, and for the rest referred him to Lieutenant Pope's communication as commander of the United States detachment, whom the governor's communication chiefly concerned.

On the 2d of May, Colonel Guillimard, the surveyor appointed in behalf of his Spanish majesty under the late treaty, arrived. On the following day, laborers and artificers were engaged in repairing the fort, and several additional pieces of artillery were mounted. On the 7th a reinforcement of forty men arrived, and on the 9th Colonel Guillimard, with several officers and a boat-load of intrenching tools, proceeded to Walnut Hills.

Ellicott lost no time in calling this fact to the notice of

the governor, and requesting a definite answer as to the time he would be ready to proceed with the running of the line.

He was informed, in reply, that the execution of the treaty would depend upon the ministers of the two nations to whom the business was intrusted, and through which channel both the commissioner and the commander-general would be informed of the time when the boundary would be run.

A company of grenadiers arrived at the fort on the 16th of May, and after a short delay proceeded to the Walnut Hills.

Philip Noland, who, from his singular management and address, possessed much of Governor Carondelet's confidence, had been some weeks in New Orleans. The governor informed him that the troubles were becoming serious at Natchez, and that he was determined to quiet them by giving the Americans *lead;* and he was asked if he would take a part; to which Noland replied ambiguously, "*a very active one.*"

On the 17th of May, more troops passed Natchez on the way to Walnut Hills. The reinforcement of that post, and the fort at Natchez, kept the inhabitants in constant fear, as they considered these preparations as designed against them.

To avert the calamities which they in consequence apprehended, many plans for attacking the Spaniards were devised and communicated to Ellicott, and rejected as premature, and calculated to involve the United States in war.

About this time, a serious difficulty took place between the Baron de Carondelet and Governor Gayoso, the true nature of which was not known, but which doubtless embarrassed their proceedings and to some extent disconcerted their plans.

On the 1st of June, a proclamation of the Baron, of the 24th of May, was communicated to Ellicott, and which, having some doubts of its authenticity, he found was not known to either Gayoso or Minor.

The proclamation, after adverting to some evil-disposed persons, who had nothing to lose, having endeavored to draw the inhabitants of Natchez into improper measures, the consequences of which would fall only on those who possessed property, whilst the perturbators would screen themselves by flight, proceeds to detail or reiterate the causes which had delayed the evacuation of the country, and the suspension of the measures for establishing the line of demarcation, attributing these delays to the imperious necessity of putting the country in a state of defence, to protect it from the apprehended attack by the English from Canada upon the Illinois, and Lower Louisiana. In conclusion, the hope was indulged that the inhabitants of Natchez would behave with tranquillity, and give proofs of their affection and attachment to the Spanish government.

In this, the governor gave proofs that he was ignorant of, or mistook, the temper and wishes of not a few of the inhabitants of the district, to some of whom nothing would have been more acceptable than the re-establishment of the British rule. The great majority of the people, however, were impatient to become citizens of the United States.

The appearance of this proclamation, so far from quieting, wrought up the public mind to the point of explosion.

At this time, an itinerant Baptist preacher, named Hannah, asked permission to preach in the American camp; but, as public worship in the Spanish provinces was allowed only to the Catholics, there appeared to be an obstacle in the way. Upon application, however, Governor Gayoso gave his consent without hesitation. As the country was in a highly inflamed state, it was stipulated by Ellicott that the preacher should not touch upon or make any allusions to political subjects in his discourse.

The novelty of a Protestant sermon drew together a large number of persons; and the preacher, being a weak, vain man, was greatly puffed up with the attention he received.

Highly elated with the reception his sermon received, which was more owing to its novelty than its merits, and emboldened by permission to speak in public, the preacher mingled with the people of the town, and his enthusiastic zeal being somewhat heightened by stimulants, entered into a religious controversy with some Irish Catholics, who, in return for the offensive manner in which he spoke of their religion, gave him a beating.

He immediately called on the governor with a peremptory demand for redress, threatening, if his request was not complied with, to seek it himself.

The governor, with great forbearance and temper, calmly desired him to reflect a few moments upon what he had said. The same language and threats being repeated, Gayoso justly became highly incensed, and ordered him into confinement.

This proceeding of the governor was construed by the inhabitants as an attack upon the privileges of an American citizen. It was the spark required to inflame the public mind and to produce the long foreseen explosion.

Early the next morning, the town was found to be in a state of great tumult and confusion. The governor and the officers of the government, with several Spanish families, took refuge in the garrison.

Thus, in a few hours, by an impolitic, but, it must be admitted, just exercise of power, the governor found his authority restricted to the narrow compass of the fort.

At this juncture, an address to the inhabitants from the Baron de Carondelet, as ill-timed and injudicious as his late proclamation, made its appearance, and, together with the late infringement of the liberty of an American citizen in the person of Hannah, the preacher, rendered the disaffection and hostility of the inhabitants general.

There was as yet, however, no system or rallying-point in the movement. Some were for attacking the fort, others for capturing the galleys and getting possession of the river.

On Sunday, the 11th of June, the day after the governor retired to the fort, a number of the most active opponents of the Spanish authority called upon Commissioner Ellicott and Lieutenant Pope, and declared their intention of commencing hostilities.

To encourage them was deemed improper, as the United States had not yet extended its jurisdiction over the country; and to offer direct opposition was impolitic, as that would have forfeited all influence and power to be useful. It was sought, therefore, to divert the attention of the people, if possible, from immediate acts of hostility, and by address and management to reduce their proceedings to some system by which they might be rendered more efficient, and at the same time might be restrained and checked if necessary.

The spirit of the people was therefore "*highly complimented*," on account of their present exertions. But, as it was necessary that the United States should have some evidence that their exertions tended to the establishment of its sovereignty, it was suggested as proper that some declaration to that effect should be signed before they could with propriety call on the United States for support.

On the following day, an interview was requested with Ellicott and Pope, by the governor, as *private gentlemen,* to see if some plan could be devised to quiet the present disturbances of the country. Lieutenant Pope refused the invitation, and Ellicott therefore informed Major Minor, the bearer of the message, that he must decline attending alone.

The following day, Gayoso informed Ellicott by letter, that there was no doubt that the inhabitants of the district were in a state of rebellion, with the probable design of attacking the fort; that several of the insurgents were riding through the country, obtaining signatures to lists already subscribed by many styling themselves "Citizens of the United States;" that he could not believe that the proceedings had the sanction of the commissioner; but should he take an active part in them, as he was represented to do, that he, Gayoso, protested, in the name of the governor-general, against his conduct, and would hold him answerable for the consequences. A *positive* answer was requested.

Ellicott replied that, under the late treaty, the people of the district had a right to consider themselves citizens of the United States; the compact between the two nations was notorious. The governor had recognized him as the agent of his government to carry that compact into effect. No human assurances could have gone further than those repeatedly made by his excellency, that the treaty would be faithfully executed. Could there have been any causes more powerful to produce the present commotion than the repeated violation of these assurances? By no principle of national law could the people of the district, now in anywise be regarded as subject to the Spanish monarchy. Conceiving themselves to be citizens of the United States, they had individually come forward to express their wishes and intentions. As an offset to the governor's declaration that Ellicott should be held responsible for his participation of the acts of the inhabitants, the latter added: "As you have assisted me in confirming the sentiment that this country belongs to the United States, on its part, as its commissioner, I protest against the officers of his majesty landing any troops or repairing any fortifications in the territory. I shall consider such conduct as a violation of the treaty, and an attack upon the interest, honor, and dignity of my country."

The governor was assured, however, that, if he had any plan of accommodation to propose, consistent with justice and honor, he, Ellicott, had every wish to enter into a discussion for that purpose.

At the instance of the governor, a private meeting took place next morning at the house of George Cochran, at which a rather angry and intemperate discussion ensued, which was near bringing it to an end. The principles of a plan of accommodation were discussed, and the concurrence of Lieutenant Pope was obtained to an attempt at conciliation by the address of Mr. Cochran and others.

The proclamation which the governor published the next day (the 15th of June), contained some expressions very offensive to the people. Although not concurred in by Ellicott, it met with no opposition from him. Its reception by the people might have been foreseen; it was torn to pieces, and treated with contempt.

The opposition now assumed a grave aspect, and acquired some form. Several companies of militia were organized, and made ready for service; and it was determined to hold a meeting of the principal inhabitants on the 20th inst.

Both parties, in the mean time, continued their preparations, and the governor exerted himself in reinforcing and strengthening the fort, his force being too inconsiderable to justify offensive operations.

One of the guns of the fort was brought to bear upon the tent of the commissioner, and a slight collision took place between the patrols of the two parties at night. Shots were exchanged, but without much damage.

On the 19th, by the request of the governor, Ellicott met him at the house of his aid, Major Minor, which the governor reached privately by a circuitous route through the canebrakes and thickets passing to the north of the plantation, and through the cornfield. The humiliating state to which he was reduced, had made, says Ellicott, a visible impression upon his mind and countenance; his situation was poignant and distressing.

He assured Ellicott, that he was sincerely desirous of coming to terms of accommodation with the people; and as he learned that the latter intended to be present at the appointed meeting of the inhabitants, desired him to use his influence to bring about a compromise.

A party of Choctaw Indians, returning from a war expedition against another tribe west of the Mississippi, arrived at Natchez at this period. Stopping as usual to pay their respects to the governor, they found him shut up in the fort: their respect for him and his people was sensibly diminished in consequence; and this incident had the effect of attaching the Choctaws to the American interest, and increasing their attentions.

On the 20th of June, 1797, the proposed meeting of the inhabitants took place at the house of Benjamin Bealk, about eight miles eastward of Natchez, near the then crossing of the Natchez trace, at the muddy fork of St. Catharine's Creek.

In consequence of the arrangements previously agreed upon by persons of property and influence in the country, little difficulty was found in prevailing upon the people to submit the future management of their affairs to a committee to be chosen by themselves.

Colonel Anthony Hutchins, contrary to expectation, took an *active, useful, and decided* part in bringing about this result.

The election was consequently held, and resulted in the choice of Anthony Hutchins, Bernard Lintot, Isaac Gaillard, William Ratliff, Cato West, Joseph Bernard, and Gabriel Benoist.

To the foregoing committee, with a singular impropriety, as would now seem, considering their official relations, and in which it seems strange they should have acquiesced, Andrew Ellicott and Lieutenant Pope were added by unanimous vote.

On the same evening the committee assembled at Natchez, and informed the governor of their appointment. The governor offered them the use of the government-house, which they declined, and then proceeded to business in a building of Mr. William Dunbar, which was in the course of preparation for the use of Ellicott, having been gratuitously tendered to him.

On the 22d of June, the committee submitted the following propositions to Governor Gayoso, and requested him to obtain the concurrence of Governor Carondelet therein :—

"First: The inhabitants of the District of Natchez, who, under the belief and persuasion that they were citizens of the United States, agreeably to the late treaty, have assembled and embodied themselves, are not to be persecuted or injured for their conduct on that account, but to stand exonerated and acquitted.

"Secondly: The inhabitants of the government aforesaid, above the thirty-first degree of north latitude, are not to be embodied as militia, or called upon to aid in any military operations, except in case of Indian invasion, or for the suppression of riots during the present state of uncertainty, owing to the late treaty between his Catholic majesty and the United States not being fully carried into effect.

"Thirdly: The laws of Spain in the above district shall be continued, and on all occasions be executed with mildness and moderation; nor shall any inhabitant be transported as a prisoner out of this government under any pretext whatever: and, notwithstanding the operation of the law aforesaid is hereby admitted, yet the inhabitants shall be considered to be in an actual state of neutrality during the continuance of their uncertainty as mentioned in the second proposition.

"Fourthly: We, the committee aforesaid, do engage to recommend it to our constituents, and to the utmost of our power endeavor to observe the peace, and promote the due execution of justice.

Anthony Hutchins, Bernard Lintot, Isaac Gaillard, William Ratliff, Cato West, Joseph Bernard, and Gabriel Benoist."

The foregoing propositions were agreed to by the governor as follows:—

"Don Manuel Gayoso de Lemos, Brigadier in the Royal Armies, Governor, Military and Political, of the Natchez and its dependencies, &c.

"Being always desirous of promoting the public good, we do join in the same sentiment with the committee, by acceding to their propositions in the manner following: By the present, I do hereby accede to the four foregoing propositions established and agreed upon for the purpose of establishing the peace and tranquillity of the country; and that it may be constant and notorious, I sign the present under the seal of my arms, and countersigned by the secretary of this government at Natchez, the 22d day of June, 1797.

MANUEL GAYOSO DE LEMOS,
JOSEPH VIDAL, *Secretary.*"

On the following day, the governor and his officers left the fort and returned to their houses.

It is worthy of remark that during the two weeks in which the inhabitants were in a state of revolt, no act of violence or breach of the peace took place.

The necessity of electing a permanent committee to aid in preserving the good order and peace of the country, was strongly impressed upon the governor, who, fully concurring in the propriety of the measure, issued a proclamation on the following day for that purpose, and the following gentlemen were chosen: Joseph Bernard, Peter B. Bruin, Daniel Clark, Gabriel Benoist, Philander Smith, Isaac Gaillard, Roger Dickson, William Ratliff, and Frederick Kimball.

The election of this committee in effect put an end to the Spanish authority in the country. All but one of the committee (Frederick Kimball, whose sentiments were doubtful, and whose residence proved to be below the line), were stanch friends to the government of the United States.

The committee held its first meeting in the house occupied by the American commissioner, on the 15th of July, having as before declined the use of the government house tendered for that purpose.

Contrary to expectation, Colonel Hutchins declined serving on the last committee, pleading his age and infirmities in excuse. He attended the first meeting of the committee, however, as a spectator, and manifested great dissatisfaction with its proceedings, which were directed first to securing the country to the United States, and secondly to the preservation of peace and good order.

Having established their neutrality, and rid themselves of the Spanish authority so far as it was seriously obnoxious to them, dissensions soon ensued between the inhabitants themselves, and rival parties sprung up, and an abortive attempt was made to supersede the permanent committee by the choice of another. The newly-acquired liberty of the inhabitants was jeopardized, and the Spanish officers looked on with complacency at a state of things which promised in the end to restore their lost authority.

By some very original and unauthorized devices, the semblance of a counter-committee was got up; but beyond denunciation, which proved harmless, and the getting up a memorial to Congress, which was disregarded, its labors were fruitless.

Although threatened at one time with an armed force of forty men, who were assembled on the Bayou Pierre, assured of the protection of the American arms, the committee pursued the even tenor of its way.

In the death of its chairman, Mr. Bernard, the committee and the whole country sustained a sensible loss.

Mr. Gabriel Benoist, who succeeded him as chairman, was a very estimable French gentleman, who came to the United States with other volunteers from France, to assist in achieving our independence; he had married the daughter of a very respectable planter settled in the country, and held some office under the Spanish government. He was obnoxious to the turbulent and disaffected, and was accordingly assailed as a French Jacobin, and vituperation revelled in the vindictive epithets bestowed upon him.

Ellicott has left in his journal copious details of these differences and bickerings. He had, however, by his too active participation in these events, considering his official relations, rendered himself obnoxious to some of the leading and prominent men engaged in them. His statements may be regarded in some degree personal, rather highly colored, and tinctured with partisan predilections, and it would perhaps be unsafe to adopt them *implicitly* as historical facts.

Let it be remembered that the country had passed under the rule of three different monarchical governments, and but recently under that of Great Britain during the period of our revolution. Many of the older inhabitants had been royalists from principle. Some of them were British officers, and continued to receive their pay and pensions even after the acquisition of the country by the United States. Not a few had migrated from the sister States, with strong suspicions of having fought on the *wrong side of King's Mountain.*

The rivalries of these for power and influence, were but the common instincts of ambitious men wherever they may be placed.

With a change of circumstances and of political institutions came also a change of views and opinions, and many of these persons became none the worse citizens, from their antecedents. The descendants of many of them, grown up with attachments to American institutions, have earned for themselves positions of respectability and influence.

It would answer no good purpose, therefore, to annoy the over-sensitive of the present age, by rending the veil which time has spread over the "bygones" of a past generation. Let them rest in oblivion.

On the 26th of July, Gayoso succeeded the Baron de Carondelet as governor-general by appointment from the Court of Madrid. On his departure for New Orleans on the 30th, he left Major Minor to represent him in the government at Natchez.

Governor Gayoso was called to rule over the district at an unpropitious time. Subjected to the superior authority of the governor-general, the Baron de Carondelet, it became his duty to execute orders and carry out the measures of the Baron, many of which, we have reason to believe, were distasteful to him. The repugnance of the inhabitants to the Spanish rule, and the impatience exhibited to throw it off before a substitute was organized by the United States, made it necessary for the good order and well-being of the country, for which he was responsible, to maintain his authority. This, under the adverse circumstances in which he was placed, rendered his situation annoying and harassing in the extreme. In his private intercourse with Ellicott and other Americans, he was ever courteous and honorable, and, apart from the duties imposed by his official station, he enjoyed for his many good qualities the respect and esteem of a large number of the most intelligent inhabitants.

He appears to have been just and upright in his administration, and to have advanced, as far as in his power, the interests of the district. The city of Natchez, on the hill, was founded by him, the land being purchased and the town laid off under his direction, and various public improvements were executed or commenced under his orders.

He survived his promotion to the office of Governor-General of Louisiana but a short time, and, in *dying poor*, he left the best evidence of these times, of his honesty and disinterestedness.

In July, 1797, the yellow fever prevailed at Natchez; one of Ellicott's assistants, and several of his men, were carried off by it. As soon as the sick could be carried, they were removed to the country, about seven miles east of Natchez. Ellicott accompanied them, and the spring, at his encampment near the present site of Jefferson College at Washington, has ever since gone by his name. Here his men were restored to health, but returning to Natchez too soon, he was himself attacked by the fever on the 7th of October.

In November, 1797, the appointment of Colonel De Grand Pré, as Governor of Natchez and its dependencies, was announced. The Permanent Committee immediately took a firm stand, and resolved that he should not be received in the capacity of governor; and that the assumption of the office by him would be regarded as a violation of the neutrality agreed upon, and be resisted accordingly.

The proceedings of the committee were transmitted to Governor Gayoso. Grand Pré, therefore, did not attempt to take upon himself the authority of his appointment, but remained quietly in New Orleans.

In the early part of December, Captain Guion, with a considerable detachment of United States troops, arrived at Natchez, and superseded Lieutenant Pope in the command.

The new commandant was much indisposed at the period of his arrival, and, although a man of superior capacity, and ardent patriotism, it is alleged that his judgment, for a time, seemed to be impaired. He was surrounded, at the period of his arrival, by many of the turbulent, aspiring, and disaffected, who took advantage of his situation to prejudice his mind against some of the best friends of the United States. Jealous of his authority, and determined not to be "*made a cipher of*," he viewed with suspicion the anomalous *Permanent Committee*, and treated it with little respect.

Taking advantage of the adverse relations between the constituted authorities, and the little cordiality subsisting between the commandant and the commissioner, some designing and ambitious persons in the country labored assiduously but ineffectually, to supersede the authority of the committee by establishing a military government. But the people had experienced too much of despotism to yield any of their newly-acquired privileges.

On the 10th of January, Governor Gayoso informed Ellicott by letter, that he was ordered to evacuate the forts at Natchez and the Walnut Hills. The event, however, did not take place for more than two months. Ellicott gives the following account of it.

"Late in the evening of the 29th of March, 1798, I was informed through a confidential channel, that the evacuation would take place the next morning before day. I rose at four o'clock, walked to the fort, and found the last party or rear guard just leaving it, and as the gate was left open, I walked in, and enjoyed from the parapet the pleasing prospect of the galleys getting under way. They were out of sight of the town before daylight."

The same day the American troops took possession of the works.

Plate I

Seal of the Province of West Florida attached to the British Patents

II. LAND TITLES.

A KNOWLEDGE of the origin and character of the various titles by which lands are held, or have been claimed in this State, cannot be without interest or utility to every planter or landed proprietor in it. The following brief outline, therefore, the design of which is to supply this information, will not, it is presumed, be deemed superfluous or out of place.

The first grant of land of which we have any account, was that most stupendous one made on the 13th of October, 1630, by Charles the First of Great Britain, to Sir Robert Heath, of which all that part of the State lying north of the thirty-first degree of north latitude, formed an *inconsiderable portion.* In 1637, Heath transferred his grant to Lord Maltravers, and it subsequently became the property of a Doctor Daniel Coxe, of the province of New Jersey; and in 1699, the same year that the French established themselves at Baluxi under Iberville, his title was recognized and reported upon as valid by the attorney-general of King William.

How the attempt of Coxe, the proprietor, to take possession and occupy it in the latter year, by sending two ships up the Mississippi under Captain Barr, was frustrated by Bienville, has been shown in the preceding historical outline.

The next grants in order, were those made by the Company of the Indies, about the year 1718, at Pascagoula and the Bay of St. Louis, on the St. Catharine, near Natchez, and on the Yazoo, of the number and dimensions of which we are not informed.

In consequence of the Indian disturbances, and of the massacre by the Natchez, these French grants seem to have been abandoned. No allusion is subsequently made to them; and those in the Natchez District, at least, appear not to have been recognized by the British government, upon obtaining possession of the country. Whether such was the case in West Florida proper, is not now certainly known. The acquisition by purchase from the early French settlers, may have been, in a few cases, the origin or basis of the subsequent British patents; as, in a late decision by the courts in Louisiana, in favor of the heirs of Pontalba, the title to the lands in controversy has been traced back to those early French grants.

From January, 1768, to September, 1779, numerous British grants were made by the Governor of West Florida; those in the Natchez District being chiefly made to officers of the British army and navy, and in many instances were of large dimensions. The largest embraced twenty-five thousand acres; two others, twenty thousand each; several were for ten thousand; and very few for less than one thousand acres. These were so located as to embrace a large portion of the most valuable lands bordering on the Mississippi, for a breadth of six or eight miles from Fort Adams to the Yazoo, and extending along the alluvial lands of the principal streams of the district.

Extracts from these grants have been given heretofore. To each was appended, by a ribbon, a ponderous wax seal, some three inches in diameter, the British arms being impressed on the obverse, with a landscape of forest scenery on the reverse, surrounded by the inscription: "Sigillum provinciæ nostra Florida occidentalis," with other inscriptions and legends.*

The conditions of these grants as to occupancy, cultivation, and improvement, were such as, if not regarded as mere words of form, to render them utterly void. Few of the lands granted were occupied or improved to the extent required, proof of which was to have been made within a stated time. They were, therefore, inchoate, if strictly construed, and were never perfected. Many of them, however, were nevertheless recognized and confirmed by the succeeding Spanish government, which, although acquiring the country by conquest, yet with great liberality guaranteed these possessions to the holders, upon the performance of certain reasonable requirements, such as presentation and proof of title, accompanied with occupancy, allowing several years for this purpose.

The titles derived from the Spanish government were of two grades; orders of survey and complete patents, the former being the incipient or incomplete form of the latter.†

To procure a grant of land, the applicant addressed a *Requête* (request or petition) to the Spanish governor, in New Orleans, and hence, from the corruption of the word, the term *ricket,* by which one class of these claims was known to the early American settlers.

If the petition was granted, an order of survey was

* See Plate I. † See Appendix F.

issued by the governor to the Surveyor-General Don Carlos Trudeau, to cause the land prayed for to be surveyed and put into possession of the petitioner. This duty was performed by the deputy-surveyor of the district, and the survey being approved and returned, accompanied by a plat, the governor thereupon granted his patent; the usual fees being paid in all the stages of the process by the grantee.

The first warrant or order of survey was issued on the 20th of April, 1784, by Don Estevan Miro, who continued to officiate as governor, and to make grants until the 29th of August, 1791. He was succeeded by Francis Louis Hector El Baron de Carondelet, by whom grants were made from the 8th of March, 1792, to the 1st of September, 1795. All the patents bear the private seal with the coat of arms of the governor, and are countersigned by the secretary Andrez Lopes Armesto. (See Plate II.)

It has been objected that the extension of the limits of West Florida, by the British government, to the Yazoo River, was an infringement of colonial charters or grants previously made, and that the titles to land made in that portion of the State were necessarily void. Spain, also, in wresting by conquest from Great Britain the same territory, not truly belonging to her, acquired no title thereto to the prejudice of the previous and rightful holders; the Spanish grants, therefore, to the same extent, were equally invalid.

This position was subsequently affirmed by the decision of the Supreme Court of the United States, and was borne out and admitted, virtually, in the treaty of peace between the United States and Great Britain, fixing the southern boundary of the independent colonies along the thirty-first degree of north latitude; and by the

See page 120

Plate II.

Facsimilies of signatures and seals of the Spanish GOVERNORS of LOUISIANA

B L C Wailes del. On Stone by M Rosenthal Cromo Lith by L N Rosenthal Phila

treaty of San Lorenzo, of the 27th of October, 1795, by which Spain finally yielded possession of this territory, to the United States.

The American government, however, with a paternal regard for the inhabitants occupying these lands, made provision for the confirmation, not only of the Spanish titles, but those of Great Britain, so far as they had been recognized by the former government, and were duly occupied.

The incomplete titles, or Spanish orders of survey, if occupied and cultivated at the date of the treaty, were also to be confirmed under the character of *donations* from the United States, when in fact the whole series, both of British or Spanish grants, of whatever grade, might so be regarded, being equally void or illegal, except so far as they were recognized by the act of Congress providing for their adjudication.

Large portions of the country being held under Spanish grants, covering lands claimed by non-resident British grantees, much uneasiness was exhibited by the holders, to whom they had been confirmed by the American government, when the British claimants manifested a disposition to test the validity of their rights, through agents, sent over from England for that purpose. Suits were instituted to eject the holders under the Spanish grants, and the anxiety of the people became so great that Congress was petitioned to compromise and quiet those claims. A report of a committee of the House of Representatives, made as late as 1814, nearly ten years after the claims had been confirmed by the Board of Commissioners, adverse to the prayer of the petitioners, which seemed to accord superior validity to the British grants, from their anterior date, was not calculated to allay the anxiety of the occupants.

The decision of the District Court of the United States, in the suit instituted by the heirs of Harcourt, and which was fully affirmed by the Supreme Court, settled the question finally, and the British grants are now no more regarded than that of Sir Robert Heath.

This decision of the Supreme Court was subsequently ably controverted by Chief Justice C. P. Smith, of the High Court of this State, when engaged, some years since, as counsel for the representatives of Campbell, who claimed a tract of land, embracing the town of Rodney, under a British patent dated 11th July, 1772. It was maintained by Judge Smith, in an elaborate argument, sustained by indisputable authority, "That the British government had the right, and had exercised it repeatedly, of dismembering or altering the limits or boundaries of its royal colonies; that the crown retained the right of property in the soil; that the extension of the limits of West Florida, from the thirty-first degree of north latitude to a line drawn due east from the mouth of the Yazoo, was a right legitimately exercised, and the grants made within those limits, by the Governor of West Florida, were consequently valid."

The rejection of the British claims should have rested, therefore, solely on their non-recognition by the Spanish and American governments, and a failure of the fulfilment of the conditions of those grants, and not upon want of jurisdiction in the British government.

So far, all grants of land were confined to districts to which the Indian title had been extinguished previous to the accession of the country to the United States.

In 1777, the British government entered into a treaty with the Indians at Mobile, by which the boundaries of the lands claimed by the French, on the sea-coast and in the Natchez District, were defined; and in the year 1779, the eastern boundary of the latter district was run, and marked by the English surveyor.

By the treaty of Hopewell, made by Col. Hawkins, the American commissioner, with the Indians at Keowee, on the 3d of January, 1786, the boundary was again established, and, finally, by the treaty held by General Wilkinson, at Fort Adams, with the Choctaw Indians, on the 17th December, 1801, was fully recognized, and a survey authorized under the superintendence of commissioners, which was soon afterwards made by order of the American government.

By the treaty of Mount Dexter, made on the 16th of November, 1805, the Choctaws ceded to the United States all the lands embraced in the counties of Lawrence, Covington, Jones, and Wayne, and those lying to the south of them, except perhaps Jackson, Harrison, and Hancock, which probably belonged to the Baluxis, and some other small tribes, which had removed or become extinct before the acquisition of the country by the United States, as it does not appear that the Choctaws claimed the lands in that quarter west of the Chickasahay River.

A further cession was made, at the treaty of Doaksstand, on the Natchez road, on the 18th of October, 1820, of the lands on the Mississippi, from the mouth of the Yazoo to a point nearly opposite the Arkansas River, comprising the counties of Washington, Yazoo, Madison, Rankin, Simpson, Copiah, and Hinds, as first established.

The residue of the Choctaw possessions in the State were ceded by the treaty of Dancing Rabbit, made on the 27th September, 1830, and the Choctaws removed to the west of the Mississippi, to lands given them in exchange by the United States.

By the treaty made at Pontotoc Creek, on the 20th of

October, 1832, the Chickasaws also ceded all their lands in Mississippi, to be *sold by the United States,* and the proceeds, deducting expenses of survey and sale, *paid to them,* and within three years removed across the Mississippi River to lands purchased by them from the Choctaws.*

By all of these treaties, from that of Mount Dexter, certain reservations were made; these consisted of improvements of some of the Indians who chose to remain —of larger reservations to the chiefs and others, and for the benefit of Indian orphans.

Besides these, Congress, in providing for the sales of the public lands, made other reservations, such as the sixteenth section of every township for schools—the grant of a township of lands to Jefferson College, and two townships for a State University.

Congress also granted two sections to the State, for a seat of government, upon which the city of Jackson was laid off.

Large grants have also been made to the State, for internal improvements; and lastly, all the swamp lands have been surrendered to it to constitute a fund for the purpose of reclaiming them from inundation, and to fit them for cultivation.

In addition to the claims derived from the British and Spanish governments, and the lands sold and patented by the United States, all the grants and reservations enumerated, constitute the basis of title by which the citizens of the State hold their lands.

The quantity of land, held by title derived from for-

* By a convention at Washington City, the 24th of May, 1834, the Chickasaws obtained a modification of the treaty to allow of grants in fee simple to all heads of families and others.

eign governments, and confirmed by the United States, amounts to 767,547 acres, 545,480 of which lie in the Natchez district, and 222,067 in the Augusta land district, east of Pearl River. The whole area of the State has elsewhere been stated at 35,520,000 acres; of this, it would appear, from data furnished by the census report of 1850, 10,490,000 acres are held by individuals, of which 3,444,000 are in cultivation.

The unimproved lands amount therefore to 32,076,000 acres, of which 25,036,000 acres are still held by the United States, or by the State of Mississippi.

III. AGRICULTURE.

THE EARLY STATE AND PROGRESS OF AGRICULTURE.

SEVERAL years elapsed, after the establishment of the French colony at Baluxi, before even the common vegetables of the garden were cultivated, and the sterile soil of the sea-shore was not calculated to invite a more extended culture, if the character and habits of the colonists, chiefly soldiers, deriving all their supplies from the mother country, had inclined them to such pursuits.

It was, therefore, not until the province came under the control of the Company of the Indies, that the tillage of the earth became to any extent a fixed pursuit. The first impulse was then given to planting by the large grants to European capitalists, who sent out laborers to open and improve their lands.

The most efficient of these were German redemptioners; but the nature of the climate, and the heavy labor of removing the dense forests, rendered the progress of improvement tedious and discouraging.

It was soon found necessary to resort to Africa for suitable operatives for the prosecution of agricultural enterprise; these were introduced by the company, from time to time, to a limited extent, and disposed of to the colonists at established and moderate rates, payable in annual instalments in the products of the soil.

These products were naturally confined, for a considerable period, to articles of necessity for home consumption, and notwithstanding some large grants were made near Natchez, and on the Yazoo, ostensibly for the cultivation of tobacco and indigo; and, although some "large plantations, with extensive improvements," were established near the former place, it does not appear that anything beyond the spoils of the chase, or the peltries procured by traffic with the Indian tribes, was exported from the country.

By the massacre of the inhabitants by the Natchez, in 1729 and 1730, these establishments were broken up, and from this period the French were too much engaged in exterminating the Natchez, and in hostile incursions among the Chickasaws, to reoccupy and cultivate, advantageously, their regained possessions.

It was, therefore, under the occupancy of the country by the English that we trace the first germ of successful and systematic agriculture in Mississippi.

The emigration which ensued, on the change of rulers, being chiefly from the Carolinas, Virginia, Jersey, and New England, was from a class differing essentially in habits from their more volatile and restless predecessors, the French, who were more addicted to the chase and to trafficking with their Indian neighbors, than to more laborious and settled pursuits.

Many of these settlers were accustomed to agriculture, and being generally accompanied by their families, resorted at once to the tillage of the earth as a means of support.

Their cultivation was necessarily rude, and their implements few and imperfect; yet their products were varied and for the purpose of subsistence ample. Almost every article of prime necessity, which the soil could yield, was produced by them to the extent of their wants.* Cattle and swine required little other attention than protection from the bear and wolf of the forest, and were raised abundantly; whilst the small farms, frequently confined to a few acres, exhibited a variety of productions that is now rarely found together in the country. Indian corn, wheat, oats, rye, rice and potatoes, cotton, flax, tobacco and indigo, were almost universally cultivated, but rarely, if at all, for exportation.

In the early stages of the settlement of the colony, many of the common conveniences of life were necessarily dispensed with, or supplied with such substitutes as ingenuity or skill could devise and fabricate from the productions of the country.

Not many years since, were to be seen the moulds in which the head of one of the most respectable and wealthy families of the present day was wont to cast the pewter platters and spoons which constituted the only *plate* of himself and neighbors. The inventories of the confiscated effects of some prominent, and as then regarded, opulent persons, yet preserved among the Spanish archives, exhibit a simplicity of attire and furniture in strong contrast with that which would now satisfy those of very contracted means or humble station.

The scarcity and high price of iron, and the consequent imperfection of agricultural implements, was perhaps most felt and least easily remedied. At that

* In 1775, Mr. Dunbar enumerates among the productions of his plantation, rice, tobacco, *flaxseed*, indigo *seed*, corn, buckwheat, barley, peas, besides *many other things*.

period cut-nails were not invented, and the wrought-nail cost a dollar a pound. Tools and all iron implements bore a corresponding price, owing, in some degree, to the high freights on heavy articles up the Mississippi; the voyage from New Orleans to Natchez, made by keel-boats and barges, requiring several weeks.

A set of plough-irons was, therefore, an acquisition of no little value. Iron entered into the composition of few of the wagons or carts, and the wheels were often made of a transverse section or disk sawed and properly fashioned from the trunk of a tree of suitable diameter.

These trucks constituted, to considerable extent, the only means of transportation of heavy articles. Even as late as after the introduction of Whitney's saw-gin, a now opulent planter, a venerable and highly respected citizen, a native of Adams County, states that, in a wagon of this kind, he hauled his crop of cotton for two years to a neighboring gin; a framework of cane serving in lieu of plank in the construction of the body.

Not many years before, the same gentleman was reduced to the necessity of fabricating his only plough by framing a common mattock into a beam, that being the only implement suited to the purpose left on his plantation by the depredating Indians.

This was only about sixty-five years since, and occurred within ten miles of Natchez, and to an individual belonging to one of the most opulent and influential families in the country at that day.

Flax was raised chiefly for shoethread and similar uses, but in some families linen cloth was made.

Leather was commonly tanned throughout the country in large troughs dug out of the trunks of trees.

From the earliest occupancy by the English, cotton in small quantities, sufficient for domestic purposes, was habitually cultivated; it was of the black or naked seed variety, was planted in hills, and cultivated with the hoe. Ffty or sixty pounds was the ordinary quantity gathered in a day. The seeds were picked out by the hand, or separated from the lint by means of the small roller gin.* It was spun and woven at home, and constituted the chief apparel of the inhabitants; the small quantity of indigo then grown, and the numerous dye-stuffs that the forests afforded, supplied all the coloring materials required for dyeing the cloth.†

Rice formed an important article of diet, supplying largely the deficiency of flour; the colonists, especially the French, accommodating themselves slowly and reluctantly to bread made from the Indian corn. It was prepared by pounding in common wooden mortars, and perhaps was not as fair as that which we now purchase, but of far richer flavor and more nutritious.

In the absence of mill-stones, when they could not be obtained, the Indian corn was reduced to meal by pounding in the same way.

Large herds of cattle were owned by the more opulent inhabitants, for which the garrison at Natchez afforded the chief market, and some were driven to New Orleans shortly previous to the change of government. The price of common stock cattle was about the same then as at this time.

* See Plate VII., Figs. 1 and 2.

† The first indigo made by Mr. Dunbar was by steeping it in barrels.

THE CULTIVATION OF TOBACCO.

When the country came under the dominion of Spain, a market was opened in New Orleans; a trade in tobacco was established, and a fixed and remunerating price was paid for it, delivered at the king's warehouses. Tobacco thus became the first marketable staple production of Mississippi.*

The tobacco plant, indigenous to the country, soon came into general cultivation.

The larger planters packed it in the usual way in hogsheads. Much of it, however, was put up in carrets, as they were called, resembling in size and form two small sugar-loaves united at the larger ends.

The stemmed tobacco was laid smoothly together in that form, coated with wrappers of the extended leaf, enveloped in a cloth, and then firmly compressed by a cord wrapped around the parcel, and which was suffered to remain until the carret acquired the necessary dryness and solidity, when, together with the surrounding cloth, it was removed, and strips of linn-bark were bound around it at proper distances, in such a manner as to secure it from unwrapping and losing its proportions.

The rope used for this purpose was manufactured by the planter, from the inner bark of the linn, or basswood, then one of the most common trees of the forest.

One end of the rope was made fast to a post, in front of which the operator, seated with the roll of tobacco

* In 1783, Mr. Wm. Dunbar, writes: "The soil of Natchez is particularly favorable for tobacco, and there are overseers there who will almost engage to produce you between two and three hogsheads to the hand, besides provisions."

on his knee, and his foot against the post, connected the other end with the carret, turning it with his hands whilst the necessary tension was maintained upon the rope, wrapped it securely and evenly from end to end.

In those days, when the roads were indifferent, and wagons and carts were few, the tobacco hogsheads were frequently geared to a horse by means of a pair of rude temporary shafts, connected with the heading, and in this manner rolled to the shipping point, or to market at Natchez; much being transported in this way from the settlements on Cole's Creek, and from greater distances.

To convey the tobacco to market in New Orleans, it was usual for several planters to unite and build a flatboat, with which one of the number would accompany the joint adventure, deliver the tobacco at the public warehouse, and, if it passed inspection, receive the proceeds, and return home by land, generally on foot; the payment being made in a written acknowledgment, or *bon*, as it was called, which entitled the holder to receive the amount from the governor or commandant at Natchez, thus obviating the labor and risk of packing the specie several hundred miles.

The monopoly of the tobacco trade was retained by the King of Spain, and the price paid for all that passed inspection at his warehouses was uniform.

The price was regarded as liberal, and yielded a fair return for its production, whilst the stability and certainty of a market encouraged an increased cultivation; the country began to prosper, and the planters were enabled to make purchases of slaves, the current price of which averaged about three hundred and fifty dollars.

There was no classification in the sale of the tobacco. If the article passed inspection, it was taken, and the quality was generally such *that for that cause* it could not be rejected. Nevertheless, it sometimes happened that an unobjectionable article was left upon the planter's hands, if, from ignorance of *established usage,* he had omitted the customary *douceur* to the inspector.

This, however, soon came to be better understood. The capacious pockets of the inspector were not worn without a purpose, and the expected purse was habitually dropped into it without at all shocking the moral sense of the wearer.

It was not necessary, or perhaps altogether proper, to couple the offering with expressed conditions; that, if not indelicate, would have been quite superfluous, it being quite safe and effectual to make the silent contribution. Nor was any particular secrecy or concealment at all necessary. This was not considered *bribery;* the king always paid his servants indifferently, and these were but the *perquisites* of office which indemnified the needy official for his poorly requited services.

Whether these usages, reacting upon the producers, had any effect upon the quality or condition of the tobacco in the end, is not, perhaps, altogether clear; but it is certain that, from some cause, either from fraud in packing, the falling off in quality, or from the competition of the Kentucky tobacco introduced into New Orleans, under General Wilkinson's contracts with the Spanish authorities, or by their connivance, the price was so reduced, that the further cultivation of it in Mississippi, for exportation, was in a few years wholly abandoned, greatly to the injury and embarrassment of the planters, who had, for the purchase of slaves, contracted debts which they now found it difficult to discharge.

THE CULTIVATION AND PREPARATION OF INDIGO.

The tobacco crop being no longer profitable, indigo, which had been cultivated for some time in Louisiana, was now resorted to.* This most offensive and unwholesome pursuit was nevertheless the most profitable one in which the planter could engage. Seed was obtained at the cost of about fifty dollars per barrel, and some of the small farmers engaged in cultivating the indigo exclusively for the seed to supply those whose larger means enabled them to erect the necessary fixtures, and to prosecute the cultivation and manufacture on a profitable scale.

Indigofera tinctoria, from which the indigo pigment of commerce is prepared, said to have been introduced from India, flourishes luxuriantly in the Southern States, where a variety termed the *Atramentum anil* is said to grow spontaneously. It was cultivated in drills, and required careful handling when young and tender, the subsequent cultivation being similar to that of the cotton plant.

When mature, in good land, it attained the height of about three feet. It was then, previous to going to seed, cut with a reap-hook from day to day, tied in bundles in quantities suited to the capacity of the steeping-vats, to which it was immediately transferred. These vats or uncovered reservoirs were constructed in pairs above ground, of thick plank dovetailed together in such a

* Indigo had not been cultivated in the Natchez District as late as 1783, and until after the failure of the tobacco business it was produced only for the seed, which was supplied to the Point Coupee and other settlements on the Mississippi.

manner as to be perfectly water-tight; the larger one, or steeping-vat, so elevated as to permit the draining off of the liquid into the smaller, or beater, in which it is churned or agitated.

This vat was usually about four feet deep, eight feet wide, and about fifteen feet in length. Two or three pairs of these vats were sufficient for the largest indigo establishments in the country. One pair ordinarily sufficed.

The vats were placed near a pond of clear soft water (spring or *hard* water would not answer), and the shallower the ponds, and the greater the surface of water exposed to the sun, the better.

Into the steeping-vat the indigo weed, as cut, was thrown, and the water pumped on to it. The steeping generally required a day; but this depended in a great degree upon the temperature of the weather during the process and that of the water used.

When the steeping was carried to the proper point, and the fermentation suffered to continue until all the coloring matter or *grain* was extracted, which was ascertained by examining the liquid in a silver cup, the turbid liquid was drawn off into the beater.

If drawn off prematurely, a loss in the coloring matter was sustained, and if deferred too long, putrefactive fermentation ensued, which injured the quality of the dye.

Attached to a shaft, revolving across the smaller vat, was a set of arms or paddles, by which the liquid was churned or agitated. In small establishments, the shaft or beater was turned by hand, but generally horse-power was connected with it.

The beating or churning process was continued for several hours, during which the precipitation was aided by adding a small quantity of lime. Other substances were often substituted, however, some using a mucilage obtained from the ocra plant, the sassafras, or from a plant known as the moave.

The grain or coloring matter being separated, as ascertained by test with the silver cup, flakes of the pigment being seen spreading or settling on the bottom, it was suffered to subside, and the supernatant liquid was drawn off through a series of holes descending towards the bottom. The indigo deposit was then removed by wooden shovels from the vat into draining-boxes lined with canvas, and placed upon beds of sand, afterwards tranferred to moulds lined in like manner, dried in the shade, and cut into cubes.

After undergoing a further curing by being laid on smooth plank shelves, where it underwent a sweat, it was packed in boxes for exportation.

A variety of a delicate light blue color was called "floton;" but that termed the "pigeon neck," from its prismatic colors, was most esteemed.

The price obtained for the best quality is variously represented, some affirming that it was from one and a half to two dollars per pound.

A second cutting of the suckers or sprouts was obtained, but the indigo produced from it was of inferior quality.

About one hundred and fifty pounds of indigo are said to have been produced to the hand.

The whole process was of the most disgusting and disagreeable character. Myriads of flies were generated by it, which overspread the whole country. The plant itself, when growing, was infested by swarms of grasshoppers, by which it was sometimes totally destroyed, and the fetor arising from the putrid weed thrown from the vats was intolerable. The drainings from these refuse accumulations into the adjacent streams killed the fish. Those in Second Creek, previously abounding in trout and perch, it is said were destroyed in this way.

It is not surprising, therefore, that the cultivation of indigo was abandoned in a few years, and gave way to that of cotton, so remarkable for its freedom from the disagreeable concomitants of tobacco and indigo culture, and comparatively so light, neat, and agreeable in its handling.

THE COTTON PLANT, ITS ORIGIN AND VARIETIES, AND ITS ENEMIES AND DISEASES.

The cotton plant, to which the generic term *Gossypium* has been applied by botanists, is of the order Polyandria, belonging to the Monadelphia class of plants.*

Although comparatively of recent introduction here, the cotton plant was known in the earliest ages in the Old World.

Herodotus describes the plant as "producing in the Indies a wool of finer and better quality than that of sheep."

Pliny mentions certain "wool-bearing trees which were known in Upper Egypt, bearing a fruit like a gourd of the size of a quince, which, bursting when ripe, displays a ball of downy wool from which are made costly garments resembling linen."

At the commencement of the Christian era, it had become an article of commerce in the ports of the Red Sea; and the remote provinces of India had at that early period acquired a celebrity for their cotton fabrics.

* See Plates III. and IV.

The popular name *Cotton*, from the Italian *Cotone*, is said to be derived from its resemblance to the down which adheres to the quince, termed by the Italians *Cotogni*.

Many varieties of the plant are described, and among them the perennial or tree cotton, which grows spontaneously in Brazil and Peru. The annual herbaceous varieties, only, are those cultivated in the United States.

The average height of the plant in land of medium quality, is about five feet. In a very fertile soil, it attains to double that height, whilst in one exhausted and sterile it becomes quite a dwarf.

Its appearance somewhat resembles that of the ocra plant, but is much more branched, and the leaves less in size and of more uniform shape.

The branches are long and jointed, occasionally bifurcated, and bearing at each joint a boll or capsule containing the wool and seed. Each boll is accompanied by a broad indented leaf, springing from the same joint of the branch, resting upon a footstalk three or four inches in length.

The woody fibre of the plant is white, spongy, and brittle, but is invested in a thick, brown epidermis, which is very pliant and tenacious.

The root is tuberous, penetrating deeply into the subsoil, and is thus less affected by drought than most other plants.

The blossom is cup-shaped, two or three inches in length, never very widely expanded, white on the first day until past noon, then changing gradually to a red—closing, gradually, for the next day or two, with a twist at the extremity over the germ of the young boll, by which it is speedily detached in its rapid growth, when it withers and is cast off, leaving the boll invested by a capacious tripartite, dentate calyx, sufficiently large to inclose it until half grown.

The calyx containing the germ of the flower is triangular in shape, and is technically known as the *square*, or *form*. In this stage of growth, these are liable to be disjointed and fall, from the long prevalence of drought; but more so when a rainy season suddenly succeeds, occasioning a second growth from the rapid elaboration of sap, which in its circulation seems not to enter into the footstalk as freely as into other parts of the plant.

The flower of the Sea Island cotton is, in its first stage, of a bright sulphur color, the boll small, trilobate, and more elongated, whilst the other varieties produce bolls of larger size, which open or divide into four and occasionally into five valves or cells.

The cotton plant commences flowering about the first of June, and ceases about the first of November, when the plant is killed by the frost.

The bolls are egg-shaped, rather under the size of the egg of the domestic fowl, pointed at the extremity, expanding widely when fully mature, exhibiting a brown tough, woody, membranous seed-vessel, somewhat horny in texture, to which the expanded locks of fibre or lint adhere.

The culture of cotton was introduced into China about the thirteenth century, and has extended largely; and the Nankin variety especially, produced there, has acquired a wide notoriety, forming a distinct fabric, which is even yet imported to some extent into the United States.

In England, although among the last countries where its manufacture was introduced, it had become well established at Manchester as early as 1640.

In 1719, it was suggested that the climate of South

Culture and Preparation of Cotton.

Plate VIII

L. N. Rosenthal's Lith. Philada.

F. Fuchs sculps.

Carolina was favorable for its production, and the first Provincial Congress of that State, in 1775, "recommended to its people to raise cotton."

Georgia is said, however, to have taken the lead in its cultivation; yet the first shipment of cotton known was in 1784, when eight bags were seized by the custom-house officers at Liverpool, it not being credited that even the small quantity of two thousand pounds had been raised in the United States. Seed was introduced into Georgia from Jamaica and Pernambuco in 1786; but the cultivation of the Sea Island variety was not established until 1789. The Upland, or the Georgia (bowed cotton), was successfully introduced about the same time.

Cotton was doubtless indigenous to America, having been found growing wild in Hispaniola and other West India Islands when discovered by Columbus; and at the period of the conquest of Mexico by Cortez, the natives made "large webs, as delicate and fine as those of Holland." Their other cotton fabrics were varied and beautiful, and constituted their chief article of dress.

When and from whence the plant was first introduced into Mississippi, is not certainly known, most probably by the early French colonists from St. Domingo, which was a touching point for the company's ships, and the place whence they derived much of their supplies. It would seem, indeed, that its cultivation here and in Louisiana on a small scale for domestic purposes preceded that of Georgia.

Charlevoix, on his visit to Natchez in 1722, saw the cotton plant growing in the garden of Sieur Le Noir, the company's clerk.

Bienville states, in one of his dispatches, dated in April, 1735, that the cultivation of cotton proved advantageous.

It is stated by Major Stoddard to have been cultivated in the colony in 1740; and Judge Martin quotes from a dispatch of Governor Vaudreuil, of 1746, to the French Minister, in which he mentions cotton among the articles received by the boats which came down annually from Illinois to New Orleans. This period is some thirty years prior to that in which it is claimed to have been cultivated in Georgia.

Among the varieties of the cotton plant may be enumerated the Sea Island, the Upland, the Tennessee green seed, the Mexican, Pernambuco, Surinam, Demerara, Egyptian, &c. &c.

The four first named are those which have been chiefly cultivated in Mississippi.

The Sea Island is confined to a very few plantations on our seaboard. It is superior to all others in length and fineness of fibre, and is on that account in much request on the continent of Europe, for delicate and costly fabrics, such as laces, and for intermixture with silk goods; it bears a high price, generally thrice as much as the best Uplands; but, being necessarily prepared for market in the roller-gin, at a heavy cost of time and labor, and being more difficult to gather, is upon the whole not more profitable than the short staple.

The Upland first cultivated here, differs from the preceding in the color of the blossom, the size and form of the boll or capsule, and in the length and fineness of the staple. Both have the smooth, black, naked seed. All other varieties seem to have a tendency to return to this by long-continued cultivation.

The Tennessee cotton has a seed invested with a thick green down, adhering firmly to it. It is difficult to gather, and superseded the latter, or black seed, for a few years, from its freedom from the rot—a disease with which the latter became infected.

They both gave way in time to the Mexican, which is now itself chiefly cultivated, or is the basis of all the varieties now in favor.

The superiority of the Mexican consists in its vigorous growth, the size of the boll and its free expansion affording a facility of gathering by which three times the quantity can be picked, as was formerly the case. The objections to it originally, and these have been in a great degree corrected, were the coarseness of the staple, and the loss sustained by its falling out, if not gathered speedily. Like the Tennessee, the seeds, although larger, are coated with a coarse, felt-like down, of a dingy white or brown color.

The Mexican seed is believed to have been first introduced by the late Walter Burling, of Natchez.

It is related by some of our older citizens, who were well acquainted with him and the facts, that, when in the city of Mexico, where he was sent by General Wilkinson, in 1806, on a mission connected with a threatened rupture between the two countries, in relation to our western boundary, he dined at the viceroy's table, and in the course of conversation on the products of the country, he requested permission to import some of the Mexican cotton seed—a request which was not granted, on the ground that it was forbidden by the Spanish government. But the viceroy, over his wine, sportively accorded his free permission to take home with him as many *Mexican dolls* as he might fancy—a permission well understood, and which in the same vein was as freely accepted. The stuffing of these dolls is understood to have been cotton seed.

Many accidental varieties have been introduced of late

years, originating in a promiscuous cultivation of different kinds, by which the pollen became intermixed, and the different qualities assimilated.

Some new and excellent varieties have thus been produced, which have been preserved and further improved by a careful and judicious selection of seed in the field. These, together with some spurious kinds, which have been palmed off upon the planter from time to time, have been known by rather whimsical and fantastic names, having little or no relation to their distinctive character. Many of them have had their day, whilst others deservedly maintain the high estimation to which their superior qualities entitle them.

The diseases of the cotton plant are the rust, the rot, and the sore shins.

The first is most probably attributable to the mineral properties of the soil, as it is local and partial in its effects; and on the spots of ground affected by it, the difference of soil is obvious to the eye. The appearance of the plant so diseased, suggests the existence of microscopic fungi, which exhaust, by their parasitic growth, the sap of the leaves, and cause them to wither and fall.

The rot, or disease of the boll, has been assigned to various causes. The first external indication of its approach is the appearance of an almost imperceptible puncture on the side, and generally near the base of the boll, surrounded by a slight discoloration or change of tint, presenting the semblance of a minute spot of grease —a character given it in the common conversation of planters, in speaking of the disease.*

The most received opinion, and that best supported is,

* See Plate VI.

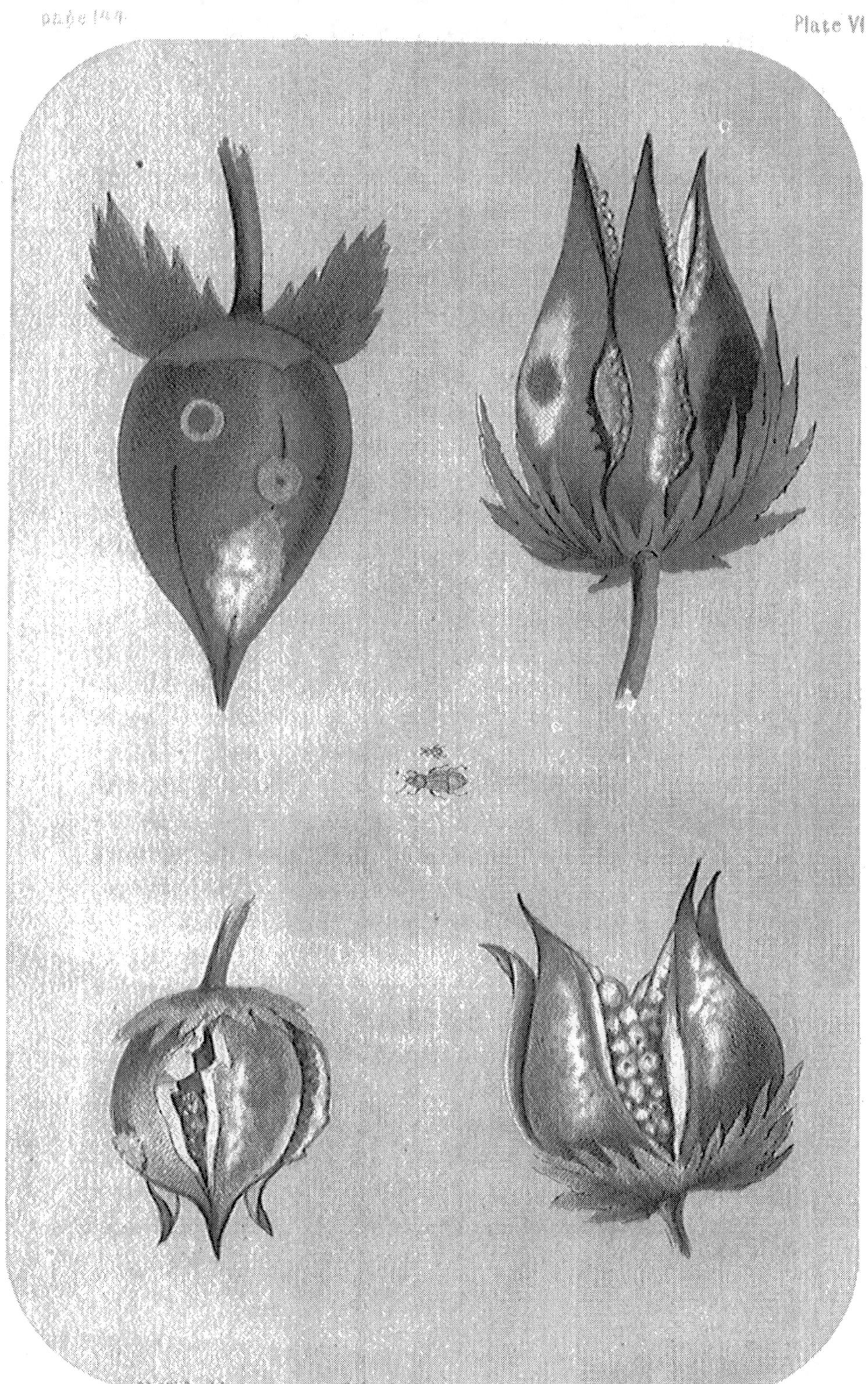

ROT IN COTTON

that it is occasioned by the larvæ of a small beetle or bug, which is hatched from the egg deposited in it, in some unknown manner, at an early stage of its growth, and which, feeding on the succulent and pulpy seed in their early stage of formation, produces the disease without immediately destroying the boll, which not unfrequently is only partially damaged, and continues to grow nearly to its mature size, but in the end becoming externally black and hard; the decayed state of the interior of the boll presenting an analogy to the peach or plum, which, though often presenting even a fair and perfect exterior, is found, upon opening, to have been long preyed upon by the curculio, or peach worm.

It is certain that the diseased and blackened boll, when broken open, often reveals a variety of small insects, sometimes in the different stages or conditions of their metamorphoses. Which of these is the real enemy can only be determined by the close and continued observation of the practised entomologist.

This disease made its appearance as early as 1810, and prevailed more or less for more than ten years, and occasionally to such an extent as almost to cause the abandonment of the cotton culture—a contingency prevented by the introduction of the Tennessee green-seed variety, which was exempt from the disease, or much less affected by it than the naked black-seed variety first cultivated.

For many years the rot was unheard of; its partial and unfrequent occurrence being too inconsiderable to create alarm, or occasion any appreciable injury.

Its reappearance in 1852, and during the late season, has, however, on many plantations, been attended with considerable damage.

The remaining disease, popularly known as the *sore*

shin, attacks the plant in its early stage. If not wholly destroyed, the bark of the stem becomes diseased and hardened, and the sap vessels dried up or obstructed at or near the surface of the ground. The disease is most prevalent during the occurrence of the cold nights of a wet and backward spring. To this cause it is attributed, and may be owing in some degree to the plant-louse, *apis pauceron,* which prevails most in such seasons.

The growth of the young plant so affected is languid and slow, and although the damaged epidermis may be repaired and overgrown by a new bark, it is questionable whether the plant ever becomes as vigorous or prolific as those that have not sustained this injury.

The cause of this malady—too early planting—suggests the proper remedy.

The casting of the forms or germs of the bolls may perhaps also be regarded as a disease attendant on a deranged circulation in the plant, owing to an unequal and irregular supply of moisture. It is manifested most generally upon a sudden transition from a very dry to a very wet season, and is consequently so far without remedy; it is, however, doubtless sometimes occasioned or aggravated by injudicious cultivation.

The enemies of the cotton plant, besides those enumerated, are chiefly the caterpillar and boll-worm.*

The ravages of the chenille or cotton caterpillar (*Depressaria Gossypioides*) has long been known in other countries. It prevailed destructively in South America and the West Indies, having been described previous to the present century, and is probably coeval with the cultivation of the cotton plant. In 1788 and 1794, two-

* See Plate V.

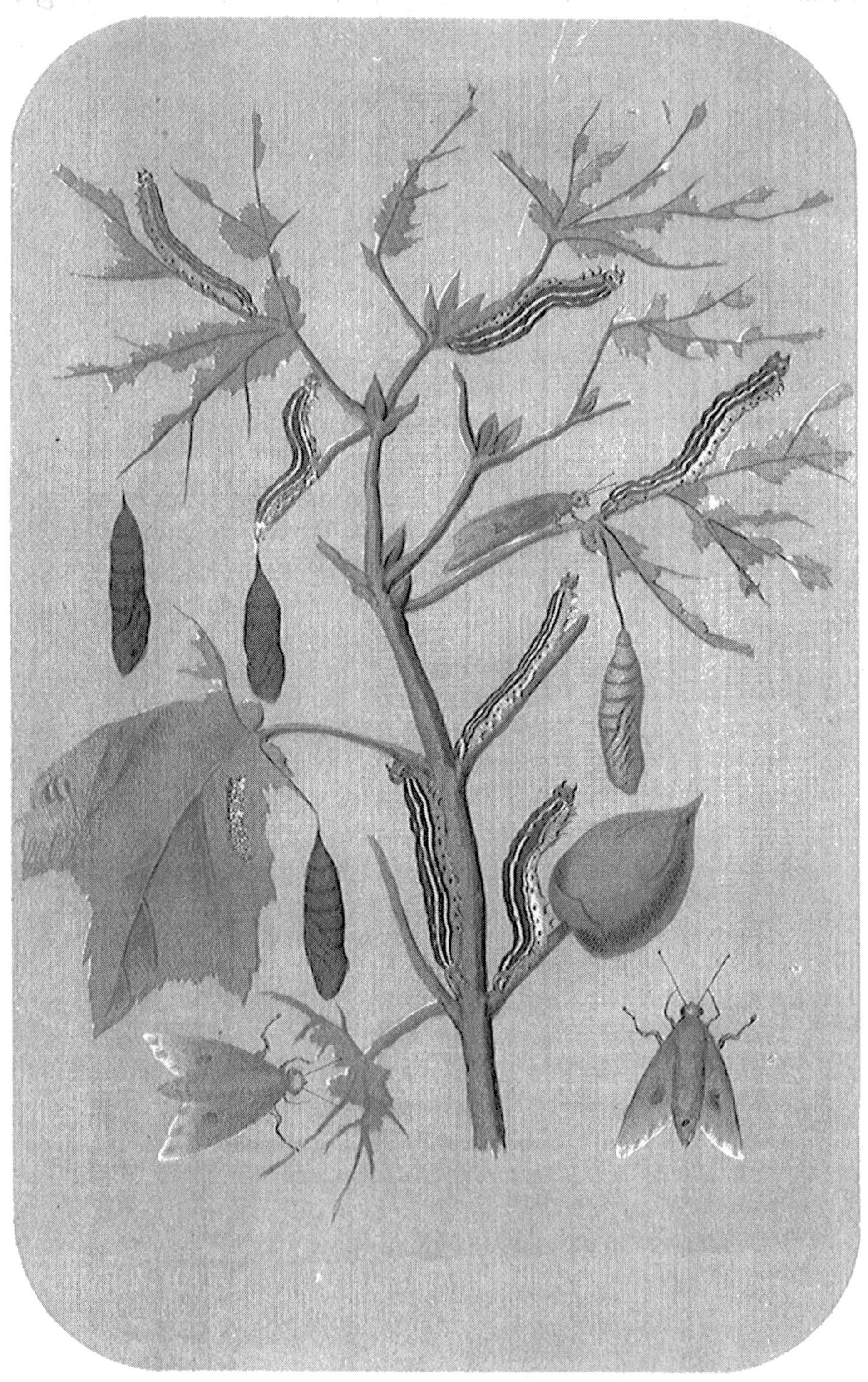

COTTON CATERPILLAR

thirds of the crops in one of the Bahama Islands were destroyed by it.

The remedy first resorted to was the burning of the cotton-stalk in which the eggs of the insect were supposed to be deposited. This seems to have been ineffectual; it was certainly so as respects the insect that occasions the rot, as, during the whole period of its prevalence in this country, the burning of the stalks was universal, and no diminution of the disease was known to have resulted from the practice.

The most feasible remedy I can suggest is one I proposed more than ten years since: it is the destruction of the enemy by means of torches at night immediately after the perfect immago or moth emerges from its puparium or chrysalis state, and flies abroad, it being well known that fire-light attracts insects of this class. If the hands on a plantation were each provided with a lighted torch of pine wood, dried cane, or some similar material, and made to pass through the fields at intervals of five or ten rows apart, shortly after twilight had closed, *myriads* of the moth would perish in the flame, each of which would have deposited its hundreds of eggs in a few days.

If this plan was *generally* adopted, and persevered in for a few successive nights *at the proper season*, its effect would doubtless be, if not entirely to destroy, at least to diminish to a very beneficial extent these mischievous pests.

The first hatching of the caterpillar in the spring could not at first be thus destroyed, or their ravages prevented; but the second *brood*, if it may be so termed, which is generally considered most numerous and destructive, and which furnishes the egg for the supply of the ensuing year, would be cut off to a great extent.

However this suggestion may be received, it is at least as practicable as any of the plans that have been proposed for the same object, some of which have been promulgated through respectable Agricultural Journals; such as the powdering the leaves of the plant with finely pulverized quicklime, or the fumigation of each separate plant with sulphurous vapor produced by burning brimstone on *chafing dishes*, each plant being inclosed, during the process, in a tight canvas hood, ten minutes being considered sufficient time for each plant! If this was at all practicable, one hand, with great diligence, might at this rate go over one acre in *fifteen or twenty days*.

The caterpillar, which does not usually appear until the cotton plant is pretty well matured, feeds chiefly upon the leaf, and the degree of damage done depends upon the period it commences its depredations; if so early that but few bolls are matured, the plant must cease to grow when thoroughly stripped of leaf.

Instances have occurred, but it must be confessed very rarely, when the growth of the plant was too vigorous, and continued too late in the season, in which a *partial* cropping of the leaves by the worm has had a beneficial effect in arresting the growth, and causing the bolls to mature and open. If their appearance is delayed until a period immediately preceding a killing frost, and during a dry season, a conjuncture not often happening, they do a benefit in removing the leaf, which, after a frost, stains the cotton and renders it very trashy, by crumbling and falling upon it.

The boll-worm is comparatively small, resembling at first the silk-worm in its early stages; its attacks are made within the calyx, and about the base of the boll, which it perforates, and when first forming and tender, it wholly devours or causes to drop off.

The insect theory, in connection with the cause of the rot, is sustained by the observations of intelligent planters made last year. It was remarked that, on lands where the different varieties of cotton had been planted separately, in alternate rows, for experiment, the most tender and succulent varieties, which would naturally first invite the attacks of insects, were those most damaged, whilst the more hardy and firmly wooded remained uninjured.

The increase of these maladies may probably be traced in some measure to the extirpation or disappearance of birds, owing chiefly to the destruction of our forests, leaving them in a degree without protection or shelter.

A beneficent Providence, in the economy of nature, designed these little winged scavengers for useful purposes. To restrain the exuberance of insect life is their peculiar office; and, so long as they are preserved and protected, their office is effectually performed. If man wantonly, and with mistaken impressions as to the extent and character of their depredations, will destroy them, he must make his account in submitting to ravages of a more formidable kind, and which may baffle his ingenuity to prevent.

This lesson has been taught with heavy cost, nowhere perhaps more clearly than on the rice plantations, where the planters would now gladly woo back the little denizens of the air, which they have frightened away or destroyed.

MODE OF PLANTING, CULTIVATING, AND GATHERING THE COTTON CROP.

There must ever be some diversity of practice, in the details of all agricultural operations. The character and situation of the land, the nature of the soil, the variations of the seasons, will influence these more or less. The following details, therefore, must be received as descriptive of the *general* practice under the most usual combination of circumstances.

We will suppose that the land has been previously cultivated in cotton, and has been already laid off and *circled* according to the undulations of the surface, at distances suited to the quality and capacity of the soil. The cotton stalk of the previous year having become sufficiently decayed and brittle, is first beaten down and broken to pieces, and left strewn upon the ground. This is done by the women and the younger hands, provided with stout sticks or clubs suited to the purpose.

Between the rows of the previous year, a furrow is now run, with a bar-shear plough without a coulter, and two other furrows are lapped upon it. In this state, it remains until all the ground is gone over, and the season for planting approaches. Two or more furrows, according to the width of the row, are then thrown up on both sides to the previous ridge, and the middles are thus broken up.

So far, the work has been done with large two-horse ploughs suited to breaking up the hard ground. In the subsequent cultivation, a lighter one-horse plough is used. Over the bed or ridge thus formed, if the rough and lumpy condition of the ground requires it, an iron toothed harrow is drawn, and the ridge is *split* or opened by a small plough, or more usually by a lighter implement contrived for the purpose, and consisting of a suitably fashioned block preceded by a coulter.

In the furrow made by the opener, the cotton seed are sown by the women from a quantity carried in the apron, gathered together at the lower end, and held by the left hand so as to form a sack which is replenished from time to time from piles of seed previously deposited in the field at convenient distances. The sowing is done adroitly at a brisk pace by a vertical or downward movement of the arm, by which the seed are strewn along the row several feet at each cast of the hand, and with the requisite regularity. A light harrow follows, to the hinder part of which is frequently attached a small roller, which smooths down and compresses the loose soil over the seed.

When the cotton has come up, and grown to the height of a few inches, in a week or ten days it begins to require thinning out and scraping. This was formerly done almost entirely by the hoe, by which the grass and cotton on the sides of the ridge were scraped away, and the cotton *blocked out* in the row by cutting it out to the width of the hoe or about twelve or fourteen inches. It is now performed by first running a bar-shear plough lightly on each side of the row, and *barring off*, as it is called, and throwing the dirt from the plant. The process also is greatly facilitated by the use of a properly constructed scraper, an implement of modern and not yet of universal, if of general use, which acts well, and saves a great amount of labor to the hoe hands.

It is desirable to follow this operation with as little delay as practicable, the ploughs on this occasion giving an inverted direction to the soil, and throwing it back to the plant with the mould-board—a process which is termed *dirting* or *moulding* the cotton. The hoes follow immediately, *thin out to a stand*, leaving one or two of the most vigorous and promising plants, freeing them from grass, and drawing the loose soil well around them for their better support.

If the planter has accomplished this much of his work *thoroughly*, and in *good season*, his crop may generally be accounted safe.

The after cultivation is varied according to the nature of the season; and the plough, hoe-harrow, or the sweep will be used as they may be found best adapted to the condition of the crop.

The latter implement is, like the scraper, of modern introduction. It resembles one of the hoes of a harrow flanked with wide-cutting blades, or wings, forming two sides of a triangle; and mounted on a plough-beam, is capable of *sweeping* the whole width of the row, or the greater part of it at once, loosening the soil and destroying weeds, vines, and everything that does not require to be turned under and effectually buried. It is a very efficient tool, and is employed with advantage, and especially in dry seasons, in keeping under the tie vine (convolvulus, or morning-glory), which, if not thoroughly done, is an after source of great annoyance and damage. This course of cultivation supposes the planter to have kept pace with the regular order of his work; but if, from a backward season and late frosts, he is compelled to replant, or if, from an unusual prevalence of rains, he is unable to run his ploughs, or, from the same cause, to scrape out his cotton in proper time, and consequently *gets into the grass*, he has necessarily to adopt such expedients as the emergency requires; and sometimes it is necessary to throw out of cultivation or abandon a part of the crop to save the balance.

The first of April is early enough to commence the

planting of cotton, which is continued to the middle of May, and occasionally later. The only motive for planting in March is to get more forward with the work of the plantation, and put in a larger crop; and this is often done at the expense of a bad stand, or having to replant, which is apt to retard and derange all the operations of the planter.

Cotton, planted in well-prepared land after the ground has become sufficiently warm, comes up sooner, grows more rapidly, and is much less liable to be injured by the "sore shins," or the plant-louse, than that which has been chilled by the cold winds and rains from getting above the ground too early in the season.

The practice of horizontal cultivation, or *circling* the rows, so as to keep them on a level on hilly and rolling land, was introduced by the late Mr. William Dunbar, of the Forest in Adams County (as Mr. Dunbar is known to have stated in conversation in the town of Washington, in 1810), at the suggestion of Mr. Jefferson, of whom Mr. Dunbar was a correspondent for many years, when the former was President of the United States. Having observed, when in France, this economical manner of cultivating the mountain sides, Mr. Jefferson recommended it as well adapted to our broken lands.

The practice was tardily adopted, and, like all similar innovations on established usages, met at first with its share of ridicule.

Many planters rely upon the eye alone in circling their lands, altering and correcting the rows in subsequent years as the direction of the rain water may show to be necessary.

The most careful and judicious class, however, have their fields carefully staked out in the first instance by means of a triangular spirit-level resting on a tripod for more convenient adjustment.

Like type-setting, cotton-picking is and must still continue to be performed by the fingers; but its rate has become as accelerated as if some new motive power was applied in the process. Fifty years since, fifty pounds a day was accounted fair work. Now the children double this; and two hundred pounds is not unfrequently the average of the whole gang of hands, to say nothing of those who pick their four or five hundred pounds of cotton (*bolls?*).

The cotton is gathered from the bolls in the field in sacks, made of Lowell cotton, suspended over the neck and shoulder, and from which it is emptied from time to time into large baskets made generally of white oak splints, and capable of holding about one hundred and fifty pounds.

It is generally weighed at noon and at night, in the field, and the baskets emptied into a wagon, hauled to the gin yard, and spread upon scaffolds, exposed to the sun, to dry. It is there picked over and trashed by the invalids, and such of the hands as are suited to this light employment.

When a long-continued drought prevails, after the frosts have checked the further growth, and the cotton becomes very dry in the field, it is not necessary to put it upon the scaffolds. If put up in bulk a *little* damp, it undergoes a heat by which the essential oil of the seed is discharged, imparting to the fibre a creamy color, highly prized by some purchasers, and which sometimes effects a good sale of a really inferior article.

This is rather a dangerous experiment, however, to make on a large scale; for, if the heat rises too high,

Plate VII.

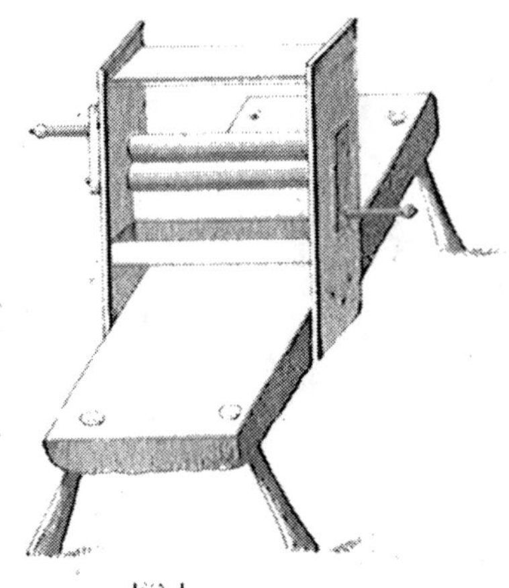

Fig 1

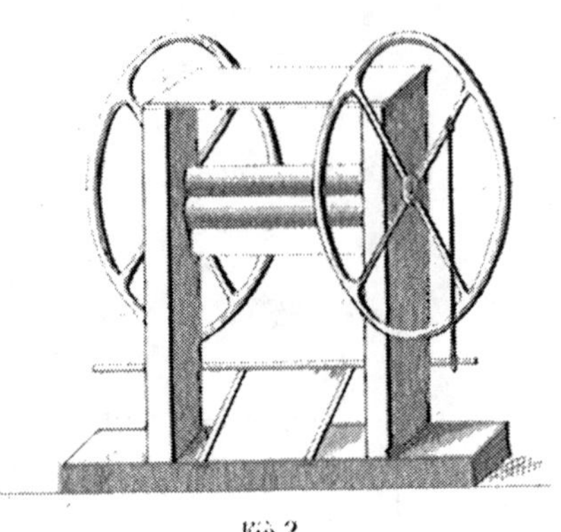

Fig 2

Fig 3

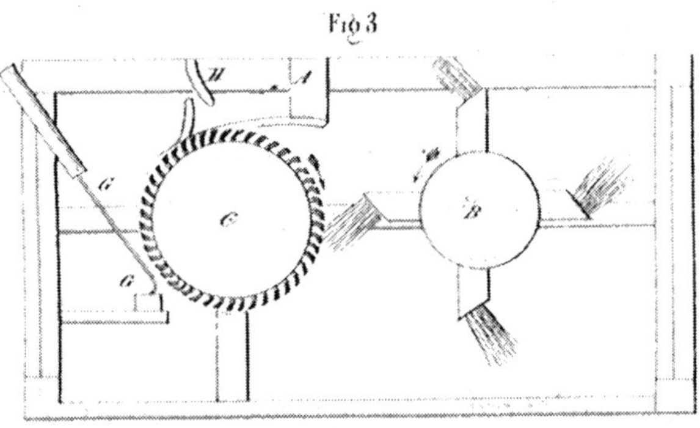

Whitrey's Gin of 1807.

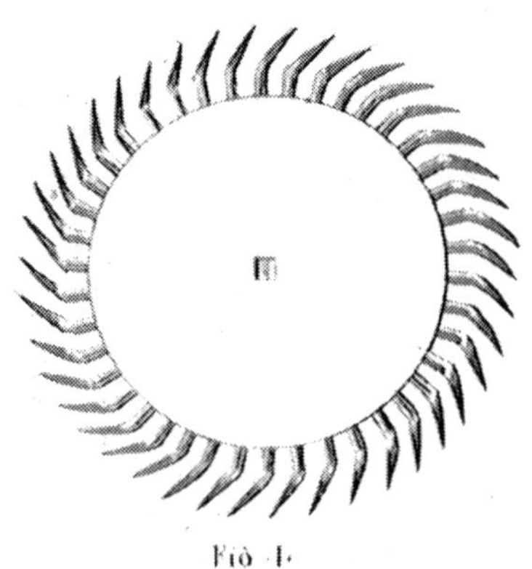

Fig 4

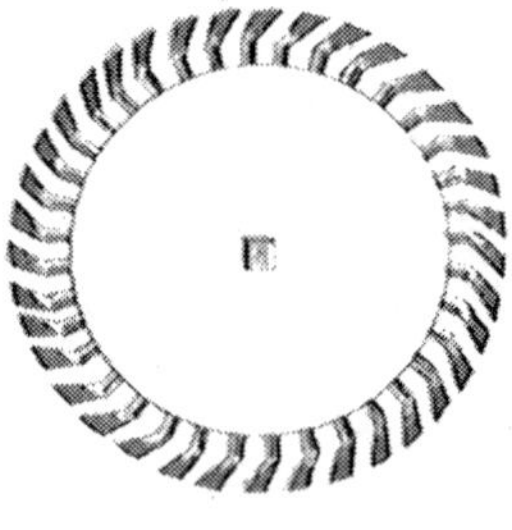

Fig 5

B. L. C. Wailes del. On Stone by M. Rosenthal Chromo Lith by L. N. Rosenthal Phil^a

putrefaction and mildew will supervene, and serious damage will result.

In an average of ten years, in which observations have been recorded, the first cotton blooms made their appearance about the first of June, and the plant was killed by frost about the first of November.

WHITNEY'S GIN—INVENTION AND INTRODUCTION OF MACHINERY.

The implements and machinery used for the preparation of cotton for market were, in the first instance, of the most simple and primitive kind. Next to the separation of the seed from the fibre by the fingers, the small roller gin was used. It was ordinarily attached to the middle of a common rude bench supported on legs inserted in auger holes (Plate VII. Fig. 1). Astride of this, two boys, seated face to face, operated each by turning a crank, one feeding the rollers with the seed cotton, the other freeing them from the lint on the opposite side, as it was drawn through, leaving the seed behind.

The rollers were less than an inch in diameter, and about eight inches long, revolving of course in opposite directions, but in close contact.

The next step, in advance, was a modification of this gin, by which the rollers were rotated by means of a treadle worked by the foot, leaving both hands of the operator free to attend upon the rollers; by which means one person was enabled to manage a single stand. This description of gin was in use in the West Indies in 1764 (see Plate VIII. and Fig. 2, Plate VII.).

Iron in the minutest particle did not *necessarily* enter into the construction of these gins, nor is it believed to be *indispensable* to this day in their improved forms.

No additional power or efficiency can be attained by the enlargement or lengthening of the rollers, and it is only by multiplying the stands or pairs of rollers, each requiring its attendants, but simultaneously put in motion by some efficient power acting upon the whole, that they have been rendered at all adequate to the demands of even moderate plantations.

The adaptation of these stands to a common power, by means of an extended cylinder or drum with which they were connected by bands is attributed to Mr. Longstreet, a merchant of Augusta, Georgia, the father of Judge Longstreet, the President of the University of Mississippi; and was introduced about 1792.

The roller gin is only adapted to the Sea Island and naked seed varieties of cotton.

The upland Georgia cotton required the preparatory process of *bowing*, in the manner that hatters prepare their felt. Hence the *bowed cotton*, formerly known in commerce.

Short as the rollers are, with the accelerated velocity given by the combined machinery and horse power, they are very liable to become sprung, and to admit the seed or any foreign substance that may be in the cotton.

A single seed so taken in will instantly scorch a notch in the rollers, and render them unfit for further use. Great pains is therefore required in picking over the cotton and rendering it perfectly clean before ginning.

The liability of igniting the lint or fibre by friction from this cause renders it necessary to employ the most cautious and expert hands in attendance upon the rollers, and to keep vessels of water constantly at hand to guard against such casualties.

New rollers have to be supplied, and it is estimated that two or three pair are daily required on an average to each stand, and one hand is kept constantly employed at the lathe to furnish the necessary supply.

Perhaps half a bag can be ginned per day with five pair of rollers under favorable circumstances; but the process is greatly retarded in damp or wet weather.

Such, until the introduction of Whitney's invention, were the miniature gins in use. The small hand gins were to be seen in nearly every planter's house, and, indeed, for many years after, were often met with on the small farms in the interior, where cotton was only raised for home consumption.

It will readily be imagined that with such means of preparing it, the culture of cotton in Mississippi was restricted to a very small space. A mere spot of ground sufficed for all that was required for domestic purposes, or which the grower could in a reasonable time free from the seed.

The long staple or Sea Island cotton had not been introduced into Mississippi; and it does not appear, from the most diligent inquiry, that more than a single small lot of only three bales, or rather round bags, was exported from the country previous to the introduction of the saw gin.

This was produced by Mr. William Vousdan, near the site of the ancient Whiteapple Village on Second Creek.

To prepare it for the roller gin, it was kiln-dried in the seed on latticed scaffolds, formed of cane, under which fires were placed.

The dawn of a new era in the agriculture of the country was, however, at hand, and was ushered in by the introduction of Whitney's gin—an invention in machinery which has not only added to the wealth of our nation, but extended the manufactures and commerce of the world in a degree without example in its history.

Eli Whitney was born in Massachusetts in 1765, graduated at Yale College in 1792, and went shortly after to Georgia, to assume the duties of a private tutor. Being disappointed in this expectation, he became an inmate in the family of the widow of General Green, and commenced the study of law under her hospitable roof.

Among other acts done in requital of the hospitality and kindness of his obliging hostess, Mr. Whitney had presented her with a tambour frame, made on a plan entirely new, and of his own construction.

This and the various toys he had made for her children, acquired for him the reputation of great ingenuity and mechanical skill, and caused the invention of a machine for the separation of the lint or fibre of the cotton from the seed, to be *suggested* to him by some gentlemen, visitors of his hostess, to whom she had considerately introduced him.

Although not seriously proposed, or with the expectation that the suggestion would be acted upon, a direction was given to Whitney's views, which neither his kind patroness nor her friends dreamed of.

His active and inventive mind was stimulated to action by the great importance of such a discovery, and he determined to grapple with the task, sensible of the vast benefits that must ensue from the successful accomplishment of the undertaking.

Never having seen in his life the cotton or cotton seed, with some difficulty, by visiting Savannah, he procured a small quantity, which he brought with him, and acquainted his friend, Mr. Phineas Miller, with his intentions, in which he was warmly encouraged, and an apartment was assigned him in the basement of the house for a workshop.

Here, with such rude tools and materials as a Georgia plantation then afforded, he went to work, and near the close of the winter had progressed so far as to render his success certain.

When the machine was erected, Mrs. Green invited to her house a number of planters from different parts of the State, to witness its operation; "and they saw with astonishment and delight that more cotton could be separated from the seed in one day, by the labor of a single hand, than could be done in the usual manner in the space of many months."*

It is not my purpose here to write the biography of Mr. Whitney. That has already been ably done by Professor Olmsted of Yale College. But it is of some interest to preserve the history of an invention to which the people of our State owe all their prosperity.

In order to gratify the curiosity which every cotton planter must naturally feel on the subject, I have been at some pains to inform myself on the subject, and have had the rare opportunity of examining critically, in all its parts, an early model of the gin on a small scale constructed under Mr. Whitney's direction, and which is now exhibited in the Crystal Palace, in New York.

I have also seen a working-stand made in 1807, to serve as a model, under a contract between Mr. Whitney and the State of South Carolina.† This latter stand has recently been used as evidence in a suit in relation to infringement of patent between two gin builders, and

* Professor Olmsted.

† Plate VII. Fig. 3. C the cylinder, B the brush, A the breastwork, H the hopper; and G G the grate.

was identified as the original gin stand of Whitney by the oath of one of his early workmen.

The model shows the progress of the invention as elaborated in the ingenious mind of its author; and his first idea seems to have been that of *carding* the lint or fibre from the seed, rather than that suggested by the use of the saw.

The cylinder in the model is divided into three parts; one-third of it at the left end is armed with stout crooked wires driven in, flattened at the sides, and the ends brought to an edge, as shown in Plate VII. Fig. 4. (The middle third of the cylinder is provided with a similar arrangement of wires, not flattened as in the first, but pointed, as in Fig. 5.) And the remainder of the cylinder is mounted with the circular saw rags, similar to those now in use.

Figure 3, of Plate VII. exhibits an end view of the stand, showing the position of the cylinder and brush, *or clearer*, as it was then termed in the specification of the patent, for which the reader is referred to Appendix G.

The gin stand made for South Carolina in 1807, consists of a frame supporting an iron form, upon which the saw cylinder and brush are hung.

An end view of the machine shows the mode of boxing the journals and retaining them in place. The seed-board of the hopper is connected with the upper part by hinges, and may be placed at any required distance from the saws. The back of the hopper descends nearly to the saws just behind the grating, and the rear branch of the grating makes the bottom of the moting trough; it also contains a movable false bottom of tin, which catches the motes.

The cylinder contains forty saws, six and three-fourth

inches in diameter, each having one hundred and six teeth; they are separated at distances of three-fourths of an inch by block tin or pewter castings.

"The seven-inch cylinder brush has six wings, each extending from one inch below to two inches above the surface, where they receive oblique tufts of bristles. The wings of the brush extend beyond the heads, and form what are called *projecting lags*.

"The machine has a large opening against the ends of the brush to admit the air freely to these lags, and thus prevent the cotton from winding upon the axis of the brush; the mote-board is made of slats two or three inches wide.

"The hopper, moting-trough, &c., form one part of the gin; and the top and ceiling, back of the openings, are each hung upon the upper bar of the iron form, and may be turned back at pleasure."

The experiments, made in the presence of the gentlemen assembled at the house of Mrs. Green, to witness the operation of the machine, as before stated, proving so satisfactory, no further doubt of the utility of the invention was entertained.

A partnership was entered into with Mr. Phineas Miller, who, like Whitney, had come out from New England to Georgia as a private tutor, and resided in the family of General Green, with whose widow he subsequently intermarried.

Mr. Miller in this manner had become possessed of the requisite funds for carrying on the business of the concern, which was, from May, 1793, conducted in the name of Miller & Whitney.

A patent was procured on the 14th of March, 1794, and Mr. Whitney established himself at New Haven, for the purpose of perfecting his invention and of availing himself of greater facilities for manufacturing the stands, which were to be shipped to Georgia to supply the anticipated demand.

"An invention so important to the agricultural interest (and, as it has proved, to every department of human industry) could not long remain a secret. The knowledge of it soon spread through the State, and so great was the excitement on the subject that multitudes of persons came from all quarters of the State to see the machine; but it was not deemed safe to gratify their curiosity until the patent right had been secured. But so determined were some of the populace to possess this treasure, that neither law nor justice could restrain them—they broke open the building by night, and carried off the machine. In this way, the public became possessed of the invention; and before Mr. Whitney could complete his model, and secure his patent, a number of machines were in successful operation, constructed with some slight deviation from the original, with the hope of evading the penalty for violating the patent right."*

The following account of the invention, and of the performance of the first machines manufactured, is given in a letter written in November, 1793, by Mr. Whitney, in answer to one received from Mr. Jefferson, who took much interest in the invention, and sought information respecting it:—

"It is about a year since I first turned my attention to constructing this machine, at which time I was in the State of Georgia.

"Within about ten days of my first conception of the plan, I made a small though imperfect model.

"Experiments with this encouraged me to make one on

* Olmsted's Biography of Whitney.

a larger scale; but the extreme difficulty of procuring workmen and the proper materials in Georgia, prevented my completing the larger one until some time in April last. This, though much larger than my first attempt, is not above one-third as large as machines may be made with convenience. The cylinder is *only two feet two inches* in length, and six inches in diameter. It is turned *by hand*, and requires the strength of one man to keep it in constant motion.

"It is the stated task of one negro to clean fifty weight (I mean fifty pounds after it is separated from the seed) of the green seed cotton per day."

The biographer of Mr. Whitney thus alludes to the unfortunate and mistaken scheme of Mr. Whitney and his partner at the outset of their business, which was to erect the machinery in different sections of the cotton region, and to engross the whole business of ginning themselves, the profits of which were very tempting, being no less than every third pound taken for toll.

"This did not at once supply the demands of the cotton growers, and it multiplied the inducements to make the machines in violation of the patent. Had the proprietors confined their views to the manufacture of the machines, and to the sale of patent rights, it is probable that they would have avoided some of the difficulties with which they had afterwards to contend."

In 1796, Miller and Whitney had *thirty* gins in operation at different places in Georgia, either by horse or water-power.

The consequence was that their patent was infringed, and they became involved from the outset in a series of expensive lawsuits to protect their rights; and it was nearly thirteen years, when their patent had nearly expired, before they succeeded in obtaining a verdict in their favor.

In the mean time, they were subjected to a series of the most disheartening losses and embarrassments.

It has been stated that Whitney did not at first use the circular saw plates in his machines, although subsequently it was satisfactorily proved in one of his suits that the idea of such teeth had early occurred to him.

The application of this form or description of the gin rag was first made by Hodgin Holmes, of Georgia, who obtained a patent for it in May, 1796.

It is related in Georgia that this form of tooth was first accidentally suggested by sawing through a board partition with a common handsaw into a room partially filled with seed cotton, into which the saw penetrated, and was observed to draw a portion of the fibre through attached to the teeth.

A gang of saws working vertically through grates was tried, but no means could be devised for detaching the lint or fibre. The saws were therefore worthless for the purpose except in connection with the cylinders of Whitney's machine; they were essentially a part of his invention.

In the celebrated decision made by Judge Johnson, in December, 1807, the Judge thus disposes of Mr. Holmes's pretensions.

"A Mr. Holmes has cut teeth in plates of iron and passed them over the cylinder. This is certainly a meritorious improvement in the mechanical process of constructing this machine. But at last, what does it amount to, except a more convenient mode of making the same thing? Every characteristic of Mr. Whitney's machine is preserved. The cylinder, the iron tooth, the rotary motion of the tooth, the breastwork and brush, and all the merit which this discovery can assume, is that of a more expeditious mode of attaching the tooth to the cylinder."

Of the merit of the invention, Judge Johnson, at that early day, in the same opinion, uses the following emphatic language:—

"We cannot express the weight of the obligation which the country owes to this invention. The extent of it cannot now be seen. Some faint presentiment may be formed from the reflection that cotton is rapidly supplanting wool, flax, silk, and even furs in manufactures, and may one day profitably supply the use of specie in our East India trade. Our sister States also participate in the benefits of this invention; for, besides affording the raw material for their manufacturers, the bulkiness and quantity of the article afford a valuable employment for their shipping."

By the introduction of this gin the value of the cotton crop of the United States was increased, in the short period of ten years, from about one hundred and fifty thousand dollars to at least eight millions. And what estimate shall we place upon the value of the invention when we view the present production of cotton?

Constituting considerably more than half the value of the whole domestic exports of the United States, it has become so identified with the wants of mankind; is so essential to the industry and capital of the world, that to withhold the produce of a single crop from our principal customer, Great Britain, would involve her manufactories in ruin, reduce her operatives to pauperism, and seriously derange all her commercial interests and relations.*

* The lives of nearly two millions of our countrymen are dependent upon the cotton crops of America; their destiny may be said, without

With what ingratitude has this great benefactor of his country and the world been treated? Millions would not adequately have rewarded him for his great boon; and yet the very name of WHITNEY has almost ceased to be used in connection with the machine of his invention, which is now known familiarly by those of the present manufacturers, and who at most can only claim some slight modification or improvement upon the original. Thus, we have Carver's gins; Bates and Hyde's, Atwood's, Parkhurst's, Taylor's, and numerous others, known only in the neighborhood in which they are made.

It is true that Mr. Whitney was not wholly uncompensated. The State of South Carolina made Miller and Whitney a grant of fifty thousand dollars, payable in four instalments. The State of North Carolina, in 1802, levied a tax on each saw employed, for the term of five years, for their benefit, and the following year Tennessee did the same for the period of four years.

Both South Carolina and Tennessee suspended the payment of the stipulated sums for some years. North Carolina, however, was true to her engagement.

In Georgia, although the patent was generally invaded, there were some who respected the invention, and *purchased* the right of using it.

One of the instruments by which this privilege was conveyed having, by rare chance, been preserved in the family of the writer, is given in the Appendix (see H.). as a document of curious interest, and as serving to show

any sort of hyperbole, *to hang upon a thread!* Should any dire calamity befall the land of cotton, a thousand of our merchant ships would rot idly in dock, ten thousand mills must stop their busy looms, and two million mouths would starve for lack of food to feed them.

DICKENS.

the exact date both of the invention and the patent, and the terms on which its use was accorded.

Whitney's gin was introduced into Georgia in 1794.

In the following year, it came in use in Mississippi, so speedily was its value made known through the whole cotton region.

In 1795, Daniel Clarke, living then near Fort Adams, in Wilkinson County, had one constructed almost entirely by a Negro mechanic owned by him, chiefly from a rude drawing and an imperfect description obtained from a traveller who had seen Whitney's gin in Georgia.

It is known that several gins were in operation in Adams county previous to the evacuation of the country by the Spaniards.*

In 1798, cotton was shipped from a gin of Thomas Wilkins, on Pine Ridge, near Natchez; it was then put up in round bags. This, next to Clark's gin, on his plantation near Fort Adams, was probably the earliest construction, and must, at the time referred to, have been in operation about two years.

In the then condition of the country, and in the absence of mechanical skill, the first machinery employed was, of course, rude and imperfect; and it is said that the first rags or saws manufactured were hammered out of hoe-blades, and had only two or three teeth to the inch. Well-made and tempered saws were worth five dollars each, separate from the other machinery. The price of *gin stands* is now about three dollars and a half per saw. The improvement in machinery having obviated the old, tedious, and expensive process, the seg-

* Mr. Dunbar mentions being from home for the purpose of inspecting a cotton gin in September, 1795; and states that, in 1797, cotton had become the "*universal crop*" of the District of Natchez.

ments of the saw are now made at a single cut, and afterwards the teeth are cut on them very accurately and expeditiously, by a machine nicely adapted to the purpose.

David Greenleaf became one of the earliest, if not the first ginwright in the country, and was unquestionably the most skilful of his day. He settled here previous to 1795, and soon after was known to have seen and examined a *model* of the Whitney gin, at the house of Philip Six, near Selserstown.

Mr. Greenleaf subsequently built a gin in the same neighborhood, on his own account, upon the land of Richard Curtiss. This was long afterwards known as the public gin of Edmund Andrews, and formed one point on the boundary line between the counties of Adams and Jefferson.

As an evidence of the skill of some of our early ginwrights, Mr. Dunbar may be quoted. Writing to a friend, in May, 1799, he says: "I have reason to think the new gin has been much more improved here than anywhere else. The latest and best gins cannot injure the cotton more than a pair of cards might do."

Eleazer Carver commenced the business of making cotton gins near the town of Washington, in the Mississippi Territory, in the year 1807.

"There were then no labor-saving machines in the country for making or preparing any parts of a gin.

"Saw-mills had not been introduced to facilitate woodwork, nor forges or foundries for the metallic parts of the gin.

"The gin-saws were made either of inferior sheet-iron, or forged from the bar by the hands of common blacksmiths, who had no better implements for finishing them than cold-chisels and files; and the making of the other parts of the machine were attended by corresponding inconveniences for the lack of workshops, lathes, and other suitable tools."

To obviate some of these inconveniences, Mr. Carver erected a small saw-mill, about the year 1810, one of the first known to him in the country.

The business of Mr. Carver in gin-building increasing, in order to have the benefit of other facilities, he established himself in Bridgewater, Massachusetts, and has continued, up to the present time, either singly or in connection with other parties, to manufacture and supply gins very extensively to the cotton-planters of the southwest.

One of his principal improvements of the cotton gin was in the construction of the grate, to prevent it from becoming clogged or choked by the lodging and collecting of the fibre in the open spaces. This was patented in November, 1838, the plan and specification of which may be seen in the *American Polytechnic Journal*, vol. i. p. 382.

Some of the merchants of Natchez erected public gins in and near that city, and at Washington and other points, in which the seed cotton was received by weight and ginned for one-tenth, calculating it to yield only one-fourth of ginned cotton.

Few planters were then so opulent as to raise cotton enough to give employment to a single gin, and those who were enabled to erect them received the crops of their less favored neighbors at the established rates. This was a profitable business, and was the foundation of the fortunes of some of the proprietors.

The cotton culture received such an impulse from the introduction of these gins, that they could not keep pace with the production. Some of them were kept running unceasingly for several years; cotton being brought to them continually from every quarter. It was frequently packed on horses in sacks, from the Homochitto and other remote settlements, a distance of twenty or thirty miles; the seed became a nuisance, and the gin holders were required to keep them inclosed to prevent the hogs of the neighborhood from feeding upon them, which was regarded as destructive to the hog.

Attempts were made to get rid of the seed by burning in the heap. No suspicion of their value as an application to the land seems to have been entertained. The stalks, also, were universally pulled up and burned on the field.

On the delivery of his crop at the gin, the planter received what was termed a cotton receipt. These receipts became literally the circulating medium of the country, protected by legislative enactment, and were recoverable with damages for non-delivery of the cotton after a period of forty days, if not otherwise stipulated.

They were received by merchants in payment of accounts, or for the purchase of goods, and were also readily disposed of at the rate of five dollars per hundred pounds of seed cotton, thus relieving the planter of all further trouble and charge; the expense of packing, hauling, storing, shipping, &c., being borne by the purchaser.

PREPARATION OF COTTON FOR MARKET, EXPORTATION, AND SALE.

Many meritorious modifications and improvements have from time to time been introduced in the construction of the gin. These consist chiefly in the size of the cylinder and brush, the construction of the teeth, and the form and arrangement of the grates, by which the efficiency of the machine has been more than quadrupled.

Gins are now constructed to run from forty to eighty saws; the sixty-saw gin is, however, most generally used, and is capable of turning out a daily average of three or four bales of clean cotton.

The cotton gin, in the form now used, is composed of a stand of about six feet in width, inclosing a cylinder and brush, arranged horizontally, and running on iron axes in composition metallic boxes. On the cylinder are arranged a series of circular saws, or *rags*, as they are familiarly termed, made of best cast-steel plates, in segments, or two parts. They are placed about one inch apart, and are so stayed and secured to the cylinder as to insure a perfect accuracy and uniformity of action.

The teeth are very pointed and oblique, and are very carefully and smoothly dressed.

The cylinder, when put in motion by a band running on a trundle-head attached to it on one side of the stand, and by which it is connected with the running gear, revolves in such a manner that the teeth pass between a corresponding series of metallic grates, curved or bent so as to conform to the circumference of the saws, and placed in such a manner as only to permit the free passage of the teeth of the saw, together with the lint which it removes in its revolutions.

The grates form one side of a movable hopper, the breastboard or *fall* in front forming the opposite; the hopper working on hinges at the bottom, by which the grates can be elevated above the saws as occasion requires.

In its working position, the teeth of the saws pass through the grates and enter the hopper just so far as to take a proper hold on the cotton with which it is kept supplied, by raking in from the pile of seed cotton deposited on the top of the stand.

In operation, the saws passing through the cotton causes it to revolve in the hopper, and form a roll from which the seed, as the lint becomes detached, falls to the bottom, and is removed by means of a spout.

In the rear of the cylinder, and in contact with it, is a circular brush of bristles supported on arms, which revolving, by means of the gearing, with a largely accelerated velocity, compared with the revolutions of the saws, whips or brushes rapidly and completely from them the lint or fibre drawn through the grates. The velocity with which this fanlike brush revolves causes a strong draft of air through the apertures in the stand, which wafts or blows the lint in light flakes or fleeces through a trunk or flue to a chamber or lint-room, made tight and close for its reception. The flues are constructed with a false floor of slats, between which much of the false seed and trash, which may have passed through the grates with the lint, falls in passing to the lint-room, and the cotton is thus freed from these impurities. It has been stated that the capacity of Whitney's gin, when first put into operation, was about one bale per day. Sixty saw gins are now guaranteed to gin five or six bales in the same period; but the average performance is not more than three where pains are taken to make a good article.

A very slovenly habit having grown up chiefly on the river plantations and swamp lands, of gathering the cotton with a great deal of dirt and trash, consisting of parts of bolls and leaf, an appendage to the gin, termed a trasher, was devised to get rid of these impurities. It consisted of a long hollow cylinder or trunk placed in an inclined position, the under side of which was constructed of coarse wire grating forming an open sieve. A long shaft extending lengthwise through the trunk, armed with short pegs, being made to revolve rapidly, the cotton, which was placed in at the upper end, was very thoroughly beaten in its passage through, and a large portion of the trash was extracted by falling through the grating.

A comparison, however, of returns of sales of clean, neatly handled cotton with those of the most dirty and foul, seems to have established the fact that dirt and trash command too good a price to be thus wasted. At least a sufficient discrimination was not made to compensate for this particularity of handling. The trashers have consequently gone almost entirely out of use.

It was thought by some that the rotary motion of the trasher gave the fibre of the cotton a twist which rendered it liable to be napped or cut by the saws in the ginning process—or at least injured for the purposes of the manufacturer.

Much progress has been made in the modes of packing cotton as well as in ginning it. In the first instance, it was put up in long round bags containing about three hundred pounds, and Sea Island cotton is still so packed. A long sack, having been well soaked and partially dried, is suspended through a round hole in the floor of an upper apartment, and kept extended by stitching a wooden hoop to the upper end, and forming a rim or ledge which supports it on the floor. The cotton is then put in gradually, whilst a man within the bag treads and rams it down with an iron bar. A small block of wood is placed in each corner and tied for convenience of handling.

In Mississippi, square bales were first made in a rough lever press. This was about the year 1779. Mr. Dunbar, who experienced the inconvenience of the machinery then used for this purpose, ordered from Philadelphia a cast-iron screw-press, which was sent out to him at the close of 1801, at the cost of about one thousand dollars; at which time he proposed to indemnify himself for the expenditure by using it in the manufacture of *cotton-seed oil.*

The lever press, however, was soon superseded by the press introduced by Greenleaf, composed of two wooden screws, which were turned alternately in the packing; this press has not yet gone entirely out of use.

The detached single wooden screw-press, with the long and ponderous A sweeps, connected with the upper end of the screw, common in Georgia, is very generally used in the eastern and northern counties of the State. It seems to be an awkward heavily-timbered structure, and never fails to excite surprise that it has not long since given place to one which is more convenient, efficient, and economical.

One serious disadvantage attending it is that, from its being disconnected from the gin-house, and frequently at some distance from it, it becomes necessary to pack the ginned cotton to it in baskets down from the lint-room in the gin-house and up to the box at the press; and, not being under the same shelter, this must necessarily be done in fair dry weather; whereas, in the other presses, the work can go on in wet weather, when the hands cannot be otherwise employed, and when, from the humidity of the atmosphere, the cotton can be more perfectly compressed.

The press invented by Dr. Newel, of Lake St. Joseph, in Louisiana, which goes by his name, has come into very general use, especially on large plantations, where heavy work is required.

It is worked by a single cast-iron screw bolted securely at the upper end to the follower, and presses upwards against a straining beam on the top of the box; the bale being taken out on the upper floor, on a level with the lint-room.

The screw ascends, without turning, through a cast-iron, movable nut or female connected with the lower beam of the press. To this nut the lever is attached, and through it also the lower end of the screw, in bringing down the follower, passes into a hollow cylinder of plank sunk into the ground. Twenty bales is perhaps the average number turned out with five hands in a day.

The objection to the press is that ninety revolutions, up and down, are required to make a bale; but the application of steam-power to this press, as has been done on large plantations, obviates this objection.

McCombs's press is worked by lever power. Two beams, the lower ends extended, and resting on rollers, stand under the press like an inverted **V** (**Λ**), on the top or point of junction of which the follower rests. These beams are drawn together by a stout cable or chain, made fast to them at the bottom, passing through blocks on opposite sides, and winding around a detached upright shaft, which is turned by power attached to the end of a suitable lever. It is a very efficient press, and is used by many. The principal objection made to it arises from the danger of the breaking of the chain or rope. The number of revolutions is fifteen to the bale.

Lewis's revolving lever-press, recently invented, seems to have brought this application of power for this purpose as near perfection as perhaps can be attained. It operates under the box by two beams placed in a manner similar to those in McCombs's press; but the ends of the levers are made to approach each other by rack and pinion work connected with the lower ends; the whole press and levers revolve around the stationary pinion. Less than four revolutions are sufficient to drive the follower up to the proper point; the whole number of revolutions up and down being only about seven.

On the principle of this press and McCombs's, there is a gain of power as the pressure is increased. By either of the latter presses, it is said, fifty bales can be turned out in twelve hours. Both of them are Mississippi inventions, introduced by ginwrights of the neighboring counties of Claiborne and Warren.

There have been many previous improvements and modifications of the cotton-press, but which, having mainly gone out of use, it is not necessary to particularize.

The boxes in which the cotton is packed in pressing, are made of wide three-inch plank, and are four and a half feet long and twenty-two inches wide, securely keyed together, and having side doors hinged on the ends to take out the bales when pressed and tied; the top and bottom of the box, either of which is called the follower, as the pressure is applied from above or below, according to the construction of the press, are made of similar timber, with seven grooves at regular and corresponding distances, through which to pass the rope.

Preparatory to making the bale, a piece of bagging of suitable dimensions is spread on the bottom of the box. A proper quantity being packed or trodden in, another piece of bagging, of sufficient size to complete the covering, is laid on, the screw or lever is put in motion, and the follower ascends or descends into the box, as the case may be, to the edge of the side doors, which are then thrown open; the ends and edges of the bagging are gathered together, and stitched with twine, and the ropes passed through the grooves and tied. The movement of the screw or lever is then reversed, the pressure removed, and the bale taken out.

Although compressed to nearly a square form, by the expansion of the rope when the pressure is taken off, it assumes a flattened shape.

Bales are estimated as averaging four hundred pounds; but, as freight is charged by the bale, many planters, especially those remote from market, prefer making them heavier, and five hundred pound bales are not unusual.

Hoop iron has been introduced of late years; but the use, as yet, is confined to a few large planters. It makes a very neat compact bale, and there is not that stretching or expansion as in the bales tied with rope. The hoops have generally a light coating of paint or varnish to prevent oxidation, and are very adroitly and speedily fastened by means of iron rivets passed through holes previously punched at proper distances.

The material used for wrapping the cotton is chiefly of hemp manufactured in Kentucky, and hence known as "Kentucky bagging." It has become so inferior of late, however, being frequently so open and slaizy that the gin mark cannot be legibly printed upon it, that it has been superseded to considerable extent by the India bagging and gunny bags, which present a neater appearance.

Five gunny bags will wrap a bale, and can be properly joined without cutting. They are, however, inferior in strength to the other materials used, and are very liable to be torn by the iron hooks used by the boat hands in loading and unloading the cotton.

The rope used is chiefly manufactured in Kentucky and Missouri, and is generally regarded as the best for

12

the purpose, inferior only to the iron hoop, which has this advantage over it, of affording greater security in case of fire on shipboard, as the cotton, in a well-compressed bale, burns slowly with a smouldering flame, affording time to extinguish it; whereas, if the ropes were burned in two, the bale bursts open, and goes off with a fierce blaze that would probably baffle all attempts to save the cargo.

Gin houses are generally built with a single floor resting on high blocks or pillars to admit of the running gear below; a superstructure with one low story, together with the span of the roof, ordinarily affording all the space required; the gin stand being at one end, and the lint room and cotton press at the other.

The running gear consists of a large central wheel, twelve or fifteen feet in diameter, the periphery of which rests upon arms framed into a massive upright shaft, which rests on an iron gudgeon, and turns in a metallic ink in a large wooden block sunk in the ground. The circumference of the wheel is provided with vertical cogs formerly made of hickory, or some hard wood, but which are now very generally superseded by iron, cast in segments of convenient dimensions, and securely bolted to the rim of the wheel; these cogs play into a wallower, or a vertical spur-wheel, on one end of a horizontal shaft, to the opposite end of which the band wheel or drum is attached; a leather band, about a foot in width, connects this with the trundle-head of the gin stand, and puts the machinery in motion.

About four mules are employed to propel the machinery. One careful experienced hand attends the gin stand, and two small boys are required to drive the mules.

The seed cotton, beyond what is required to keep

the gin employed, is generally put up in separate cotton houses, as a measure of precaution to guard against its loss in the event of the burning of the gin, which not unfrequently happens from the friction of the machinery, carelessness, or by the act of the incendiary.

The great majority of gins are propelled by horse-power. Steam, however, is coming very much into use on the large river plantations, and the gin houses are constructed of enlarged dimensions and at considerable cost; two or more gin stands sometimes are placed in the same building.

In Washington County, there has recently been erected a very spacious and complete gin house, containing four eighty-saw stands, in which a very complete steam-engine supplies the power by which the seed cotton is elevated, ginned, and pressed, and the bales lowered.

At the expense of some tediousness of detail, all the principal machinery employed in preparing the cotton crop has now been sufficiently described to afford the uninitiated a reasonable knowledge of all the processes it undergoes in fitting it for market.

The bales are now weighed and numbered, and the name of the proprietor, or of his plantation, or both, is printed or marked on one end. Formerly, the weight was also added.

The cotton is then hauled in wagons or carts, with ox or mule teams, chiefly the former, to the nearest and most convenient shipping points, from which it is consigned to the agent or commission merchant of the planter.

That on or convenient to the Tombigbee River goes to Mobile; the residue to New Orleans, accompanied by bills of lading given by the boats, a copy or duplicate of which is retained by the shipper.

The smaller planters find a market nearer home, and generally prefer selling at the shipping port, chiefly at Yazoo City, Jackson, Vicksburg and Natchez, and at Aberdeen and Columbus on the Tombigbee.

A considerable portion from North Mississippi goes to Memphis, Tennessee. That which goes to New Orleans and Mobile, is delivered at the cotton presses, or is deposited on the wharves, and thence hauled on drays to the warehouses of the consignees.

Each bale is then sampled by cutting into the edge and drawing a small portion of the cotton, which is classified and put up in packages of cartridge paper, and exposed in the counting-room of the merchant to the inspection of the cotton-brokers, who are employed to purchase for the manufacturers, or those who speculate in the article.

When sold, it is reweighed, and sent to the steam-presses, where it is recompressed and reduced to equal dimensions on the sides for greater economy of space in storing on shipboard.

If carefully and correctly weighed, there will generally be a gain on the gin weights in favor of the planter of two or three per cent.

Accounts of sales are returned to the planter, and the proceeds credited to him, deducting two and a half per cent. commission for selling and the incidental charges, such as freight, drayage, storage, weighing, and river and fire insurance; the latter being covered by what are termed open policies, kept by the merchant with the insurance offices, and which embrace all consignments except those on which the shipper prefers taking the risk himself, and notifies the consignee accordingly.

MAIZE, OR INDIAN CORN—VARIETIES—CULTIVATION AND PRODUCTION.

It is needless here to discuss the question of the eastern or western origin of this most nutritious and invaluable grain. That has already been satisfactorily done, and the evidence justifies us in placing it among many other similar contributions for which the Old World is indebted to the New.

It is certain that the first Europeans that set foot in Mississippi found it generally cultivated by the Indian tribes.

In the progress of De Soto's expedition, it was noticed as "of such luxuriant growth as to produce three or four ears to the stalk."

With us, as an article of food, it has become by far the most important that our soil produces.

The varieties which seem best adapted to our climate are the Tuscarora, the Gourd Seed, and the White and Yellow Flint.

Other varieties thrive well, but being less generally applicable to the varied uses of the grain, are not established as a common production.

Among these are the White Flour corn, the Sweet Rareripe, or Mandan, the small Flint "*pop-corn*," and some fancy kinds, such as the Golden Grain, &c., which are occasionally introduced.

All these kinds are valued for particular qualities, which are combined in none, and are more or less in favor with different planters, according to the uses or purposes for which they are designed, or as they accord with the standard of excellence which each one, in the diversity of taste or judgment, may have formed.

Generally, they are kept distinct, and preserved at least in their original purity, if not improved.

Some planters, who are noted for good management and good living, cultivate at least two or three kinds, which are not suffered to become mixed, so as to have the benefit of all the distinctive qualities of the grain in all the forms in which it is used.

Too many, however, content themselves with a *single* kind, if such may be said of a heterogeneous mixture of every variety that results from indiscriminate cultivation.

As a stock corn, the gourd seed, from its easy mastication, is perhaps generally preferred, a preference, notwithstanding the property and the size of the ear and grain, to which it is not fully entitled, being perhaps the lightest and least nutritious of all the varieties.

The white flint is unequalled for bread, which, when properly prepared, approaches most nearly that made from wheat; and for that famed Maryland and Virginia dish, "*great hominy*," a luxury which few substantial planters will forego at their tables, is indispensable.

Its great hardness forms the objection to its use for stock, particularly for old horses and oxen—an objection which, however, may be obviated by soaking it in water for a few hours.

It is a heavy corn, and contains a large proportion of nutriment; is perhaps as little affected by weevil as any other, and withstands the drought better than any other kind; and it is admitted that it yields most fodder.

The Tuscarora, which is an intermediate variety, originating doubtless in a mixture of the white flint and gourd seed, and in which the opposite and objectionable properties of these are in a measure overcome, is decidedly, for common purposes, the most valuable, as it is believed to be the most generally cultivated variety; for the size of the ear, the smallness of the cob, and perhaps the yield per acre, it is unsurpassed.

It requires careful selection, having a tendency, in rich land, to run too much to stalk or to return to one or the other of the varieties in which it originated.

Contrary to the too generally entertained opinion that all our seeds *run out* in time, and require continual changes from abroad, this corn has been cultivated for more than thirty years on the same plantation, in which time it has been greatly improved.

The Flour Corn is highly esteemed by many for bread, being very white, and pulverizing readily in the mill to a soft impalpable meal, free from the gritty character of that from the flinty varieties. Its chief excellence, however, is found in its superiority for use in the green or immature state, as the *roasting ear*, being unequalled for the pulpy sweetness and tenderness of the grain when so dressed.

It is claimed, for some of the yellow varieties, that they are the most nutritious, as evidenced by the relative weight of the grain and the percentage of alcohol produced by distillation; they are, however, unsuitable for bread, having a raw dough-like taste, and are believed to be unwholesome, intestinal diseases being sometimes traced to their use.

Corn with us is cultivated chiefly in the drill, being planted on the ridge or in the water furrow, according to the character of the ground, whether flat and low or high and rolling; the success of either mode depending somewhat on the moisture or dryness of the succeeding season.

The most usual time of planting is about the first of March; the only motive for planting earlier being to get out of the way of the cotton crop; the cultivation of which is too much embarrassed by a late crop of corn.

The plough is the principal implement employed in the cultivation, and it is rarely gone over more than twice with the hoe.

The blades are generally in a condition to be gathered for fodder between the *laying by* of the cotton and the commencement of the picking season.

The tops or top fodder are very rarely saved, as in the northern States; and the blades, after being dried in the field, and tied in bundles, are put up in stacks in or near the barnyard, but more usually in convenient places in the fields where they grow.

Some planters gather their corn in the latter part of August, or before the press of the cotton-picking season. If it is suffered to remain in the field, as it frequently is, until the approach of winter, it is usual to bend down the stalk below the ear, as in that inverted position it is better protected from the weather, the shuck, or husk, very effectually shedding the rain, and preventing the mildew and sprouting of the grain. It is also less exposed to damage from violent winds, which frequently occur about the period of the autumnal equinox, and better protection against the depredations of the woodpecker, blackbird, and other enemies, is thus afforded.

The proper time and mode of housing corn, with reference to the ravages of the weevil, have long been a contested question among planters.

Many store it away in open, well-ventilated cribs, with latticed sides. Others sprinkle the different layers of corn, always put up in the *shuck*, with a weak brine, or strew the berries or leaves of the China tree, or the bark and leaves of the sassafras, through the mass in the same way.

None of these expedients have proved effectual, and I am inclined to think, from conversation with many judicious, practical planters, that the cribs cannot be too close or dark.

It is the result of their experience, also, that the *destruction* of the weevil, which is deposited in the field, is best accomplished by gathering the corn when quite wet, immediately after a rain, and housing it in that state. Sufficient moisture is retained to occasion a degree of heat in the mass, adequate to the destruction of the weevil, either in its mature or larva state, without at all damaging the corn. The close, dark crib secures it then from further damage, as very few weevil will find access to it.

It must be understood, however, that the corn is not to be exposed to rain after being pulled from the stalk, or when lying in heaps on the ground. If so, it becomes saturated, and, if put up in that state, would infallibly mildew and spoil.

In gathering corn in the field, it is *slip-shucked*, as it is termed; that is, the footstalk is broken off within the shuck, so as to leave the outer coarse and weathered folds attached to the stalk, the ear remaining enveloped in two-thirds of the inner sound and softer folds or layers, which serve not only to protect the corn from shelling off and wasting in the hauling and housing, but supply a large store of valuable forage for mules and cattle, even more nutritious, when properly treated, than the blades themselves.

It is difficult to estimate the average production per acre, throughout the State. Perhaps it is as low as twenty bushels. Thirty bushels are accounted a very fair crop, and forty a large one.

The total production of corn in the State, in 1849, was stated at 22,446,000 bushels, equal to about thirty-seven bushels to each individual inhabitant.

Mississippi ranks only as eleventh as a corn-producing State, making a little over a third of the quantity produced in Ohio and Kentucky. Three other States, including the adjoining State of Tennessee, make double the quantity. If our corn crop was suitably distributed, it might perhaps afford a scant subsistence, but the river counties are largely indebted to the Western States for their supply.

WHEAT, OATS, RYE, BARLEY, RICE, ETC.

Of these less cultivated and comparatively less important cereals, some of which are imperfectly adapted to our climate, this notice will be quite brief.

The humidity of the climate, especially of the southern and western counties, subjects wheat to the smut; and the want of water-power, and suitable mills for preparing the flour, together with the facility of procuring it from the wheat-growing States, at a cost below that of producing it, prevents its cultivation in this quarter.

In the northern and eastern counties, where these considerations do not apply to the same extent, and where there are in many neighborhoods convenient, and in some cases very efficient, merchant mills, it becomes more an object of attention. The quality and weight of grain in that quarter, and the yield per acre, are spoken of favorably; but of this I have been unable to procure more minute particulars.

The quantity raised in Mississippi, in 1849, was 138,000 bushels.

Oats, of which, in the same year, there were produced 1,500,000 bushels, are better adapted to our climate.

Of the two varieties, Spring and Winter Oat, the latter, known also as the Egyptian or Black Oat, is cultivated chiefly for pasture, and may be grazed with little deterioration of the crop until the first of March. It succeeds well, and would be more cultivated if the abundant production of Indian corn, in the general estimation of planters, did not render it unnecessary. It is, however, much more extensively sown than the census returns would indicate; as, being in a great measure designed for winter grazing, perhaps not half the quantity grown is harvested.

Some planters are in the habit of sowing the winter oat between the cotton rows, when they go over their fields the last time with the hoe-harrow. The seed lie dormant whilst the ground is shaded, and do not germinate until the cotton plant is killed by the frost. The oats are not sufficiently advanced, therefore, to injure the crop, or to present any impediment to the gathering of the cotton. After supplying the winter grazing, the green crop is turned in, in the spring, by which the land is thought to be enriched; the oat also protects the ground from washing into gulleys by the heavy winter rains.

Rye and barley may be said to be grown almost exclusively for pasturing. By the last census returns, about 10,000 bushels of the former, and only 229 bushels of the latter, were the amount produced in 1849. The former is adapted to every part of the

State. Barley I have only seen in the northern counties. In Washington County, it is said to thrive as well as in Kentucky.

A class of grain-bearing plants, which can hardly be said to be cultivated, at least to any extent, but which are often found growing in vacant spaces in the fields, frequently, from a chance scattering of the seed, have a value for some purposes which should entitle them to more attention. I allude to the *Holcas bicolor*, Guinea Corn, or Chicken Corn, as it is variously termed, and the allied species, the Broom Corn, and another kind known to me only as the "Hebron Corn." These all resemble the maize in the stalk and blade, growing equally as high, the stem more slender and of a tougher and more reedy character. The grain is produced on large heads, on the extremity of the stalks.

The first two species are too common and well known to require further description; the latter, or "Hebron Corn," grows in a compact and heavy cluster, the stalk generally curving downward a few inches below the head, which grows to maturity in an inverted position; the grains in each head are very numerous, and more than double the size of those of either of the other species.

These all afford a valuable grain for young poultry; but their chief value consists in shading and fertilizing the land, and more especially for stopping washes and gulleys in the fields, which is done very effectually by the matted roots, and for which purpose it is coming to be the practice of many planters to strew the seed of the Guinea corn about the ends of the turn-rows and heads of hollows, a usage much to be commended.

Of rice, the census returns give about 2,700,000 pounds, as the crop of Mississippi in 1849. It is very generally cultivated in the southeastern counties, rarely, however, beyond an acre or two on a farm, although there are some plantations of considerable extent, as on the tide-waters of the gulf, one of which was observed on Back Bay, a few miles in the rear of Mississippi City.

The Upland variety is chiefly cultivated, and is in some cases partially irrigated.

It is principally cleaned by pounding by hand. A mill was met with, however, in Marion County, where both the hulling and winnowing were very effectually performed by water-power, on a scale adequate to the wants of a considerable neighborhood. The flavor of the newly-prepared rice met with in those counties is much richer and sweeter than that which we ordinarily purchase.

SUGAR-CANE.

The sugar-cane is cultivated to a limited extent in some portions of the State. By the census returns, it appears that the crop of 1849 was equal to 388 hogsheads, and about 18,000 gallons of molasses.

Molasses has been made as far north as latitude 33° 40′ north, in Chickasaw County, where an experiment of three years has encouraged the belief that sugar can be profitably produced there to the extent of the local demand.

Sugar has also been made in Hinds County on a small scale for experiment, and small *patches* of the cane become more common as we approach the sea-shore.

East of Pearl River, and south of Covington County, many of the most substantial planters make all the sugar and molasses required for their own use, and some to spare to their neighbors.

The cane is obviously becoming gradually acclimated, and may at no distant period be grown advantageously throughout the greater portion of the State, for home consumption.

The sugar-mills are, of course, rude, and of small dimensions, consisting, in fact, of little more than the rollers for grinding the cane, which are made of seasoned oak timber, and stand generally in the open air; a common shed suffices for a protection of the kettles, which are common iron ones, such as are used for stock.

There are two of these mills in Pike County, and as many in Amite, where molasses has been made. In Marion County there are some eighteen or twenty, and several in Perry.

Should the ravages of the army worm and the rot continue to increase, and the present price of cotton not be maintained, the period is not remote, perhaps, when the cane will, to considerable extent, supersede the cultivation of cotton on the river plantations as high up as Natchez or Vicksburg.

SWEET POTATO—BATATUS EDULIS.

The esteem in which the sweet potato is held may be estimated by the extent to which it is produced, 4,742,000 bushels, worth more than two millions and a quarter of dollars, being the crop of Mississippi of 1849.

In the production of this esculent, Mississippi ranks fourth among the States of the Union; Georgia, North Carolina, and Alabama only excelling her.

Five varieties are cultivated with us, which will be

mentioned in the order of their excellence, as generally estimated. First in quality, as in extent of cultivation, stands the Yam, which, if surpassed by some in average size, is approached by but one in delicacy of flavor. Its shape is oval or roundish, with a smooth exterior, and yellowish tint. It is as prolific as any other, and keeps remarkably well.

The next in place is the Spanish, or White potato; it is long and crooked, with large veins or nerves running lengthwise on the exterior, by which it is universally characterized. Another characteristic, which distinguishes it from all others, is an aptitude of the flesh, or meat, if I may so designate it, when cooked, to divide or separate in layers or flakes lengthwise, the fibre at the same time being destitute of any stringy property.

Early in the season, it is rather too milky to suit the taste of many, but when thoroughly cured, it becomes very sweet and rich, differing somewhat in flavor from the yam. It grows to a large size, and, singularly enough, notwithstanding its excellence, it seems to be greatly neglected of late, and is not now often met with.

The Bermuda potato has a deep crimson or purple skin; but the interior is very white. In form, it is more cylindrical than the yam, somewhat elongated, and is regarded by some as the largest and most prolifie variety. Its flavor, however, is coarse and flat.

The Red is the earliest variety introduced here. It was formerly very generally cultivated; it is inferior to the foregoing in size, and not now very much in use.

It is rather dry and mealy, and is best early in the season, when newly dug, and it is perhaps the earliest to mature.

The Poplar Root, which somewhat resembles the yam in outward appearance, but not generally so round, with a smooth skin, and the color rather a deeper yellow, was introduced ten or fifteen years since with high commendations. It proved a watery, insipid kind, however, and is now generally banished.

Up to the period of 1810 or 1815, the yam potato was rarely seen; the old red and white Spanish being altogether cultivated—the former much the most extensively.

The Bermuda is the most recent introduction.

All the varieties of the sweet potato succeed best in a loose sandy soil, although the yam is said to flourish in the prairies of the eastern counties. I have seen one of that variety raised near Macon, which weighed ten pounds.

The proper time for planting is about the first of April, and the most approved mode of raising the yam is to *spread* the small roots or potato plantings on a rich bed about the first of March, covering them with three or four inches of loose rich soil. When the sprouts make their appearance above the surface, they are drawn and set out in newly-made ridges after or during a rain.

These beds continue to throw out a succession of sprouts, which may be planted every favorable season as late as the first of August, and if well worked, and the weather be not too dry, will make good potatoes. It is said the red potato does not succeed so well when planted in this way.

At some seasons, the sweet potato is sufficiently matured for early use by the first of September; but it is attended with great waste to commence on them so soon, as it is thought the tubers grow more in October, after the vine begins to decline than before.

The best time for digging potatoes is the first good dry mild weather succeeding the first frost that kills the vines. They are then better *ripened,* freer from water or sap, and consequently keep better. They should not be suffered to remain undug until the ground freezes, as they will become frostbitten and rot.

The most approved mode of preserving the sweet potato, is to place them in piles or heaps of about twenty-five bushels each, on raised ground, with a flooring of corn-stalks and straw, the sides being lined with the same material, the whole covered with three or four inches of earth or sod, a small aperture being left near the apex of the cone for the escape of the moisture which passes off from the potato when undergoing the sweat, which always takes place soon after they are placed in bulk.

Put up properly in this way, they will keep perfectly sound and sweet until June or even later.

The potato *patch* affords a good gleaning to the fattening hogs, which are usually turned upon it, and find in the small tubers, cut and waste potatoes, a favorite food, on which they thrive rapidly, and is a good preparation for after feeding on corn in the close pen.

Some planters put in a large crop of sweet potatoes for this purpose, and when corn is scarce give no other food. The meat is said, however, to be less firm, and the lard more oily, than that of the corn-fattened hog.

THE IRISH POTATO—SOLANUM TUBEROSUM.

The Irish potato is not extensively cultivated, and seldom beyond the limits of the garden.

Two varieties—the Meshanic, and the Purple Eye—are those which seem to be most approved, the red being rarely planted, under the common belief that the white varieties succeed the best. For what we do plant we are dependent every year almost entirely on those brought down the Mississippi from the Western States.

A course embracing the planting, cultivation, and after treatment, which has been tested many years, may be confidently recommended as one attended with much success.

In suitable weather, soon after the first of January, on the even, clean, but unbroken *surface* of the ground appropriated for the purpose, place the cuttings, with the eye upwards, three inches apart, in rows two feet distant from each other. Cover *well* with light rich vegetable compost. Well rotted corn-blades, straw, or leaves from the woods are well suited for this purpose. Draw over this a moderate ridge of earth. As soon as the tops show themselves generally above the surface, an inch or two high, ridge up with earth, again covering the top entirely, and repeat this in ten days or so, when the tops appear the second time. This will give a ridge of sufficient size, and *completes* the cultivation.

About the middle of April the potatoes are fit for use, and are to be dug daily, as required.

About the first of June, especially if the season be dry, the tops begin to fail and gradually die; the grass and weeds which spring up between the rows must not afterwards by any means be removed; otherwise, when deprived of the shade afforded by the top, the potato will become partially scorched or baked in the ground by the intense summer heat, which makes them watery, and causes them to rot. Protected by the grass and weeds, they remain fresh and sound, and will keep in excellent condition until frost.

It is generally conceded that the Irish potato cannot in our climate be kept through the summer out of the ground. For this reason, and possessing no value for stock, together with the preference which most southerners give to the sweet potato, it is not more cultivated.

The crop of 1849 was about 260,000 bushels.

There is a considerable consumption of the Irish potato in our cities and towns convenient to the river, which are obtained from the Western States, at a price much below what they can be produced for here.

PULSE.

The bean is not cultivated at all in Mississippi as a field crop. Several varieties of the cornfield pea, however, are extensively grown.

One million of bushels is reported as the production of 1849; but, when it is remembered that a very large portion of the crop is consumed by stock in the field—that being cultivated with us mainly for the amelioration of the land, the period for gathering coming on also in the press of the cotton-picking season; and that consequently a large proportion of planters save little more than is necessary for seed, it will at once be perceived that the quantity stated in the census returns, as the production of Mississippi, is *very greatly* below that actually raised.

The chief varieties cultivated are the Cow Pea (phaseolus), the Crowder, and the White Pea.

The first is supposed to be indigenous to the United States, as it was found in cultivation among the Indians by the first English settlers in Virginia. The color of this pea is a dark yellow inclining to red, and tinges the water in which it is boiled a dark color, inclining to purple. It is of coarse flavor, and fit only for stock.

The Crowder is considered more prolific. The pod is larger and longer, and the peas, which are numerous in each pod, cylindrical in form, the ends truncated or flattened by compression one against another, growing in close contact. It is for this reason very subject to mildew and rot in wet weather—an objection from which the other named varieties are in a great measure exempt.

The last mentioned, or White Pea, introduced within a few years, and not yet very generally, seems to remain sound in the field for a length of time, and can therefore be housed at the convenience of the planter. Besides this good property, it forms an excellent dish for the table, being light in color when dressed, and even of more delicate flavor than the marrowfat pea of the garden. There is reason to believe that if it could supersede the other varieties, the prejudice against the pea, arising from the frequent loss of stock of all kinds from feeding too freely upon it in the fields, would in a great measure be overcome, these casualties arising probably from the unsound and consequently unwholesome condition to which the Crowder especially is subject.

The pea is most usually sown broadcast between the corn rows at the time it receives the last working with the plough or harrow; sometimes in the rows at an earlier stage of the growth of the corn—a practice that many object to, as it impedes the gathering the fodder which becomes entangled by the vine.

A new variety, said to come from Oregon, has been introduced the present year, and highly recommended as a fertilizer of the soil.

In the first stage of its growth, the Oregon pea stands

erect, and is not unlike the cotton plant, branching somewhat in the same way, the stalk near the ground being at least an inch in diameter. After attaining the height of about three feet, it bends to the ground, which it soon covers with a heavy mat of tangled branches or vines.

The hull or pod is perfectly cylindrical, nearly straight, and not exceeding three or four inches in length, quite black, and well filled with a small green pea, resembling in form and size the ocra seed.

From the size and strength of the stalk or vine, the ploughing it in the green state is quite impracticable. It returns, however, a large amount of vegetable matter to the ground, and on this account will probably be found to excel the common pea vine. The pea itself seems to be too small and insignificant to be of any value.

GRASSES.

Of our grasses, no attempt will be made here to give even a catalogue. Only a few of the most characteristic and useful will be noticed.

Foremost of these, although an introduced species, stands the Bermuda. It is rather a later grass, and revels in the hot, dry weather of midsummer, when most of our other grasses fail.

It will bear two or three heavy cuttings, and produces an almost incredible quantity of delicate nutritious hay, excelling, it is believed, in this particular, any other grass.

Like the sugar cane, it has not yet been so far naturalized as to perfect its seed, and is therefore propagated wholly by transplanting. The facility with which it extends itself by means of runners, which trail to a great length over the ground, striking root at every joint, from which spring also numerous narrow fine blades, forming a thick, matted, luxuriant growth, soon spreads it over a considerable space. Indeed, this property, its tenacity of life, and the depth to which it drives its rootlets, render it a terror to many planters almost as great as the bitter coco, of the sugar plantations in Louisiana.

It is true that it is rather troublesome to contend with in the cultivation of a corn or cotton crop on ground on which it has become thoroughly established; but with proper management it can be eradicated.

Shade is inimical to its growth, and any crop that will cover the ground very densely through the summer and fall, will in a year or two destroy it.

It is emphatically the best grass for our climate, and the only one that fully withstands the scorching heats and severe droughts of our summers.

Forming a dense compact sod, it is destined to be the chief agent in reclaiming those extensive tracts of broken lands in the river counties, once unsurpassed for fertility and productiveness, but which, by negligent or injudicious cultivation, have become defaced with unseemly gulleys and gaping ravines, to arrest and fill up which, must be the first step in reclaiming them.

The Natchez grass, a native which derives it name from first being noticed about the commons of that city, is found overspreading the bluff lands of the river counties. To what extent it has spread in other sections of the State, I am not fully prepared to say. It is a coarse luxuriant grass, growing in tufts or bunches, and bearing its seed in a head, enveloped in a black powder, or smut, which renders it unsightly and disagreeable. It appears to stand the drought well, and, notwithstanding it is coarse and tough, cattle seem to thrive upon it.

The crab grass (*panicum sanguinale*), which has a very wide geographical range, is perhaps the most abundant and persistent species here. It is that with which the planter has chiefly to contend in the cultivation of the cotton and corn crop. It has ample time to come to maturity after the cultivation of the latter has ceased, producing generally a heavy and luxuriant crop between the corn rows, from which most of the crab-grass hay saved is *pulled* by the hand.

There are many other native grasses, such as the crow-foot and other yard grasses, but none of them has assumed any importance for producing or saving of hay.

The timothy, blue grass, and orchard grass, receive some attention in the northern part of the State, but are rarely met with in the other portions of it.

The white clover is pretty generally distributed, grows luxuriantly in good soil, and might be turned to good account but for its objectionable property of salivating stock, especially horses, when grazing upon it.

Experiments have been made in the *cultivation* of red clover with the use of plaster of Paris with very satisfactory results.

STATISTICS.

PROGRESS AND CONDITION OF THE PLANTING INTEREST.

Having passed in review the chief products of agricultural industry of the State, I subjoin a set of tabular statements, compiled from the United States census returns, and from other sources, to exhibit, in a condensed view, the progress and present condition of the planting interest, and which will afford some reliable data for estimating its future prospects. The progressive increase of the population of the State is also given for convenient reference, in connection with the agricultural statistics.

Population of Mississippi, decennially ascertained.

1800.	1810.	1820.	1830.	1840.	1850.
8,850	40,352	75,448	136,621	375,651	606,555

Statement of the Cotton Crop of the United States for the last ten years, with the Receipts, Average Price, and Value at New Orleans.

Year.	Receipt of first bale in New Orleans.	Receipts to Sept. 1, in New Orleans.	Total receipts in New Orleans.	Average price per bale.	Total value in New Orleans.	Total crop of the United States.
1843	Aug. 17	292	910,854	$32	$29,147,328	2,030,409
1844	July 23	5720	979,238	24	23,501,712	2,394,503
1845	July 30	6846	1,053,638	32	33,716,256	2,100,537
1846	Aug. 7	140	740,669	44	32,589,436	1,778,651
1847	Aug. 9	1089	1,213,805	29	35,200,345	2,347,634
1848	Aug. 5	2864	1,142,382	27	30,844,314	2,728,596
1849	Aug. 7	477	837,723	50	41,886,150	2,096,706
1850	Aug. 11	67	995,036	49	48,756,764	2,355,257
1851	July 25	3155	1,429,183	34	48,592,222	3,015,029
1852	Aug. 2	5077	1,664,864	41	68,259,424	3,262,882

Cotton Crop of the United States, of 1849, *in bales of* 400 *pounds.*

Alabama	564,429
Georgia	499,091
Mississippi	484,293
South Carolina	300,901
Tennessee	194,523
Louisiana	178,737
North Carolina	73,849
Arkansas	65,346
Texas	57,596
Florida	45,131
Virginia	3,947
Kentucky	758
Indiana	14
Total (statement per census returns)	2,468,624
Total, per annual statement New Orleans price current of Sept. 1, 1853	2,096,706
Discrepancy	371,918

Comparative Summary of Cotton Crop of the United States, from New York Shipping List, in bales of 400 *pounds.*

	1850.	1851.	1852.
New Orleans	933,369	1,373,484	1,580,875
Alabama	451,748	549,449	546,029
Texas	45,820	64,052	85,790
Florida	181,204	188,499	179,476
Georgia	322,376	325,714	349,490
South Carolina	387,075	476,614	463,203
North Carolina	12,928	16,242	23,496
Virginia	19,940	20,820	25,783
Elsewhere	979	175	9,740
Total crop	2,353,257	3,015,029	3,262,882

Agricultural Productions of Mississippi from Census Returns of 1840 *and* 1850.

Year.	Bales of cotton.	Bushels of corn.	Bushels of wheat.	Rye and oats.	Bushels sweet potatoes.	Pounds of rice.
1840		13,161,237	196,626	680,068	1,630,100	777,195
1850	484,293	22,446,552	137,990	1,515,894	4,741,795	2,719,856

Live Stock in Mississippi, from Census returns of 1840 *and* 1850.

Year.	Horses.	Mules.	Cattle.	Sheep.	Swine.
1840		109,227*	623,197	128,367	1,001,209
1850	115,460	54,547	733,970	304,929	1,582,734

Agricultural Productions of Mississippi in 1849, *per Census Returns of* 1850.

COUNTY.	Bales of cotton.	Bushels of corn.	Bushels of wheat.	Bushels of oats.	Rye and barley.	Pounds of rice.
Adams	17,473	334,353		6,660		
Amite	7,847	380,917		15,310	16	151,603
Atala	5,631	522,503	1,109	15,244	78	27,015
Bolivar	4,723	107,075		60		
Choctaw	4,458	404,244	8,082	36,794	162	23,350
Chickasaw	9,644	771,452	7,802	25,623	182	7,540
Covington	1,164	108,920	104	9,417	101	41,235
Coahoma	2,430	134,815		255		6,727
Copiah	9 ,318	436,485		42,174	5	241,685
Claiborne	20,795	488,003		13,924		20
Clark	1,817	174,235	215	2,690	20	6,690
Carrol	17,989	727,340	744	82,122	308	39,070
De Soto	20,278	741,519	4,482	68,278	107	10,275
Franklin	4,347	189,195		4,995		83,220
Green	81	41,275		115		30,810
Harrison		9,524				81,380
Hancock	70	22,825		305		129,420
Hinds	19,829	853,305		61,689	90	105,650
Holmes	12,635	543,155	1,814	48,177	611	72,550
Itawamba	5,519	533,507	4,430	26,592	119	473
Issaquena	8,461	143,130		1,045		
Jefferson	16,193	417,745		14,035		
Jones	250	60,988	11	3,411	5	74,555

* Horses and mules.

Agricultural Productions of Mississippi in 1849—Continued.

COUNTY.	Bales of cotton.	Bushels of corn.	Bushels of wheat.	Bushels of oats.	Rye and barley.	Pounds of rice.
Jasper	1,422	209,691	194	14,923	80	39,110
Jackson		29,848				113,975
Kemper	5,115	504,685	238	40,495	60	
Lawrence	3,304	229,129	2,820	14,281	21	76,103
Lafayette	10,387	562,530	14,749	57,964	887	45,985
Leake	1,644	180,637	321	9,071	358	70,040
Lauderdale	4,195	324,459	2,808	21,771	129	102,203
Lowndes	15,127	871,864	1,166	41,120		5,850
Marion	1,411	130,504	10	5,806	30	134,540
Madison	14,863	785,485	331	76,964	628	54,821
Monroe	17,814	901,136	7,485	62,696	644	4,436
Marshall	32,775	1,236,006	19,326	147,232	2,232	82,683
Noxubee	12,555	895,713	1,853	52,631	134	123
Neshoba	1,422	153,235	1,703	9,197	260	14,050
Newton	1,474	165,186	305	12,861	5	32,330
Oktibbeha	5,479	389,796	2,094	24,124	100	7,189
Pike	4,128	245,751		27,366	51	290,550
Panola	8,918	451,909	4,809	45,062	359	15,889
Perry	388	58,360		1,705	9	88,000
Pontotoc	9,017	667,012	8,339	30,331	334	32,131
Rankin	2,676	217,673		11,626		66,105
Smith	1,111	128,641	212	8,251	103	36,195
Scott	881	95,500		3,865		57,590
Simpson	1,851	165,099	113	6,199	7	83,207
Sunflower	1,900	33,390				
Tishomingo	3,945	526,769	8,559	50,704	406	10,600
Tunica	717	94,735		680	50	50
Tallahatchie	4,977	190,930	203	10,962	16	282
Tippah	12,098	865,131	22,011	83,440	475	32,333
Winston	3,091	326,408	6,235	34,221	269	44,394
Washington	26,178	424,600		1,400		
Warren	18,513	451,875		7,790		580
Wilkinson	26,381	504,795		19,450		17,690
Wayne	1,217	84,280		580		6,300
Yazoo	22,052	556,505		30,270	36	16,210
Yellobusha	14,314	640,775	3,313	59,335	347	5,135

Agricultural Productions of Mississippi in 1849.

COUNTY.	Sweet potatoes.	Irish potatoes	Peas and beans.	Butter and cheese.	Pounds of sugar.	Gallons of molasses.
Adams	35,220	4,380	12,847	22,753		480
Amite	111,335		24,485	42,607		
Atala	112,153	6,289	2,190	90,193	120,000	12
Bolivar	29,066	2,042	806	15,732		
Choctaw	88,674	1,395	18,479	94,836		
Chickasaw	111,815	3,796	12,789	140,032		
Covington	51,849	1,043	14,897	23,642		115
Coahoma	22,837	2,621	2,430	35,150		
Copiah	117,006	10,858	52,208	73,720	1,000	1,110
Claiborne	83,854	10,336	65,217	83,013		
Clark	78,675	280	485	50,476		
Carrol	176,360	6,393	65,315	139,965		
De Soto	137,170	16,846	38,231	191,175		
Franklin	44,039	1,208	19,000	23,190		
Green	17,236		780	10,710		
Harrison	19,395	435	735	205		
Hancock	33,925	330	1,070	3,405		750
Hinds	240,435	18,711	79,001	114,327	1,000	1,680
Holmes	124,892	10,319	53,856	131,968		
Itawamba	105,692	3,132	20,166	161,376		
Issaquena	18,595	1,829	2,240	23,535		
Jefferson	77,129	10,635	46,079	85,874		
Jones	32,615	84	4,660	6,895		
Jasper	78,945	525	1,821	18,680		
Jackson	29,669	880	2,389	10,517		
Kemper	175,960		4,444	187,175		
Lawrence	66,139	1,413	12,413	34,463	2,000	5,999
Lafayette	105,700	7,620	31,566	180,430		
Leake	46,534	1,309	3,957	33,373		140
Lauderdale	111,444	3,765	15,411	69,922		
Lowndes	98,418	1,014	6,439	145,347		
Marion	62,405		22,340	14,705	4,000	5,945
Madison	175,230	9,806	45,957	111,481		
Monroe	168,860	6,481	48,896	117,500		
Marshall	216,640	21,513	52,458	278,540		
Noxubee	96,035	5,239	4,345	171,500		
Neshoba	55,696	1,034	1,185	40,050		
Newton	58,047	194	2,292	55,518		
Oktibbeha	66,490	2,262	5,214	66,658		
Pike	64,040	126	6,841	48,664		
Panola	74,583	6,933	29,108	95,283	10,000	
Perry	44,980	270	6,428	16,000	150,000	230
Pontotoc	116,371	2,297	3,546	130,030		

Agricultural Productions of Mississippi in 1849—Continued.

COUNTY.	Sweet potatoes.	Irish potatoes.	Peas and beans.	Butter and cheese.	Pounds of sugar.	Gallons of molasses.
Rankin	68,206	1,467	8,000	54,034		
Smith	46,450	660	3,527	25,620	100,000	508
Scott	34,367	35	808	14,008		
Simpson	40,280	672	21,589	26,143		235
Sunflower	9,410			5,655		
Tishemingo	73,990	9,566	8,578	132,900		
Tunica	7,270	2,768	368	8,855		
Tallahatchie	38,052	3,836	9,703	29,164		
Tippah	125,675	7,915	9,484	216,464		
Winston	87,173	2,213	8,901	100,869		
Washington	22,315	10,000	13,433	17,710		
Warren	71,374	20,630	23,319	88,664		
Wilkinson	33,727	740	13,069	10,965		
Wayne	37,605			7,510		
Yazoo	128,272	10,014	41,140	59,633		
Yellobusha	135,424	5,263	65,824	173,901		200

IV. GEOLOGY.

INTRODUCTORY REMARKS.

ADDRESSED, as the present report is, mainly to those engaged in agricultural pursuits—a class which, however intelligent or educated, it is no disparagement to suppose, in common with many others, not deeply versed in the principles of geology, or conversant with its teachings—a familiar style, and an avoidance of technicalities as far as practicable, will obviously be regarded as most appropriate.

Whilst scientific details will, therefore, in a great measure, be omitted, explanations will, to some extent, be unavoidable, which, to the well-read and practised geologist, would seem commonplace and unnecessary.

This earth is not composed, as some may suppose, of a heterogeneous and chance agglomeration of rocks and minerals; but these are found distributed through the different strata with an order and consistency that indicates design, and a conformity with fixed laws.

These laws, properly understood, present the only safe guide to those who engage in exploring the earth's crust for its treasures.

Apart from the speculations as to the composition of

the earth's centre, of which, practically, we know nothing, the investigations of geologists as to its exterior coating or crust, so far as it can be explored, have resulted in establishing, out of several different systems that have been proposed, certain principal divisions, separated by such striking differences of character as to be easily distinguished, and which for convenience it has been found desirable to adopt.

These are composed of groups of allied or analogous strata, supposed to have been produced under similar circumstances and about the same epoch, and are designated in general terms, as the Primary, the Secondary, and the Tertiary formations; and, although they have become less adequate to represent the present state of geological knowledge, are sufficiently definite for the present purpose.

The Primary is composed of the primitive, earliest existent, or *hypogene* rocks, so called, as being formed most remote from the surface.

They are of a crystalline structure, and are referred to an igneous origin, and, so far as known, are destitute of organic remains, indicating a commencement anterior to that of animal or vegetable existence.

The Secondary succeeds in the ascending order, and is composed of marine and fresh-water deposits. Arenaceous, argillaceous, and calcareous rocks form the principal masses, and are associated with beds of chert, ironstone, and coal. The strata of this formation are characterized by innumerable organic remains of fish, mollusca, crustacea, &c., belonging wholly to extinct species, and especially by numerous and gigantic forms of saurian reptiles, indicating that the portion of the earth which, during this period, had emerged above the surface of the waters, was too frequently subject to inundations and atmospheric irregularities to be occupied, to much extent, by a higher order of beings.

With this period, also, two distinct assemblages of terrestrial plants appear to have flourished and become extinct, embracing the flora of the Carboniferous era. With the cretaceous system (including the Maestricht beds), which sometimes connects it with the succeeding formation, ends the series of deposits which are ranked as strata of the Secondary period of geology.

The Tertiary formation comprehends all those varied stratiform deposits, more recent than the Secondary, which underlie the modern group, and are characterized by distinct species of fossil animals and plants; presenting the striking feature of repeated alternations of marine deposits and those of fresh water.

During this period, there appears to have been a constantly increasing provision for the diffusion of animal life. Its most ancient deposits contain organic remains related to those of the Secondary period, and the most recent contain many existing species of animals associated with forms now extinct.

Mr. Lyell has subdivided the Tertiary into the Eocine, the Meocine, and the older and the newer Pliocene, founded on the relative proportions of the extinct and recent species of shells which they contain. In these divisions are found also the unconsolidated rocks, such as the sands, clays, and marls, as well as lignites and conglomerates.

Above these principal divisions we have the Quaternary, embracing the modern group "to which belong all those formations now completed, or in progress, upon the face of the earth or in its waters, which contain the remains of man, or of his works, or the remains of plants or animals of *existing* species, unmixed with any that are extinct."

Some geologists include under the Quaternary division some of the upper strata of the Tertiary; but in a more restricted and accepted sense, it will be used here to comprehend only the Post Pliocene deposits, and will include the modern diluvian or northern drift, which here separates the Modern group from the Tertiary; the ferruginous sands and clays, presumed to have had a contemporaneous origin; the recent lacustrine marls, the series closing with the alluvium of the surface.

The foregoing description will be better understood by referring to the section of geological strata represented in PLATE IX., in which, however, many of the subordinate strata, according to the different systems, have been omitted as not essential to the illustration.

Although all the foregoing principal divisions or formations are found to exist in all the countries that have been geologically explored, it is not to be inferred that all the strata of which they are composed pervade the whole globe. Many of them, on the contrary, are absent in different countries, owing to the relative position of the earth's surface, and the distribution of land and water at the period of their deposition. They are represented, therefore, in the order they assume in point of time, being governed by the mutations which the earth has undergone, and the paroxysms of upheaval and subsidence, more or less active and general, which, at remote and widely separated periods, have repeatedly occurred.

But, although important strata, or even entire groups, may be missing or non-existent in some quarters, in none is their relative order inverted or transposed; but they maintain an undeviating succession consistent with the period of their formation; and thus it is that all minerals are not to be found or expected alike in all situations, or where the strata to which they properly belong do not and cannot in the nature of things, exist.

The thickness of all the strata taken collectively, as estimated on the section before referred to, Plate IX., amounts to several miles. Now, as the deepest shaft yet sunk into the earth in mining operations is said not greatly to exceed half a mile, it may be asked how it is that geologists have arrived at a knowledge of so much of the earth's crust as they claim to have acquired?

If the different strata had remained undisturbed in the position in which they were first deposited, we must have remained forever ignorant, not only of the character and thickness of these strata, but of their very existence. But, in those great convulsions which the earth has undergone, in the upheaval of entire and lofty mountain ranges, the pre-existent and superincumbent strata have been tilted up, dislocated, and inclined with their edges to the surface, as is represented in the section Plate X., Figure 1.

This section will illustrate the fact that, in travelling over a country that has been so convulsed, across the strata, or in a direction from A to B, the different strata will be passed over successively as they appear upon the surface.

Now suppose that, along this distance, a series of natural sections, such as the channels of streams or ravines, should occur at different intervals, or that at the points C, D, E, wells or shafts should have been sunk, these several strata would be revealed, and the dip or angle of inclination, ascertained, and consequently the thickness of each or of the whole from B to F might be readily determined.

This is still more satisfactorily exhibited in the deeply-cut channels of rivers running in a direction transverse from that of the strata for many miles, which often occurs, by which the whole may be distinctly brought into view, in regular order, as represented in PLATE X., Fig. 2. This is well exemplified in the Niagara River below the falls, as noticed by Mr. Lyell.

Thus it is, by accumulating and collating such data, derived from various and distant quarters, aided also by the chemical composition of the rocks and their imbedded fossils, that our knowledge of the structure of the earth is acquired.

The geological structure of this State embraces the Quaternary and Tertiary formations, and merely enters upon the higher strata of the Secondary, including, perhaps, the *equivalents* of the mæstricht beds, and to a limited extent those of the Cretaceous group.

The name of this group is derived from the chalk which, in Europe, constitutes its prominent feature. Here it is characterized by yellow, ferruginous, and green sands, and micaceous shales, associated with and replaced by limestones, approaching to a chalky aspect, but affording neither real chalk nor flints.

Its thickness has been estimated as varying from three hundred to six hundred feet.

Its organic remains are nearly all marine, and are entirely distinct from those of the Tertiary above.

The older rocks of the Secondary and those of the Primary formation are not found at all in the State, except in the transported fragmentary pebbles and boulders of the diluvium or northern drift.

With these preliminary explanations, which could not be more briefly stated, and which, however familiar to many, may be essential to a general understanding of the subject, I shall proceed to give a detailed statement of the rocks and minerals that have been observed, with reference to their character and position.

LOËSS, OR LOAM.

A prominent and interesting feature, which distinguishes the counties bordering upon the Mississippi below the Yazoo, is found in that considerable deposit superimposed on the diluvial gravel, and which enters into the more easterly range of counties only along the margins of the Homochitto, Big Black, and Yazoo Rivers. Its average width, on the east side of the Mississippi, does not exceed twelve miles, and it is not met with at all on the western side, at least below the high lands of Arkansas.

In the escarpment of the Mississippi Bluffs, and in other natural sections, it is seen frequently of the thickness of fifty or sixty feet, thinning out as you recede from the river, until it is lost, and the red sands and pebbles on which it rests, appear upon the surface.

European geologists describe it, under the name of Loëss, or Lehm, "as an alluvial tertiary, sedimentary deposit, consisting of very fine, well-washed, yellow, calcareous loam, occurring over considerable tracts, and found reposing on every rock from the granite of Heidelberg to the gravel on the plains of the Rhine."

Here it has not the character of a local alluvium, and is probably due to the same causes that have spread the gravel and pebble deposits so widely over our surface.

In March, 1846, being desirous of drawing the attention of Mr. Lyell, then on a visit to this State, to this peculiar and interesting deposit, he accompanied me on an excursion to one of the large ravines in Adams County, where it is exposed to the depth at least of fifty feet. Speaking of the result of this examination, in his travels subsequently published, he remarks that "the resemblance between this loam and the fluviatile silt of the valley of the Rhine, generally called Loëss, is most perfect."

Its imbedded fossils are chiefly bleached helices or snail shells, together with mammalian remains, hereafter to be noticed in detail, under the head of the Palæontology of the State.

At every bluff on the Mississippi, from Fort Adams to the Yazoo, and in the hills in the rear, this loam is seen, and the roads leading into the interior cut into it deeply and expose it on every hand.

On the declivities of the hills bordering the Yazoo, and its tributaries on the east, it is frequently seen and has been observed in the bluffs at Memphis, but much diminished in thickness of the deposit.

Its highly calcareous properties, its abundance, distribution, and locality, entitle it to a further notice, which it will receive among our other Marls.

SANDSTONE—DAVION ROCK.

Among the few consolidated rocks which our Alluvio-Tertiary formations afford, susceptible of use as building materials, we have three or four varieties of limestones, and sandstones of as many aspects.

The Davion Rock of Fort Adams is an argillo-silicious composition, of a dingy white color in the mass, containing a small proportion of sand, cemented together and tinged by a brownish-red metallic oxide, which pervades it in irregular and distorted veins, and which, forming the hardest portions of the mass, gives the weathered surface a very rough and nodular character.

It is traced in a direction north of east, and is seen cropping out at the crossing of the Natchez and Woodville road, in Section 8, Township 2, Range 2 West.

Beyond this, continuing in the same general direction, its character becomes gradually modified, being much more silicious and uniform in character, and freer from the oxide; the iron it contains consisting of an inconsiderable amount of pyrites, in small detached nodules.

Occurring in considerable beds five or six miles northeast of Woodville, of a quality supposed to be suitable for building purposes, considerable tracts of the government lands on which it was situated were entered about twenty years since, and some quarries were opened, and the stone used to a small extent in Woodville and the vicinity. These quarries have never been regularly worked, and are now, from some cause, rarely resorted to.

Crossing the Homochitto near Wilson's Ferry, the ledge is intersected by the Natchez and Liberty Road in Franklin County, on or near Section 47, Township 5, Range 1 E. The more compact and arenaceous portion of the stratum is here about three feet in thickness, with about the same thickness, above and below, of the more argillaceous and crumbling material, which, in wet weather, forms a very tenacious white pasty clay, rendering this a very formidable pass to the wagoners on the road, who have given to the ridge on which this ledge runs the name of the *Devil's Backbone.*

This rock seems not to be continuous or traceable more than ten or fifteen miles further in this direction, and is found of its best quality at Dixon's Quarry, Section 40, Township 6, Range 2 E., between Well's Creek and Morgan's fork of the Homochitto. It was here that the stone used about the arches and for the lintels of the windows in the Catholic church in Natchez was obtained.

GRAND GULF SANDSTONE.

The next and only other point at which the sandstone appears on the banks of the Mississippi, is at Grand Gulf in Claiborne County. Here it presents an entirely different aspect from that at Fort Adams.

Specimens of this rock, superior in hardness to granite itself, have attracted the attention of mineralogists by its anomalous character, and resemblance to some of the primitive rocks, and the appearance which it sometimes presents of having been subjected to igneous action.

It is variable in color and texture, many specimens having the appearance of aggregated grains of coarse, angular, black and bluish sand incorporated in a matrix of a white porcelain or enamel-like character, and approaching to a fine brexia in its composition—a quality which has occasioned it to be spoken of frequently, in common parlance, as *petrified* rock.

The range of this rock is between the Big Black River and the Bayou Pierre (on both sides of the latter in some localities), and extending eastwardly to the vicinity of Raymond and the Mississippi Springs, near which it occurs of a softer and more uniform character or texture, and from whence that employed in the basement and pavements of the State House at Jackson was obtained.

It is still quarried for building purposes there, and at different points in its course. One house has been seen built wholly of it, obtained on the Bayou Pierre.

It has been found a convenient material for the foundations of houses and the construction of chimneys, and in early times it was frequently used in the neighborhood for mill-stones. The abutments of the new bridge at Grindstone Ford, on the Bayou Pierre, are built of it quarried on the spot, and at Grand Gulf it has been freely used in paving the streets or side-walks.

This rock presents itself in mass in the escarpment of the bold promontory on the Mississippi, about a mile below the mouth of the Big Black River, and immediately above the town of Grand Gulf, against which the current of the river sets in full force, and by which it is deflected by its effective resistance in such a manner as to create the extensive and formerly dangerous whirlpool or eddy which gave name to the place.

At many points within the scope I have mentioned, this rock crops out in the beds of the watercourses, and upon the sides of the ridges, exhibiting, as in that in the Mississippi bluff, such an identity of character as to induce me to characterize it wherever met with as the Grand Gulf rock.

On the Tallahaly, a branch of the Bayou Pierre, near Colonel Dabney's, Township 4, Range 3 W., in Hinds County, it is abundant, and has been freely used for the foundations and chimneys of negro quarters in that neighborhood.

At the Mississippi Springs, the attendant clays, or decomposed portions of the imperfectly formed rock, are very similar to those of the *Backbone* in Franklin County, before mentioned.

The course of this ledge seems arrested at this point by the limestone intervening between it and Pearl River, and which seems to range from the lime quarry of Mr.

Marshall to that formerly worked by Mr. Long, about eight miles south of Jackson.

The sandstone, it is presumable, takes a more southerly range, passes under Pearl River into Rankin, where it probably forms the natural pavement which has attracted much notice as a supposed work of art.

Slabs of this sandstone, very similar to those described in Rankin County, have been seen in considerable quantity, both detached, and resting in their native beds on the White Oak, a considerable tributary of the Bayou Pierre in Copiah County.

These were about five inches in thickness, of a smooth even surface, separated into rather regular angular forms, the under side only being uneven and cellular, from resting on the diluvial gravel on which it lies.

Several extensive ranges of similar rock occur in Atala County, having a direction from N.E. to S.W. It is of more uniform texture, finer grit, and greatly harder and more durable, than that of any other deposit observed.

Considerable quantities of massive sandstone is found near Rocky Ford in Pontotoc County, on both sides of the Tallahatchie.

Of the other sandstones noted, I have to mention that in the forks of the Chilly Creek in Section 35, Township 4, Range 1 E., in Tippah County. The rock designed for the Washington Monument, contributed by the State, was procured here, and sent to Natchez to be cut by the sculptor, Mr. E. Lyon, and rejected as too hard and cellular. It is a silicious coralline rock, of extreme hardness, partially agatized. From the description given me by Mr. Campbell, who was employed in getting it out, it was probably one of a group of *boulders* or erratic blocks, the whole not extending beyond a quarter section. I learned, however, from Mr. Tucker, who lives in the neighborhood, that there is another similar group on another stream in the same vicinity.

About a mile east of Ripley, in the same county, I was shown a small bed of calcareous sandstone containing a variety of shells, among them the turretella and cerethium, the latter of a large size, the cavities of the shells being frequently filled with a drusy spar. It is rather cellular, occasioned by the decomposition of the fossils, and contains some minute shark's teeth. It is probably the rock spoken of by some as a species of the millstone grit.

FERRUGINOUS SANDSTONE—IRON.

The most generally distributed form of silicious rocks is the iron sandstone in its various conditions.

From the thin plates or sheets resembling pot metal, to the coarser and more massive forms, it is met with in most parts of the State.

In several of the counties where this rock is convenient and abundant, and in blocks of sufficient dimensions, it has been used for the base or foundation of the court-houses and other public buildings, and occasionally chimneys have been constructed of it.

On some of the head branches of Coles Creek, in Adams County, it is seen in considerable quantities.

In Pike County, it is found a short distance below Holmesville, forming a bluff bank on Bogue Chitto, piled up to the height of ten or twelve feet.

In Leake County, the road leading to Columbus crosses a considerable ridge, on which it abounds, as it does also near De Kalb, in Kemper County.

It is seen in the eastern part of Lafayette County, on the road leading to Pontotoc.

In Panola County, and in Tallahatchie County, it is of frequent occurrence.

All the stone of this character, seen north of the Tallahatchie, exhibits more or less mica in its composition. The mica, not noticed south of this was also observed in the sands and clays in Marshall County.

These are a few of the localities in which this Iron sandstone is most conspicuous.

But I have nowhere met with it more massive and abundant than near Grenada in Yellobusha County. Some of the conical peaks of the hills are there covered or paved with it, in rounded mammillary and botroidal forms.

Very frequently it occurs in the characters of a conglomerate or pudding stone—a concrete formed of the rounded cherty pebbles of the drift, and either massive or in thin and widely spread sheets, the latter forming a species of hard pan, in which latter character it is found resting upon beds of Yellow Ochre, as at the base of the Natchez Bluffs, and again twelve miles below, at the White Cliffs on the Mississippi.

At the latter point, this rock presents another character, and affords a rare exhibition of fulgorites on a magnificent scale; the tubes singly or grouped together in great masses, of large caliber and considerable length, resembling cannon or organ-pipes. These tubes, however, are of many sizes, varying from an inch to a foot or more in diameter.

A few miles north of Ripley, in Tippah County, on a ridge where this ferruginous sandstone abounds, fulgorites, of a smaller size than those of the White Cliffs, are numerous, and appear to have been collected, with other fragments of the rock, and piled up so as to form a mound supposed to be one of the monumental tumuli of the aborigines, and similar in character to the Cairns of Scotland.

The formation of these fulgorites has been attributed to lightning.

Under favorable circumstances, these ferruginous conglomerates are continually forming. An old horseshoe, or any scrap of iron cast by chance in coarse sand or gravel, particularly if intermixed with soil containing calcareous matter, soon forms a concrete, and illustrates the chemical affinity by which the particles coalesce.

Iron, which enters largely into the composition of the matrix, at least, is one of the most generally diffused of all solid minerals. It forms a constituent part of many animal and vegetable substances, and is also deposited from chalybeate waters.

And here, it may as well be mentioned in what other forms it is found to exist in the State.

Besides the pisiform or argillaceous oxide occurring occasionally in certain soils in considerable amount, of no appreciable value, but rather a pernicious ingredient, injurious to most crops, the bog ore, which is attributed by mineralogists to vegetable depositions, exists in many situations, generally in the wet bottoms of watercourses, where the earth is of that whitish, tenacious description usually characterized as *Crawfish land.* It has been met with on the Amite, Pearl, and Leaf Rivers, and doubtless exists in many similar situations. That on Leaf River is said, by a gentleman practically acquainted with the subject, to compare favorably with similar ore worked in New Jersey.

A mile or two west of the residence of Mr. Frederick Braugher, in Tippah County, a conglomerate or pudding-stone occurs, composed wholly of pisiform iron. The nodules, formed of concentric layers, are of more than the ordinary size.

Iron ore of different character, and of good quality, is said to be sufficiently abundant for profitable working, not far distant from De Kalb, on Section 34, Township 10, Range 17 E., in Kemper County, on the Paticfaw. I have not yet had an opportunity of visiting the locality, and my information in regard to it amounts to this: that, being considered by an experienced iron-master, as superior to that which he had worked in Tennessee, he purchased the land, and a company was chartered by the Legislature of this State for working the ore, some years since; but, from some cause not stated, the enterprise has not been carried into effect.

A hydrated peroxide of iron termed limonite, is found in the talus of the Natchez Bluff.

These limonites occur in round balls, or of more flattened ovoid forms, assuming sometimes varied and fantastic shapes. They rarely exceed five or six inches in diameter, and are generally much smaller. Whatever shape they may assume, or however irregular or contorted, they are always hollow, the crust or shell inclosing either sands highly mineralized with sulphate of iron, or with ochrous earths generally of a red or yellow color, which impart a vivid tint to the interior surface of the shell. On one occasion, a crystal of gypsum, or selenite about two inches in diameter, was found inclosed in one of these. The exterior of the shell is generally of a rather dull brown, but the fracture exhibits a more lustrous and metallic aspect.

These limonites are found in considerable numbers loose and detached, and are often in an entire condition as well as in broken fragments, seen agglutinated together, and forming with the associated pebbles, the composition of the conglomerate of the locality.

LIMESTONE.

Limestone is not known to make its appearance on the Mississippi but at one point.

At Vicksburg, it presents itself in the channel of the small stream bordering the city on the north, and in the face of the bluff is traceable for half a mile or more above.

The stratum appears to repose upon a yellow marl, and to be divided by it into three layers of some three feet each in thickness, the whole including the intervening marl, not exceeding ten feet.

The lower member of the stratum, which is of a bluish tint, affords an excellent material of variable thickness, not exceeding a foot, perhaps, in blocks of any extent.

The upper members consist of a yellowish, imperfectly formed, and perishable rock of little value.

This rock is seen occasionally from Vicksburg, exposed along the Walnut Hills to Haynes's Bluff, or Old Fort St. Peter's on the Yazoo River, and probably extends higher.

Towards the interior, it crosses Big Black River, and crops out at Steward's quarry, on the Jackson and Vicksburg Railroad, on Section 28, Township 6, Range 2 W., in Hind's County, a few miles west of Clinton; also at Marshall's Quarry, on Section 17, Township 5, Range 1 W., near the Mississippi Springs.

It occurs again at the former quarry of the late John

Long, near Pearl River, eight or nine miles south of Jackson.

A cut on the railroad between Jackson and Brandon, on the plantation of Mr. Chambers, in Rankin County, also exposes the lime-rock, not, however, as at Marshall's or Steward's quarries, or at Vicksburg, in a continuous and connected stratum, but rather as a congeries of angular disjointed blocks, variable in size and form, and rarely of dimensions suitable for building purposes, but well adapted for burning into lime. (See Plate XI., Fig. 1.)

Besides the extensive use made of this rock in paving the streets of Vicksburg, it has been quarried near St. Peter's and taken to Yazoo City.

It is also used by the marble cutters in Vicksburg, for monumental tablets, as well as for lintels, door-sills and steps, being considered as equal to any other limestone of this formation in the United States, ordinarily used for these purposes.

On the recommendation of the late Edwin Lyon, the sculptor at Natchez, founded on the examination of specimens submitted to him, a block intended for the National Monument has been obtained from Steward's quarry, for the Grand Lodge of Mississippi.

At this quarry, also, the stone used by the contractors for the Lunatic Asylum, in the construction of that building, was obtained, being regarded as greatly superior to the sandstone used in the State House.

The rock at Marshall's is of equally good character, but the facilities of transportation not being equal to those at Steward's (situated immediately on the railroad), Mr. Marshall converts his into lime.

In the further prosecution of the geological survey,

other beds of limestone, of equal value for building purposes, will doubtless be found in other quarters.

Limestone of a different character, known commonly as the white, or rotten limestone, exists in immense deposits, particularly in what is termed the prairie lands, in which it is met with frequently cropping out on the surface, but, from the deficiency of hardness, and an aptitude to decompose and fall to powder, by exposure to the atmosphere, is rather to be classed as an indurated marl, than a consolidated rock.

Experiments in building have been made with some of the most compact and harder descriptions of this rock, which although readily cut into blocks in the moist state in the quarry by the ordinary cross-cut saw, was found to harden when properly dried, and some very imposing and extensive edifices were erected of it in St. Stephens, in Alabama, about the year 1818. It was found, however, very liable to exfoliate and crumble from the effects of damp and frost.

Whether this can be prevented, and if an exterior coating of hydraulic cement will remedy this defect, is perhaps, worthy of experiment.

Less widely and more sparingly distributed, we find calcareous tufa, claystones, or concretions, deposited by the calcareous, or *hard* water of some of our springs percolating through the marly soil.

Of the latter character, in nodular or cylindrical forms, it is associated with all of our newer marls.

Lime, in the form of a sulphate or selenite, has been revealed in the cut of the railroad near Clinton, in Hinds County, occurring in flattened crystals with pointed ends, sometimes several inches in diameter, and in vertical plates seaming the gypseous marl of the locality.

Crystals of selenite have also been found ten or fifteen

feet below the surface, in digging cisterns, about half a mile northeast of the State House, in Jackson.

At Ball Prairie, about six miles west, selenite is abundant on the surface.

Agaric mineral, or mountain milk, occurs in the fissures and seams of all the lime-quarries before mentioned, and when first exposed, is of the appearance and consistency of newly-mixed plaster of Paris in small portions, but soon acquires great hardness.

CLAYS, OCHREOUS EARTHS, AND SANDS.

Considerable deposits of potter's clay are found in many situations.

That in the bluff at Natchez, and at the White Cliffs, twelve miles below, where it is abundant, has been tested at a pottery in Natchez, and found to be of a superior quality.

A pottery is in operation in Marshall County, and one was formely established at Brandon. There are doubtless others in the State, there being no deficiency of material for their supply.

A fine description of a very white plastic clay, of uniform texture, and well adapted for modelling, is also found at the White Cliffs, in Adams County, in Wilkinson County, and elsewhere.

A medallion, modelled by Mr. Lyon, the late sculptor, in Natchez, from a specimen furnished him, and which was obtained on the lands of Dr. Holt, in the suburbs of Woodville, is deposited in the State Cabinet at Jackson, with other specimens in the crude state, as well as several variegated and differently colored varieties obtained elsewhere.

Yellow ochre is also frequently found below the diluvial gravel, generally covered with a lamina of hard pan or thin crust of conglomerate, and sometimes containing iron in botroidal and dendritic forms.

It occurs at the White Cliffs very pure and in large quantity, but is only exposed at extreme low water. During the embargo which preceded the war of 1812, two ships from Boston were loaded with it from that place.

Used as a pigment, it combines readily with oil or water; and when burnt gives a lively red color.

On the lands of Dr. White, Section 35, Township 3, Range 3 W, in Hinds County, my attention was called to a mineral earth occupying a spot of small extent on the surface, to which stock of all kinds resorted for the salts which it seems to contain, and which they lick or eat freely, and all with impunity except the hog, which is said to be destroyed by the use of it.

Dr. White has observed that it has the effect of changing the skin of the hog to a red color; that the carrion crow seems to reject the carcass, which resists putrefaction to a considerable degree, and dries up, and cures, as animal matter is said to do in some parts of Mexico.

Other deposits of similar character have frequently been met with of limited extent. They are generally entirely destitute of vegetation, and in their natural state neither corn nor cotton will grow upon them.

The application of cotton seed and a crop of pea vine renders them temporarily productive, and the growing crop, when so improved, has been observed to resist the drought in a remarkable degree.

Many of our streams are characterized by the great deposit of fine white sand which they afford.

Pearl, Leaf, and Chickasaw Rivers, in some parts of

their course, are of this character, as well as some of the minor streams in the western counties.

The different branches of Cole's Creek, in the Counties of Jefferson and Adams, are remarkable in this respect; and the crossing of them is rendered difficult and dangerous after the occurrence of every freshet, in consequence of the extensive beds of quicksands in their channels.

Sand for building purposes, is to some extent a merchantable commodity, and is supplied in New Orleans from Ellis Cliffs.

These cliffs are some two miles or more in extent, and about two hundred feet high, presenting in some parts perpendicular sections of pure sand and clays. Boats continually ply from that point, and gangs of hands are continually engaged in loading flats for the New Orleans market.

One contract for sand from the White Cliffs, for the Custom-house in New Orleans, amounted to upwards of twenty-eight thousand dollars, and in this connection it may be mentioned that several boat-loads of pebble and conglomerate were obtained from the talus of the Natchez Bluffs for the foundation of the same building, and for that of the State House in Baton Rouge.

Taking the State at large, the ferruginous sand deposits greatly predominate; they are seen on the Mississippi only at Fort Adams overlying the diluvial gravel. They spread widely over the County of Wilkinson, and are exposed in heavy deposits in every ravine or natural section, associated with the plastic clays, conglomerate, and gravel; passing thence eastwardly through Amite, Pike, and Marion Counties.

They can be traced almost uninterruptedly east of Pearl River from the sea-shore to the Tennessee line, intervening, as it were, between the prairie lands and the western alluvium. Sections on the railroad near Brandon are given in PLATE XII., Figs. 2 and 3.

It would be tedious and unnecessary to enumerate all the localities where these deposits have been encountered in force. The following are some of them :—

On the shore of Lake Borgne a few miles west of Shieldsborough. In Hancock County, seventeen miles north of Habolochitto Bridge. In the northwest corner of Perry County, near Leaf River. In Marion County, west of Pearl River, four miles from Columbia. Near Col. Dabney's, Township 4, Range 3 W., Hinds County.

Three miles east of Hooper's Ferry, on Pearl River, in Leake County, on the road to Tacinto Post-office. Near De Kalb, in Kemper County. About seven miles south of Macon, in Noxubee County. Near Grenada, Yellobusha County. Near Pontotoc, and a few miles west of Ripley, in Tippah County.

In sinking wells at Oxford and other places, the sand encountered at some depth often presents delicate roseate and lilac tints.

MARLS OR MINERAL FERTILIZERS.

The term *marl* is often very vaguely applied by different writers; and the names variously given to the mineral substances sometimes used as renovators of the soil, do not always convey a clear idea of their distinctive character or properties.

In Europe, a non-calcareous earth is used as clay-marl; and slate-marl, gypseous marl, bituminous or fetid marl, and variegated marl, &c., are frequently spoken of; the latter, a marbled earth containing sulphate of iron, and certainly very unfit to be *used* as a marl, however it may be called.

The green-sands of New Jersey, from being similarly applied, have come to be classed by many among the marls, although, when pure, possessing no calcareous properties.

Shell marl seems too indefinite a term, as the marls of this character are various, and may belong either to the secondary or tertiary formations, or have a marine or fresh-water origin; the marine shell-marls themselves differing essentially in their qualities.

Properly speaking, marl consists of calcareous and argillaceous earth combined in various proportions; and, as the former or latter prevails, so is it beneficially employed on clays or sands.

Mr. Ruffin, than whom no one is more familiar with the calcareous fertilizers of our country, and who from his close and extended observations both in Virginia and South Carolina, is the most competent authority on the subject, in view of the confusion which has existed, adopts, in his application of the term, "any compound or mixture of earths of which *carbonate of lime* in any form constitutes either the sole or chief value as manure, and is in such large proportion as to be of important value, and of which compound the mass is soft enough to be excavated and broken down with ordinary digging utensils."

The application of marl as a stimulant of the soil, is of very ancient date, the use of it being mentioned by Pliny, and other ancient Latin writers, as highly beneficial in its effects; and clays and marls have been long and extensively used for this purpose, in England and elsewhere.

In the United States, marls have been freely applied in New Jersey, Delaware, Maryland, and Virginia; and more recently, and to less extent, in South Carolina and other States.

In New Jersey, the green-sand *Marls*, so called by Professor H. D. Rogers, have been in use for more than forty years.

As the green-sand has been discovered to exist under "various geological relationships," besides those it presents in New Jersey, as it does in Virginia, Maryland, and Delaware, and having recognized its presence in this State associated with the tertiary marls and the sulphate of lime, I am inclined to follow the example of Professor Rogers, in his report on the Geology of New Jersey, and to embrace those substances among our marls, giving the term a wider acceptation than that to which it is restricted by Mr. Ruffin, as not only locally more convenient, but as sanctioned by popular usage and understanding, as comprehending all those mineral substances or compounds, commonly applied to the soil with a view to its greater productiveness, and not requiring previous preparation, such as the burning to lime or grinding into plaster.

I propose, therefore, for the present, and until further researches and developments may render a different arrangement expedient, to consider our Marls as constituting the following varieties:—

1. *Lake Marl.*—That found in limited lakelike depressions; the beds of former lakes or ponds of an origin either preceding or subsequent to the diluvial period; and which is characterized by the fresh-water shells, described under the head of Palæontology, including Planorbis, Cyclas, Paludinas, Lymnæa, &c.

2. *Diluvial Marl*, or the Loëss; a finely comminuted, pulverulent, silt-like loam, containing thirty per cent. or more of carbonate of lime, the shells, which are numerous, being exclusively terrestrial, embracing many species of helices or snails.

3. *Marine Marl*—such as that at Vicksburg—varying somewhat in character in different localities, but all including marine shells, with specific distinctions, but of allied genera.

4. *Gypseous Marl*—such as those near Clinton and Jackson, in Hinds County—containing crystallized gypsum or selenite, and resembling somewhat in appearance the *chocolate-colored* green-sand marls described in New Jersey.

5. The tertiary *green-sand marl*—as existing at Jackson—containing an immense quantity of shells of the eocene period, differing from those at Vicksburg, and including species that are new and undescribed.

6. The *Indurated Marl*—the white or rotten limestone so called, found chiefly in the prairie region—of a pale blue color when first dug out in its moist state, below the surface, but which bleaches and crumbles to powder by exposure to atmospheric action.

7. The *Cretaceous Marls* of the Tombigbee and its tributaries, varying in character, and containing, in some of the beds, more or less green-sand, and characterized by fossils of the cretaceous group.

It will be seen, in the chapter on analysis, that few of these marls have been chemically examined, and the reasons have before been stated. As yet, they have received little attention from our planters; and I can learn of very few experiments which have been made with them.

As these will probably become of much value hereafter, and exert an important influence upon the agricultural prosperity of the State, it will not be considered out of place to quote, from Professor Rogers's report on New Jersey, a description of some of the properties, and the value and effect of some of these marls in that

State, in order that those interested in the matter may be induced to introduce them into use here.

Dr. Emmons, who was connected with the agricultural department of the New York survey, made analyses, several years since, of some of our marls sent him for that purpose, and in giving the results in his *Quarterly Journal of Agriculture*, published at Albany, he remarks, "that from these examinations it would appear that the South is really rich in fertilizers, and that there is no necessity for her lands becoming poor and barren; and of one of the specimens analyzed, he adds, that it will be found a valuable fertilizer, as it contains almost half the amount of potash which the green-sands of New Jersey do, that are so remarkable for giving fertility to the exhausted lands of that State."

The improvement of the soil produced by the marls in New Jersey is said, by Professor Rogers, to be very permanent, changing the natural growth from *Indian* and other grasses to white clover. They have been very profusely applied in some parts of that State, one hundred loads or even more to the acre, being no unusual dressing.

The chief value and usefulness of the green-sand is ascribed to the potash, which is always present and essential in some proportion to its composition. Its astonishing potency has been shown by the luxuriant harvests derived from fields wholly uncongenial to vegetation, by the application of *sea-beach sand*, a substance still more arid than the soil itself, but which contained a very small proportion of the alkaline granules disseminated very sparingly through it.

Twenty loads of marl per acre, may be regarded as a bountiful dressing, and marling at a cost of five dollars per acre has been considered equivalent in its effects to the application of barnyard manure, at a cost of *two hundred* dollars.

A marl is *mentioned* by Professor Rogers, as containing less than sixty per cent. of green-sand, which had the disadvantage of a slight impregnation of sulphate of iron or copperas, and he states that the privilege of digging it at the pits sold readily at thirty-seven and a half cents per load. It was largely transported in wagons to a distance of twenty miles, and retailed at the rate of ten cents or more per bushel.

In respect to *calcareous* marls, they generally require some time, after their application to land, to become effectual; they are best spread on the surface before winter, leaving them to be acted upon by the rain, frost, and air, before ploughing in. They are most advantageously applied to land when in grass, and are improved by repeated harrowing and rolling.

They should be applied cautiously to clay lands. Sandy lands will bear a larger quantity.

Some consider that the best mode of using marls is to form a compost of it with alternate layers of stable-manure, or of marsh muck, peat, or other vegetable matter.

In the application of marls, it is important to avoid those containing any astringent matter. Such are seriously detrimental to the soil, and noxious to all vegetation.

This pernicious property may be distinguished by an acrid, inky taste, and by a white effloresence resembling frost which often overspreads the marl in dry weather when exposed for some time to the atmosphere; this is generally sulphate of iron, derived from the decomposition of pyrites in the associated clays.

The intermixture of this deleterious ingredient in the

marl is very obvious in that of the eocene beds at Vicksburg, as seen in the *frosted* surface of the detritus forming the talus of the bluffs above the city, denoting the presence of copperas or vitriol.

These may, however, be neutralized by the intermixture, in the compost heap, of a small proportion, about one per cent., of newly burnt and caustic lime thoroughly disseminated through the mass.

Those who desire to try the effects of marl upon their lands, and have had no experience in such matters, cannot do better than to consult Ruffin's Essay on Calcareous Manures, and his Report on the Agriculture of South Carolina. His great experience, his extended research, and withal his long-continued and successfully conducted experiments with the marls of Virginia, have caused him to be looked upon in the light of a public benefactor, and procured for him recently a very complimentary election as an honorary member of the United States Agricultural Society, in consideration, as it was flatteringly announced, "of the incalculable benefits conferred by him upon the whole farming interest of Virginia by his genius and industry."

The indurated marl, generally known as the *rotten limestone*, is described by Dr. Troost, the late eminent geologist of Tennessee, as "having an earthy appearance, interspersed with minute particles of mica and grains of green-sand sometimes so small as to be perceptible only by the aid of the magnifying glass.

"It is soft, and, when exposed to atmospheric influence, disintegrates, crumbles to dust, and forms a more or less plastic paste with water.

"When properly mixed with soil, it is very beneficial to agriculture. Of this fact, the farmers of Pennsylvania are well convinced, and hundreds of loads are taken from New Jersey where similar marl exists, to improve their farms. The same is the case with the farmers of Maryland, who send at great expense to the Eastern Shore for that substance."

We possess inexhaustible stores of this marl in our State, but, the land being remarkable for its sterility where it most abounds and crops out upon the surface for want of the proper admixture of soil, it is not properly appreciated, or rather, it is regarded as a nuisance.

Some of the railroads, now in progress in the eastern part of the State, will traverse the whole extent of this marl region, laying it open, and exposing it in every cutting where it is not already spread out upon the surface invitingly to view.

When we reflect upon the great value of this material, applied in connection with the marsh muck, the pine straw, or the peat of the sandy flats of our southern border, is the expectation too extravagant that, at no remote period, we shall see the cars freighted with thousands of tons of this marl, wheeling it to the gulf shores to convert their arid wastes into garden spots of fertility and productiveness?

COAL, OR LIGNITE.

The great coal deposit lies between the two systems of rocks known as the Old and the New Red sandstones, and the great mass of bituminous coal, susceptible of being profitably worked, is found below the latter.

An inferior kind of non-bituminous coal, worked on the continent of Europe only to supply the local demand, is found in a newer group of rocks called the oolite.

Lignite, or wood coal, partially carbonized, belongs to the tertiary strata; it is considered by some as an imperfect coal, not yet mineralized; whilst others doubt whether it ever becomes true coal.

There are several kinds, variously known as Bovey Coal, Erdkohle, Moor Coal, &c.; these generally burn with a flame, but neither swell nor cake like the true coal.

The foregoing is the language of different writers on geology.

With this knowledge, and a recurrence to the explanatory remarks which introduced this division of the present report, and a reference to the geological section (PLATE IX.), an inference may be drawn as to the probability of discovering this mineral in the State, and as to its character and quality if found.

In the reconnoisance that has so far been made, Lignite has been found in many situations, and satisfactorily ascertained to exist in others; but as yet with no results as to character or position contradicting or impairing the evidences of geological research or of past experience. I am aware that different expectations have been entertained, and it would assuredly be very agreeable to me to have it in my power to announce a different conclusion.

The most considerable deposit of lignite, by far, which has come under my observation, is that at Vicksburg. This I had a favorable opportunity of examining on the 10th of October, 1852, owing to an unusually low stage of water in the Mississippi, it being rarely exposed to view.

On that occasion, I measured five hundred yards on its surface, along the margin of the river, and obtained specimens of it for the cabinets at Jackson and Oxford, where they may be seen.

When quite moist or newly taken from the water, it is quite sooty in its character, soiling the hands equally as much, and its whole appearance seemed to answer the description of the Erdkohle of Werner. Dried in the shade, it loses the smutty property in a considerable degree, and becomes comparatively compact; exposed in a moist state to the sun, it flakes off and falls to powder.

The bed forms the base to the talus of the river bluffs, and is of course covered to within a short distance of the water's edge, or to that portion of it recently swept by the current of the river, with the detritus which crumbles from the sides of the bluff, consisting in the inferior portion of the mass, of a dark brown shaly clay, saturated with sulphate of iron, resulting from the decomposition of pyrites, the clay being so highly charged with the mineral as to exhibit in dry weather a white efflorescence on the surface, resembling frost.

Sharks' teeth, large oyster shells, madrepores, and the eocene shells of the formation washed from the upper strata, are intermixed and imposed upon the shale.

The thickness of the bed I had no means of ascertaining, no excavation having been made; the outer edge terminates abruptly, and the perpendicular face is washed by the river, which flows along the margin to a great depth.

I observe that the proprietor of this bed, who resides in Virginia, is making arrangements for sinking a shaft, and testing its quality.

All the other beds of lignite which I have observed, or the existence of which I have ascertained, are of a more recent formation, and lie above the Eocene.

That near the Big Black, Section 47, Township 13, Range 2 E., in Claiborne County, visited in June, 1852, reveals itself on the bluff bank of a small branch, about five feet above its bed, and some fifty feet below the general surface, filling a space of about two feet between two strata of the Grand Gulf sandstone. The horizontal range of its outcropping could not be traced more than thirty feet; the deposit is quite compact, and has the appearance of decayed vegetable matter greatly compressed by the rock in which it is imbedded, and the superincumbent soil.

Traces or impressions of water plants, or flags of inferior growth resembling blades of grass, are detected in it.

The deposit on the lands of General Miles, near Chula Lake, Section 7, Township 14, Range 1 E., in Holmes County, has been frequently spoken of by those who have seen it, and in favorable terms. I have not yet examined or procured specimens from it.

In the same county, and not distant from this, is another bed on Funnigusha Creek, to the east of the crossing of the old road near Coconover's old stand.

In Hinds County, Mr. Fairchilds informs me, that in sinking a well on Section 11, Township 4, Range 3 W., he encountered a bed of considerable thickness, thirty-five feet below the surface. Similar deposits have been noticed by myself or others in the following localities: In Rankin County, near Partin's Ferry, on Pearl River. On Section 30, Township 11, Range 12 E., near Philadelphia, Neshoba County. On Snow Creek, Section 7, Township 4, Range 1 E., seven miles south of Salem, in Tippah County; and at McElroy's mill on Turkey Creek, in Yellobusha County.

Traces of lignite are also seen on the Homochitto, a

few miles south of Meadville; in a small branch about a mile northeast from the State House at Jackson; and in a cut on the railroad, near Brandon, Rankin County. (See Plate XII. Fig. 2.)

IRON PYRITES, GOLD, COPPER, AND LEAD.

How frequently the discovery of gold and other valuable metals has been authoritatively announced in the State may be remembered, perhaps, by those who have practised upon the credulity of the community in the form of a newspaper hoax, calculated to create a sensation for a time, and most conveniently fill a vacant corner in a paper which dearth of news, or want of other matter may have left unoccupied.

Last year, an imposing statement, which went the rounds in the public prints, sent some hundreds to the pine hills in Marion County, to search for an imaginary placer.

Just now, another discovery is sprung—the scene, a little removed to the neighboring County of Jackson; and the most *unmistakable signs* of the existence of gold are given, even to the width of the *vein* and *dip* of the stratum.

Vein rock, properly so called, is not to be found, in all probability, within two hundred miles of the locality, and the formation of the district consists of loose and unconsolidated sand-clay and gravel.

However abundantly diluvial gold sands may *possibly* exist, the *veins and the dip,* at least, are purely imaginary.

The introductory explanations which have before been given, and again referred to, in the case of coal, apply equally here.

Gold, silver, and copper belong properly to the primary formation; and the carboniferous limestone, that on which the coal measures repose, lying low down among the secondary strata, is the chief depository of lead.

Gold, unlike silver, copper, or tin, is rarely met with in veins, but is disseminated in small quantities in the rocks in which it occurs, chiefly quartz.

There is, therefore, but one deposit in the State, the diluvium or northern drift, in which any of these metals could be expected in the most limited and diffused particles. Gold has been found in minute grains (exceedingly minute) in the quartose and agatized pebbles of that deposit.

Pyrites, that deceptive mineral which is generally found to be at the bottom of these reputed and delusive discoveries, is, on the contrary, generally diffused. It is found in rocks of all ages, and abundantly in those of the recent formations.

It occurs in subglobular nodules in the cretaceous rocks, in the white limestone or indurated marl, the sandstone, and associated with the lignite of the tertiary.

Its colors are chiefly bronze, brass yellow, and steel gray, and its structure is either capillary, cellular, hepatic, and radiated, of which latter character are the nodules spoken of.

Its composition is iron, 47.85, sulphur, 52.15; but as an iron ore, owing to the combination with the sulphur, it is worthless.

That occurring in the primitive rocks contains a percentage of gold sufficient to justify its separation, but in that of the recent formations gold is not to be expected.

By different processes, sulphur, alum, and copperas are extracted from it; the two latter profitably, when found in large and convenient deposits; all the copperas of commerce, and much of the alum, being derived from this mineral.

Exposed to the action of the atmosphere, it decomposes and falls to a black powder.

The brilliant fracture of the nodular varieties, and their brassy or golden color, are well calculated to deceive the inexperienced, and it has, in consequence, received the popular sobriquet of "*fool's gold.*"

When in charge of the Land Office, west of Pearl River, many years since, many tracts of the public lands were sold on the faith of this mineral; and frequently, when specimens brought to the office for exhibition were unwrapped, no little surprise was experienced by the deluded parties, to find the precious mineral reduced to a black powder, and the paper in which it was inclosed corroded and dropping into fragments from its caustic character.

In June, 1852, it was stated, in a paper published in Louisiana, on the authority of a letter received there, "that a Mr. ———, living on Black Creek, in Marion County, had found a gold mine where he could *get it by the cartload*, but concealed a knowledge of its locality. He was closely watched by numbers of people, but no clue had been obtained to guide them to the bed of treasure. It was further stated, that a company had left with the intention of camping out and searching for the gold."

Happening to be at Columbia near the supposed locality two months after, I met with some of the persons interested in the discovery. The situation was still concealed, and supposing, as usual, the mineral found to be pyrites, stated my impression, and desired to examine a specimen, but none could be procured.

All, I was informed, had been sent to the Mint at New Orleans, where I was assured it had been assayed and pronounced pure copper.

I learned, in conversation with different persons, who knew something of the matter, that the particles found were of various sizes, from that of a small shot to that of the size and form of the "*end of a man's thumb.*"

It was said to have been picked out of the gravel on the side of a ridge, not in the bed of a creek. It had, it was said, the appearance of the droppings of melted metal, could be cut with the knife, was malleable, and emitted no sulphurous fumes in the furnace; in short, had none of the distinguishing characters of pyrites.

After the assay, the belief in gold was abandoned, and the copper hypothesis adopted.

Some tradition of the neighborhood represented the discovery not to be a new one, and alluded to an old bell-maker of the vicinity, who, some twenty or thirty years before, had been in the practice of using it for the brazing of his bells.

May these particles not have been the droppings from the brazier's furnace, of copper obtained in a more commercial way?

A belief has been current in the country for more than forty years, that lead mines do exist in the State, and small fragments or cubes of galena have in that time been frequently picked up in various quarters.

I have long been aware that such fragments have been found, associated with the Indian relics dispersed over the country and disintombed from the burial-places of the aborigines, and have entertained the opinion, in common with many others, that these were worn and regarded to some extent in the light of amulets or ornaments, and were buried among the cherished trinkets and other articles of personal property, with the dead body, as has been the practice of savage nations.

There is sufficient proof existing in the character of some of these relics, that the Indians once occupying this region, both the Mound-builders, and those of more modern tribes which succeeded them, had an intercourse with the primitive regions of Arkansas and Missouri, where the crystalline rocks and galena abound, and that some of these have been fashioned into articles of ornament for personal decoration.

It has not been my fortune to encounter the galena in other circumstances than the foregoing, but evidence that I cannot discredit, as to its existence in many situations in larger quantities than can be reasonably accounted for in this way, leads me to attribute its presence to diluvial action. If the first mode of transportation is inadequate to account for it, none other than this seems to remain.

A consideration of the force and energy of this agency, in connection with the northern drift or diluvium so called, hereafter treated of, and the materials unquestionably borne hither by its power, will probably satisfy the most incredulous that it was adequate to transport all the lead that can be found in the State.

This conjecture is strengthened by the fact that in those localities where it is said most to abound—that is, in Lawrence, Noxubbe, and Tippah counties—it is represented as occurring in intimate association with the cherty pebbles, the well-known detritus of the drift period.

Among the localities in which the galena has been found may be instanced the White Cliffs, and St. Catherine, in Adams County; on the Bayou Pierre, in Claiborne County; near Lauderdale Springs; near Philadelphia, Neshoba County; in Lawrence County, twelve miles east of Monticello, on the head of Dry Creek; in Kemper County, Section 34, Township 10, Range 17 E., twelve miles from De Kalb; and in Tippah County, a few miles northwest from Ripley.

DILUVIUM, OR NORTHERN DRIFT.

All diluvial action, of which we have evidence at different geological eras, was formerly referred to one violent and transitory period, and that attributed to the Noachian deluge; and hence the term diluvium, which was first applied by Dr. Buckland to all the superficial beds of gravel, clay, and sand on the surface of the earth; in the distribution and rapid accumulation of which, and the distinctive and foreign character of the materials deposited, we have proof of a violent irruption of water.

Although this hypothesis has been long abandoned, and the theories once entertained in reference to the phenomena of drift greatly modified, the term is still retained, but usually coupled and connected with others, conforming more in their signification to the present views entertained on the subject.

These deposits are referred to now as the Erratic block group, the Boulder formation, and the Northern drift, and are attributed to the most recent of the series of Cataclysms which have left their impress upon the globe.

The enormous size of many of the erratic blocks and boulders, the astonishing distances the pebble and smaller detritus have been transported, the mode of their distribution, and the eminences on the earth's surface which they have surmounted, indicate a force, or power employed in producing these effects, surpassing in energy any physical process now in action.

Some, however, yet maintain a belief in a more tranquil and gradual accumulation, by causes now operating with existing intensities.

As there are doubtless many who have not investigated this subject very thoroughly, or have made themselves familiar with the various theories that have been advanced, it may be as well to state that the transportation of the materials composing the diluvial beds is now *generally* attributed to the combined action of ice and water.

It has been said that investigations into the character of the drift have been too much neglected, and that the accumulation of facts connected with it, where circumstances favor the examination, is highly desirable.

Constituting an important and very interesting feature in the geology of the State, the character, composition, and distribution of the deposit will be here noticed. The reader can adopt his own hypothesis, as to its origin and the agent of transportation.

These deposits include the clay, sand, and gravel, containing existing species of testacea, and the remains of extinct mammalia.

The loam, or loëss, before spoken of, and again referred to as a diluvial marl, is of course embraced, as affording no proofs of long submergence, but on the contrary many of rapid accumulation. This is evident in the character and dispersion of its fossils through the stratum, and in its homogeneous character; for it is difficult to suppose it to have preserved that aspect if formed by the inconceivably slow process of deposition as river silt; a process, according to the calculation of eminent geologists, taking the ascertained rate of deposition of the Mississippi River at the present day as the basis of the calculation, requiring tens of thousands of years to accomplish; during the whole of which extended cycle, therefore, some dozen existing species of helices, which we find distributed from the lowest to the uppermost portions of the deposit, would seem to have constituted the almost exclusive fauna of the earth subject to have been drifted into it.

It seems more reasonable to imagine it to have been swept from the surface of pre-existing land, *teeming* at the time, with these terrestrial testacea, by the drift with which it is found associated.

Having no rocks in place here susceptible of retaining the scratching or grooving made by the moving block in passing over them, as in the more Northern States, and by which the direction of the drift has been determined, we have here to conjecture the course from the position of the *possible* original localities of the transported detritus, and the direction of the mountain ranges from which they are supposed to be derived.

In reference to the character of the small pebbles and boulders of the deposit, specimens of which were sent to Dr. Locke several years since, he remarked that they were very interesting, as tending to prove the wide dispersion of the drift, many of them being identified with the rocks found in place by Dr. Owen and himself in the survey of Iowa and Wisconsin.

It is probable, however, that we need not look so far for the primitive beds of these rocks if we suppose them to have pursued the usual course of diluvial currents, that is, a southeasterly direction. We may, perhaps, find their origin in those insulated mountain ranges, the Ozark Mountains and the Washita Hills in Arkansas and Missouri, distant two and three hundred miles only in a direct line from the western border of our State, near our principal diluvial beds.

This hypothesis is in accordance with facts at variance with the supposition of a more northern origin. Some of these are that the northern and northeastern counties of the State seem, in a great part, if not wholly, destitute of drift of the character of that of which I am treating. The channel of the Ohio River seems entirely without it, as is that of the Mississippi from the mouth of the Missouri to the vicinity of Memphis; the character of all the gravel I have observed in the Ohio and in the Mississippi between the points mentioned, being of a calcareous or imperfectly formed argillaceous description; whilst in the vicinity of Vicksburg and Natchez, and not extending below the White Cliffs, twelve miles only below the latter place, are found the heaviest deposits of the cherty and primitive formed diluvial gravel, and of the largest description in the whole course I have indicated. To the west, the lower Red River and Washita are destitute of these deposits, near Shrevesport, on Red River; and on the upper Washita, they are said to abound.

Assuming Port Gibson as about midway, measuring across the *stream*, we shall find a nearly continuous belt, averaging some sixty miles in width, extending through the State in a southeasterly direction, widening or contracting occasionally in its course, and perhaps with some skips or interruptions, such as are to be expected in deposits of this nature.

I am persuaded that the width of the stripe or belt may be traced through the State at the crossings of the eastern streams, Pearl, Leaf, and Chickasawhay Rivers.

It is, however, in the character of the pebbles and *boulders* of the formation, if they may so be called, that the unmistakable evidences of its foreign origin are seen.

These consist, in great part, of that description of rock known as chert or hornstone, an impure flint, often containing, or bearing the impressions of, fossil shells or corals, but most usually of crinordeal forms, the separate joints or fragments of encrinital stems, the latter occurring frequently, separate from the matrix, in the character of pebbles, being wholly converted into the same cherty rock, or into a yellowish jasper, and in some instances, into Carnelian or Chalcedony.

Associated with these are found the quartz rocks in various modifications, as ferruginous, milky, and limpid quartz; jaspers, yellow, red, and banded, as well as the black variety known as Lydian Stone or touchstone, together with several varieties or modifications of agates, chalcedony, and carnelian.

Porphyry has been occasionally seen, but is rare.

Among these are also found petrifactions of coral, shell, and wood in rare and varied conditions of mineralization, not merely silicified in the simple state, as ordinarily seen, but often agatized, opalized, and converted into carnelian, jasper, and jet.

As every particular regarding the character and composition of the drift seems to be a desideratum, it may not perhaps be amiss to be more minute in these details.

The chert and jasper pebbles, without possessing any very marked or determinate forms, are neither distinctly angular nor much rounded, although palpably waterworn; the black variety, or Lydian Stone, is an exception, however, being generally somewhat flattened with rather smooth faces, but otherwise irregular in outline.

The larger and coarser quartzose and jaspery agates, and, in rather less degree, the carnelians, are variously contorted, the agates frequently of rough exterior, and many of both cellular.

The quartz pebbles, on the contrary, whether of the limpid, milky, or ferruginous varieties, uniformly occur in symmetrical convex disks, sometimes nearly circular, but most generally of an ovate form.

The carnelians vary in color from the brown or sards to the white or chalcedony, but are generally of an amber or pale red, and rarely afford a facet over an inch square, although occurring sometimes three or four times as large.

The sards are generally smooth, flat, and present a much larger surface, possessing a somewhat conchoidal fracture, and the edges are generally of unequal thickness.

The finer varieties of agates are of a closer texture, and freer from flaws than the carnelians, being of the composition of chalcedony, striped with variously-colored veins, or concentric rings, and sometimes clouded, and are known as sard agates, or sardonyx, in contradistinction to the larger and coarser kinds first mentioned, in which the crystalline quartz and jasper are generally combined in variable proportions.

The sard agates are fully equal to the German or oriental agate in beauty and texture.

All these varieties are susceptible, in the hands of the lapidary, of being formed into handsome gems. Many of them have been cut and polished, and are much admired.

As these pebbles have all been subjected to an equal degree of attrition, the ultimate variety of form is doubtless owing to their distinctive crystalline structure.

In illustration of the degree of force necessarily employed in the transportation of the materials comprising the drift, it is proper perhaps to speak more definitely of their dimensions.

Blocks of chert, of cubical or angular forms, which have either not been rolled, or have, since their deposition, been broken into these forms by their natural lines of fracture, are occasionally found measuring two cubic feet or more; and a block of pure milk quartz weighing about ten pounds has been obtained.

The largest boulder seen, was found six or seven miles north of Vicksburg, near the base of the range of bluffs known as the Walnut Hills. It is of a symmetrical, ovate form, very similar in shape to the ferruginous quartz pebbles before spoken of, and approaching them somewhat in mineral composition, and of somewhat greater convexity of form. It measures about three feet in length by more than two in its greatest transverse diameter; the weight being conjectured to be at least five hundred pounds.

Another angular block of perhaps equal dimensions has been seen in another locality.

The general limits of distribution of this drift have before been stated. The heaviest deposits that have come under my observation, both as to the extent of the beds and dimensions of the boulders, are those on Big Sand in Claiborne County, some twenty miles northeastwardly from Port Gibson. This is exposed for several miles along the widely cut bed of the creek, and in several others in the vicinity, extending to and along the Bayou Pierre.

Others, not much less considerable, are found on St. Catherine's Creek, near Washington, and on some of the small branches of Cole's Creek, in Adams and Jefferson Counties.

An extensive gravel bar, extending over a surface of more than three hundred acres, is seen at Diamond Island, in the Mississippi, fifteen miles below Vicksburg.

Another, of nearly half the extent, is seen at Natchez Island, six miles below the city.

On a bar at the base of the Natchez Bluff, and on another in the Mississippi River, about five miles below Rodney, considerable deposits are found, the latter only exposed at low water.

On these river bars, the finest and largest of the sard agates and carnelians have been obtained.

Many other extensive beds have been noticed more in the interior, but have not been much explored, and it is not necessary to specify others.

Petrified wood has been spoken of as constituting some of the ingredients of the drift. I would not be understood, however, as referring it all to that origin. On the contrary, petrified wood is of very general occurrence over a large portion of the State, and will be further noticed under the head of Palæontology, hereafter to be treated of.

I incline to the belief, however, that the silicified palms or endogenous woods, which have so far been found only within a limited compass, not exceeding an area perhaps of ten miles in extent, are derived, like the boulders with which they are associated, from a foreign source.

These endogens have all, more or less, a rounded water-worn character, and being confined, so far as yet observed, to a single locality, may have formed part of the freight of an extended ice-floe, which, grounding in that quarter, discharged its contents upon the surface.

A variation in the character of the predominating rock or fossils composing the beds of drift in different localities has been observed, suggesting a conclusion that separate fields of ice, starting from various points, charged with the detritus of dissimilar formations, or not wholly alike in their mineral characters, may, in the termination of their course, have thus distributed them.

These palm woods differ both in their specific character and in their forms of silicification.

More than twenty species have been obtained, and constitute one of the most novel and interesting features in our palæontology. Some of these are beautifully agatized, some converted into jet, and others into a fine, close-grained, fawn-colored jasper.

Rounded, boulder-like masses of a foot in dimensions, and others of less diameter and eighteen inches in length, have been obtained.

It is, perhaps, scarcely necessary to add that the drift is differently disposed, not merely in beds or depressions, but heaped up in elevated knolls or moraine-like ridges and positions, attributed by Sir Charles Lyell and other eminent geologists, to the lateral pressure of moving ice.

These deposits always occur between the vegetable soil and the rocky strata of all ages, that constitute the geological basis of each section of country.

To the north of St. Peter's, Nicolet found it overlying the primary rocks to the south, and on both sides of the Mississippi it covers siluvian rocks. On the upper Missouri it rests upon a cretaceous formation, and upon the tertiary.

SPRINGS AND WELLS.

The section of the State embracing the pine region is bountifully supplied with springs of pure freestone water; and in the southernmost counties water is also obtained in wells of such moderate depth that they are, for greater convenience, habitually used.

Twenty-five feet may be stated as the average depth at which permanent streams are attained in Amite, Pike, and Marion; and on the flat lands nearer the seaboard, wells rarely exceed fifteen or twenty feet, the water being drawn by the pole and sweep.

In the alluvial lands of the river counties, springs are much less common, though not entirely deficient, and well water is freely obtained at about sixty to eighty feet.

In both, however, the water, although cold and limpid, is highly impregnated with lime, and is termed *hard* water, as unsuitable for washing, and not much less so for culinary purposes.

Being also regarded to some extent as unwholesome for drinking, cistern water has come into very general use, especially in towns and villages, as more salubrious.

The wells at the University of Oxford were sixty to seventy feet deep, and afforded a plentiful supply of good water; but having failed in the spring of 1852 (attributed to the shock of an earthquake felt very perceptibly at that place on the 23d of January, 1852), another well was sunk in the June following, to the depth of 145 feet before water was obtained, the whole distance through coarse silicious sand, of various colors, with thin strata of white clay; but no fossils were obtained.—(*Dr. Millington.*)

Along the whole extent of the Yazoo and Tallahatchee valleys, and the whole front below, on the Mississippi, copious springs or subterranean streams issue from the base of the bluffs; the water, however, flowing from beds of ochreous earths, and pyritous clays, is largely charged with sulphate of iron, and its habitual use is highly pernicious.

The undermining effects of these streams, some of them

of considerable volume, issuing not much above the low-water level of the Mississippi, and washing out the beds of sand, through which they flow, have produced considerable basin-like subsidences, and occasioned a peculiar indented configuration of the bluff margin, such as a striking example is afforded of in the *punch-bowls* just above Natchez.

Where the tertiary strata are exposed, or approach near the surface, as in portions of Hinds, Madison, and other middle counties, springs, at least such as are constant, are almost entirely absent; but well-water is frequently obtained from twenty to thirty-five feet below the surface. If obtained at the greater depth of fifty to eighty feet, it is generally fetid and unfit for use, being derived from the black offensive muck of the tertiary strata.

The shallow wells in use, are rarely permanent, seldom lasting more than a few years, when others are dug in situations previously experimented on with the auger.

The water is evidently derived from the surface, percolating through the upper strata to the pipe-clay and sand, which gives it, frequently, a somewhat turbid or milky appearance. An instance occurred, in the southern part of Hinds, where a fair quality of water was abundantly obtained at fifteen feet, within a few yards of the spot where a well had been recently sunk eighty feet to the black mud, and consequently abandoned.

This black, fetid muck of the prairies, seems extensively dispersed, and has been encountered at various localities, from the vicinity of Oxford to that of Brandon, at a depth of from fifty to eighty feet—a difference not greater, perhaps, than that of the inequalities of the surface. The same may be said of the eastern part of Neshoba.

The prairie district is lamentably deficient in good water. Where Artesian wells are impracticable, water is brought to an *attainable distance* by boring.

In Okolona, a boring has been made to the depth of 470 feet, which supplies a well sunk to the depth of ninety feet, the water rising to within seventy-five feet of the surface.

In Noxubbe County, these borings are very numerous. They range from one hundred and fifteen to six hundred feet in depth, the water rising variously to from fifteen to eighty feet of the surface, to meet which, the wells are sunk to the requisite depth, from which the water has then to be elevated in the ordinary way, by the windlass.

In one instance, water was brought to within three feet of the top, from a distance of three hundred and five feet; the boring was then continued to four hundred and forty-eight feet, but the water rose no higher.

Cisterns are frequently excavated in the white-lime rock of the prairie, requiring no walling or cement, and supplied either by these borings or with rain-water.

Tanks or ponds, for the supply of water for stock, have also been made in the rock, but, it is said, have not proved very reliable.

Franklin Springs, situated at the head of Wells's Creek, of which it is the principal source, on Lot 5, Section 37, Township 7, Range 1 E., is the most noted natural object in the county of that name. This was the earliest resort, as a watering-place, in the State. Thirty-five years since, these springs enjoyed some reputation; but as little improvement was made for the accommodation of visitors, and as they were not known to possess any medicinal properties, they were supplanted by Columbia Springs, in Marion County, and for a long period had gone out of use.

For two or three years past, they have again been attracting some attention, and buildings of a limited extent have been erected.

The peculiarity of these springs consists in the volume of water forced upwards from a considerable depth, by an evidently great pressure. The pool or basin formed by the principal spring, is used as a bath. It may not be inaptly likened to a natural Artesian well, with a tube or perforation about four feet in diameter, which has not been fathomed.

A person leaping into this with some force, may sink a short distance below the surface, but will be forcibly ejected. In a quiescent state, one cannot sink below the armpits. Poles twenty feet in length have been inserted in it, with no other apparent resistance than that presented by the ascending column of water.

The water is pure and limpid, but, owing to a quantity of decayed and finely comminuted vegetable matter, and sand held in suspension over the aperture, the vision can penetrate but a short distance into its depths.

The temperature of the bath, with the thermometer plunged some distance below the surface, was 64° Fahrenheit. In the open air, before immersion, it stood at 72 degrees.

As connected somewhat in character with these springs, and situated some eight miles below, near the stream of which they are the source, but on elevated pine lands, may be mentioned two wells (in the same county) about a mile or so distant from each other, in which, on penetrating a thin stratum of hard pan, the water in each instance rushed up with such violence, for a depth of forty feet, that the digger was extricated with difficulty. The water continued to stand at that elevation, and, although surrounded at no great distance by springs of pure freestone water, was so strongly impregnated with lime and iron as to be unfit for use.

MINERAL WATERS.

Mineral water is found in many parts of the State, and is generally sulphurous or chalybeate.

Several springs have enjoyed for a time, a reputation which made them the resorts of fashion and pleasure, or attracted the invalid by the virtues attributed to them.

The first of these, in point of notoriety and fashionable resort, was Stoveall's Spring, near Columbia, Marion County, Section 24, Township 4, Range 19 W.

The next in order were the Brandywine Springs, on the waters of the Bayou Pierre, about twenty miles east of Port Gibson, in Claiborne County.

These, which were in high favor some twenty years since, as well as the Columbia Spring, were of sulphur water, and have long since ceased to be frequented, and the buildings, once familiar with gay and joyous throngs, have fallen to decay, and have nearly all been removed.

The Mississippi Springs, formerly known as Bankston's, near Clinton, in Hinds County, next attracted attention. Extensive buildings, but of rather a temporary and perishable character, were erected, and the place enjoyed for several years a liberal patronage, until it was in a great degree supplanted by its more popular and widely known rival, Cooper's Well, distant only about two miles, on Section —, Township 5, Range 2 W. The water of this well has acquired a high character for its curative effects in a certain class of diseases, and its reputation is attracting numbers afflicted with such disorders, even from distant States.

The water is unlike any other hitherto discovered here, the chief ingredient being sulphate of lime.

This well, situated in a cove, at the foot of a very high gravelly ridge, is 107 feet deep. A stratum of sandstone (found also on the surface) and one of conglomerate or pudding-stone, were penetrated.

The temperature of the water, ascertained by me in May, 1852, was 66° Fahrenheit, the mercury standing at 88° in the open air, before immersion.

Dr. Smith, in his analyses of the previous December, reports the temperature at 64° Fahrenheit; that of the air being at the time 50 degrees; showing a difference of two degrees between winter and summer, owing, doubtless, to the exposure to the different medium of the atmosphere of the surface, colder at one period and warmer at the other.

Analyses of this water, and of such other mineral springs as could be procured, will be found under the proper head.

Among others which have for some years past attracted many visitors, may be mentioned the Lauderdale Springs and the Artesian Springs of Madison County.

Ocean Springs, on the sea-shore near Baluxi, has the latest notoriety, being opened to visitors for the first time last summer, and seems likely to be much frequented as a summer resort.

There are many other mineral springs which have not yet come into general notice; some still unimproved, and known only to or frequented by persons in the immediate neighborhood; a mere mention of some of these will complete the list; among them are the reputed alum springs of Madison, Marion, and Pike Counties; a white sulphur spring in Neshoba County; and the springs in Marshall and Lafayette, the properties of which I have not learned.

ARTESIAN WELLS.

Artesian wells, so called from the province of Artois, in France, where they are generally supposed to have been first constructed, are of such a description, that, by boring into the earth to the requisite depth, water is obtained on the surface or escapes from the orifice in a jet to a variable height above it, and this result is due to the principle that water will find its own level.

Success, therefore, is not to be expected alike in all situations, and such borings are to be undertaken only in those formations, or under certain conditions of geological structure, in which the strata are so disposed in reference to their dip or inclination, and their character and consistency, as to render this practicable.

Plate XI., Fig. 2, exhibits a section of such a stratification as answers these conditions.

The whole series is seen so curved or inclined by some subterranean movement as to present a concave surface or basin-shaped structure: *A* represents a stratum of such consistency or character of rock as to retain the water falling on it, upon its surface; *B* a stratum of sand and gravel, or of such other porous materials as will absorb the water which falls upon and is conducted into it by *A*, and which is prevented from rising above by the retentive strata of clay, or any impervious rock, represented by *C*. Borings from the surface, as at *E E*, penetrating into the water-bearing stratum *B*, will afford an escape for the water through the superficial deposits *D*, to the surface, or to the level of its source, the water itself being the motive power, and the elevating force being restrained or counteracted in the degree of the resistance the water encounters in passing through the strata, the weight of the column ejected, and the atmospheric pressure above the surface.

It is obvious, therefore, that borings into *A*, in the direction of its outcropping, or into the basin itself, if it were filled with superficial deposits to a higher level than the source of the subterranean fountain, would not be attended with success.

Other agencies may co-operate, it is true, in producing this effect, as the carbonic acid gas, which, in its escape from its invaded sources, forces the water up with it.

In the remarkable well at Kissingen, in Bavaria, a column of salt water, discharging one hundred cubic feet per minute, is thus ejected with such force as to elevate it fifty-eight feet above the surface from a depth of sixteen hundred and eighty feet.

Similar effects are produced by the same agency, but in a less stupendous degree, in the salt wells on the Kanawha, in Virginia; and in the sulphur well, bored in the bed of the Scioto River, near Columbus, Ohio; the water is driven up with great force by its own gas, from a depth of two hundred and fifty feet.

The Geysers, or intermittent hot springs of Iceland, afford another example of the elevation of water by natural means, the elevating agent in that case being the pent-up vapor generated by internal volcanic fires.

The popular belief that Artesian wells are of very modern origin is unfounded, as, according to several ancient writers, they appear to have been known at an early age.

The well at Lillers, has been in use since the beginning of the twelfth century, and has afforded, during a period of seven hundred years, a constant and undiminished supply of water.

The wells at Elbeuf, Tours, and Rouen have, during a long period, been equally constant; and the inference is that such fountains are inexhaustible.

Until recently, the well at Grenelle, a suburb of Paris, was regarded as the most stupendous and successful experiment of the kind. Eight years were occupied in its construction. It is about eighteen hundred feet in depth, and affords about half a million of gallons of water in twenty-four hours.

It is surpassed, however, by the salt well at Kissingen, before mentioned, which was commenced in 1832, and not completed until 1850. Its depth is 2,325 feet, and the cost of construction, including fixtures, exceeded thirty thousand dollars.

In addition to those already mentioned, the most considerable undertakings of the kind in this country are the following: Belcher's Well, at St. Louis, Missouri, which, in April 1853, had attained the depth of 1,590 feet, the boring being still prosecuted day and night, by steam-power; and the well at Charleston, South Carolina, in which, in May 1853, more than a thousand feet of boring was accomplished, and the work was rapidly progressing. Ultimate success was anticipated.

The geological structure of a considerable portion of Alabama and Mississippi also is favorable to these enterprises.

In the former State, there are said to be not less than *five hundred* of these wells, and their depth rarely exceeds six hundred feet.

In our own State, the number approaches, perhaps,

one hundred. In Lowndes County alone, there are more than thirty of these, chiefly on the east of the Tombigbee River.

Details as to the locality, depth, and volume of water discharged, &c., of a number of these, were obtained when on an excursion to that county.

These are all of quite moderate depth, ranging from one hundred and fifteen to three hundred and seventy feet.

The most remarkable of these is that formerly known as Bexley's, which, from the very inconsiderable depth of one hundred and ninety-six feet, throws up one hundred and sixty gallons per minute.

The next, as regards the volume of water, is that of Fernande's, the depth being one hundred and ninety feet, and the discharge one hundred and fifteen gallons.

The highest jet above the surface is fifteen feet, given by the wells of Jordan and Cannon. In the others enumerated, it ranges from three to five feet.

The public well in Columbus is the deepest, being three hundred and seventy-one feet; it discharges thirty gallons per minute, four feet above the surface, the temperature of the water being 65° Fahr.

From Dr. Spillman, of Columbus, to whom I am indebted mainly for the foregoing details as to the wells in Lowndes County, and for other attentions, I derived the following particulars as to the stratification disclosed by the boring of the public well in Columbus; the Doctor being the only person, so far as I could learn, who had bestowed much intelligent observation on the subject in that quarter, or had taken note of such observations. The details were more minute, as furnished, than I have given them, but in the absence of similar observations in reference to other wells, the omission of the minute divisions of the strata are unimportant.

Artesian Well at Columbus.

Stratum.	Feet.	
A	50	Ferruginous clays and pebbles.
B	160	Green-sand, composed of chlorite of iron, &c.
C	83	Incoherent micaceous earth, of light ash color, with lignite and pyrites alternating.
D	7	Hard brown-colored argillite.
E	18	Fine ash-colored grit, with particles of mica.
F	12	Yellow-colored hard argillaceous earth.
G	28	Tough, brown, argillaceous earth, difficult to bore.
H	13	Compact green-sand to water, temperature 65° Fahr.
	371 feet.	(See PLATE XI., Fig. 1.)

At Aberdeen, Monroe County, which is about six or seven miles west, and about twenty-four north of Columbus, the public Artesian well in the town is five hundred and twelve feet deep, and affords about ten gallons of water per minute. It is strongly chalybeate, imparting a deep copper tinge in a short time to the tin and earthen vessels in which it is kept.

But few attempts have been made, I believe, at Artesian wells west of the dividing ridge between the waters of the Tombigbee and those of Pearl River.

About twenty-five years since, one was commenced in Natchez, in which, however, a moderate depth only was attained, the obstacle being, it is said, the quicksand encountered—a difficulty which the undertaker had neither the experience nor the ingenuity to surmount.

In 1848, the Rev. Mr. Lambuth, residing on Section 2, Township 7, Range 2 E., ten miles south of Canton, in Madison County, bored to the depth of two hundred and eighty feet, when, on penetrating through a sand-

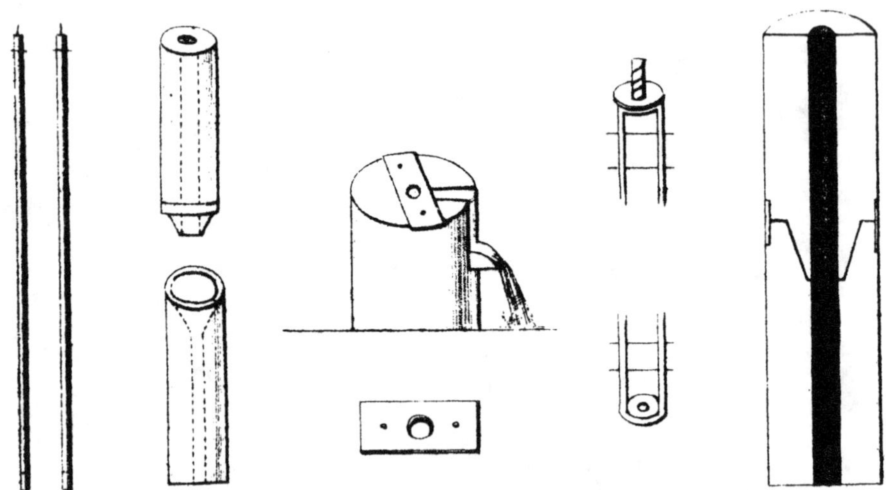

ARTESIAN WELLS

Process and implements for boring.

B. L. C. Wailes del. On Stone by M. Rosenthal. Chromo Lith. by L. N. Rosenthal Phil.

stone not exceeding a foot in thickness, the water rushed up to within eighty feet of the surface, with such force as to clog up the boring, which had not been tubed.

Near the same place, two years later, he repeated the experiment with the same result.

In a third attempt, an imperfect tubing, formed of plank, inserted down to the rock before penetrating it, enabled him to continue the boring; and at the further depths of fifty and one hundred feet respectively, other water-bearing strata were encountered, each of which afforded an obvious increase of water, which had risen near the surface when the auger was broken, and could not be extracted.

In 1852, he renewed his experiments on the public square in Canton, one hundred and two feet below the level of his former attempts.

Allowing for the difference of elevation, he found a general correspondence in the strata penetrated. A depth of 280 feet was attained, when the rush of water became so great as to fill up the imperfect and badly adjusted tubing, which at that point, by an untoward accident, became hopelessly crushed and deranged.

In neither of these borings were the cretaceous rocks reached, but the tertiary green-sand marl, with fossils similar to those found at Jackson, I understand, was penetrated.

The process of boring, as I witnessed it in Lowndes County, is easy; the apparatus is simple, and attended with but moderate expense or consumption of time. (See Plate XIII.) A tripod, formed of common poles, about thirty feet high, sustains a block over the aperture from which the boring rods are suspended, and which are managed by two laborers, who walk around at opposite ends of a short movable lever, connected with the iron bar, or *sinker*, which forms the upper section of the rods, and is provided with a series of holes, at suitable distances along its entire length, about ten feet, through which the lever is keyed, and by means of which it can be shifted and adjusted at a higher elevation, as the auger descends.

To the lower end of the sinker, wooden rods, in sections of about twenty feet in length, tipped with iron to admit of being screwed together as the work progresses, are attached; and these are elevated, as occasion requires, by the rope by which they are suspended, passing through the block, and connecting with a windlass, which may be worked, if necessary, by horse-power.

A bored log is usually inserted down to the indurated marl or lime-rock. This is necessary to prevent the loose incoherent earth or sand of the upper strata from caving in or being washed away. The log has an aperture sufficient to admit the free passage of the auger and rods, and is driven or forced down in one or more sections of twenty feet, suitably united, to the requisite depth, which is sometimes near a hundred feet.

When the compact rock is penetrated, and sandy, incoherent strata met with, tubing becomes necessary; sheet-iron is generally used for the purpose, but cast-iron pipes are considered more suitable.

Thirty feet a day can be bored in the soft lime rock, but not more than ten in the sand-rock or green-sand. Fifty feet is sometimes accomplished the first day.

The ordinary charge for boring is thirty-three cents per foot for the first three hundred feet; for the next two hundred feet, fifty cents; and over five hundred feet, one dollar per foot.

The tubing with sheet-iron, is estimated to cost fifty cents per foot.

The cost of the whole apparatus necessary for boring, including windlass and other tackle, need not exceed three hundred dollars.

The subjoined table, of some of the wells in Lowndes County, exhibits a great inequality, both in depth and volume of water. All these are situated on the east side of the Tombigbee River, and, in the absence of other data, afford no satisfactory indications of the inclination of the strata.

It is a matter of regret, that my inquiries, when visiting the prairie district, were not productive of more reliable information, on a subject of such prominent interest to a considerable portion of the State.

Many of those who have engaged in the execution of these enterprises, have taken little note as to the dip, thickness, or character of the various strata encountered in these borings, and their observations have not generally been such as to indicate the likelihood of success, or to enable them to form any reasonable inference as to the probable depth of the water-bearing strata in other localities. The work is, therefore, often prosecuted as a hap-hazard adventure, and success is regarded as wholly fortuitous.

I hope I shall succeed hereafter, in acquiring further information of more practical value, on this interesting subject.

As far as the facts collected in the vicinity of Columbus, authorize a conjecture, it may be inferred that the dip of the strata is to the southwest, at the rate of about twenty-five feet to the mile.

In the present stage of our investigations, and the experience we have acquired, it is perhaps idle to speculate at this time upon the probability of finding water-bearing strata above the cretaceous rocks which would fulfil the conditions of Artesian fountains.

It has been the opinion of some, that the burrstone sands were of this character; but, however promising the indications may sometimes have been, this belief, as yet, is not known to have been verified.

In the boring at Charleston, South Carolina, these sands have been passed, and the cretaceous rocks penetrated to a considerable depth, without a satisfactory result.

Table of Artesian Wells in Lowndes County, east of the Tombigbee River.

PROPRIETOR.	Quarter of section.	Section.	Township.	Range.	Depth.	Rise above the surface.	Gallons per minute.
Public well in Columbus	W. ½ S. W. ¼	16	18 S.	18 W.	371	4	30
Bexley or Richardson	W. ½ S. E. ¼	19	17 S.	17 W.	196	5	160
A. Moore	E. ½ S. E. ¼	8	18 S.	18 W.	197	3	15
William Winston	W. ½ N. W.	8	18 S.	17 W.	200	4	30
W. Covington	N. W.	24	17 S.	18 W.	185	4	75
C. R. Jordan	N. W.	1	19 N.	15 E.	260	15	4
Rhasa Cannon	N. W.	11	19 N.	16 E.		15	10
E. W. Kirkland	E. ½ S. E.	7	18 S.	17 W.	265	4	60
F. Exford	W. ½ N. W.	14	18 S.	18 W.	206	4	10
C. McLarin	E. ½ N. W.	14	18 S.	18 W.	246	3	20
S. G. Wells	W. ½ N. W. ¼	18	18 N.	17 E.	115	4	15
J. J. Fernandis	W. ½ N. E.	31	17 S.	17 W.	190	3	115
J. M. Wyne	E. ½ N. W.	23	18 S.	18 W.	190	4	35
E. C. Eggleston	S. ½ N. W.	18	18 S.	17 W.	185	3	40
B. Barry	W. ½ S. W.	1	18 S.	18 W.	178	4	30
W. Dowsing	W. ½ S. W.	10	18 S.	18 W.	256	3	25
James Miller	E. ½ S. W.	25	19 N.	17 E.	203	5	2
Robert Jameson	W. ½ S. E.	28	17 S.	17 W.	145	4	50

PALÆONTOLOGY.

Palæontology is that branch of natural history by which we gain a definite knowledge of organic remains, or of the fossil and extinct animals and plants which have been aptly termed the medals of creation, and the embalmed memorials of a former world.

It furnishes a certain clue and guide in our geological researches, and enables us to identify the different formations in very distant localities when the distinctions founded solely on mineral characters would fail.

The discovery was made, about half a century since, by William Smith, a land surveyor, and now recognized as "the father of English geology," that certain groups of fossils were peculiar to certain strata; a knowledge which has since been improved by Sir Charles Lyell, in his division of the tertiary strata, as has before been stated. In this division, the testacea or shells, found to exist in greatest abundance and variety, and of wider and more general distribution, have been adopted, to the exclusion of the remains of plants and vertebrated animals, which are comparatively of too few species and are confined to fewer localities.

More than three thousand species of fossil shells have been ascertained. Of these, about eight hundred perhaps belong to the pliocene, one thousand to the miocene, and twelve hundred to the eocene divisions of the tertiary; and, although some species may be common to all, or run into the other divisions, yet a large proportion of them may be regarded as the exclusive and characteristic fossils of each.

It is by noting the existence of these in new and distant localities, and by the discovery of new and undescribed species, that our knowledge is extended, and hence it is that our eminent geologists impress upon those engaged in such investigations the importance of collecting all these relics, none of which, however mutilated or imperfect, are regarded as too trivial to be preserved.

These remarks may tend, perhaps, to modify, in some degree, the lightly formed opinions of those who have been accustomed to regard the collection of fossil remains, especially of minute shells, as a puerile pursuit or a frivolous recreation of the idle; and the study of their nature and history as tending to no useful result.

The discovery of the skeletons of gigantic mammalia, such as those of the Mastodon or of kindred species, may excite a temporary interest among the curious; but the less striking discoveries, due to the labors of the naturalist, are too generally disregarded and unappreciated.

Few States in the Union are so rich in organic remains as Mississippi, and a description of some of these, and the localities in which they occur, will here be given.

So far as our secondary formations have been explored, they afford no fossils of an earlier origin than those of the cretaceous period. I except, of course, the *transported* exuvia of the drift, and which will be noticed in that group.

The organic remains of the cretaceous system, it should be remarked, are almost wholly marine; no land or fresh-water shells or bones of mammalia having yet been formed among them.

At the Plymouth Bluffs, on the western side of the Tombigbee River, about five miles above Columbus by land, Casts of the Ammonites of large size, as well as those of the Inoceramus, or Catillus Cuveri; and the nautilus, bellerophon, and bacculitis faujasii, are numerous in the lowest exposed strata of micaceous shale and green-sand, which forms the base of the talus, and in which the Exogera Costata are profusely deposited, having fallen from the superior strata in the escarpment of the bluff where they are seen horizontally disposed in place.

From the character of the bed in which they are found, it is difficult to extract the casts from the matrix, and but few, chiefly those of the Catillus, were obtained.

The exogera, however, are of different character, being mineralized nearly to silicification. The shells detach themselves readily from the strata, and are found also strewn profusely on the surface of the adjacent prairies, and in the small superficial channels and ravines at a prairie bluff, two miles further, near the Oktibbeha Creek, where the gryphæa globosa and a peculiar small hook-shaped fossil, the Hamulus onyx, are also found, the latter similarly dispersed in great quantities.

At the base of this bluff, near the water's edge, ledges of conglomerate, formed chiefly of the exogera, are exposed, and at Plymouth Bluff the pecten quinque costatus was found among the other fossils.

Near Aberdeen, ammonites, changed to a compact calcareous rock, have been found of large size. I met with some considerable sections of these, divided by the transverse plates or partitions of the cells, and susceptible of being fitted together or reunited at their joints or lines of separation.

The lamna cuspidata of Agassiz, has also been found in the prairie rock near Aberdeen.

At Okolona, the gryphæa globosa was seen in the white limestone excavated from the deep well in that place; the shells all having a black slaty appearance, attributable, perhaps, to the presence of the pyrites in the rock.

Beyond Prairie Mound, and about fifteen miles from Pontotoc, near the base of a long hill, which the road ascends, the prairie rock is seen to crop out, and the exogera are again abundant; and at this point a considerable number of belemnites were obtained, numerous fragments of them being strewn by the roadside.

Several miles further, after surmounting the hill or ridge spoken of, in the bank of a branch of the Chowapa, the exogera are again seen, and nearer to Pontotoc, two or three miles to the south, they are found in massive beds, forming a conglomerate rock extending with little interruption several miles, the general range bearing nearly east and west, and on the northern declivity of the ridge, resembling a prolonged indented parapet.

The spatangus, a small species of which occurs at another more easterly locality nearer Pontotoc, enters partially with the exogera, and a proportion of minor fragmentary shells, into the composition of the conglomerate, in and near which, some very minute sharks' teeth were also found.

Near Tocshish, the old missionary station, some twenty-five years since, and before the Indians had removed from the country, some very conspicuous and extensive ranges of a similar conglomerate were to be seen rising several feet above the surface, suggesting the idea of an ocean reef, or an ancient sea margin. I could not learn with certainty whether these ledges yet exist. The practice which has obtained in that section of burning this shell rock into lime, has most probably consigned them to useful and economical purposes.

The occurrence of the vertebra, and some of the other bones of the Mosasaurus, found in digging cisterns, and in the Noxubee Creek, near Macon, renders it probable that there is a formation in that section equivalent to the Maestricht beds, separating the cretaceous and tertiary series, this reptile belonging to the former group, and being characteristic of the beds spoken of.

Further investigations, which have as yet been prosecuted only to a limited extent in that quarter, will probably reveal some of the characteristic shells usually associated with these remains, and which are common neither to the cretaceous nor to the tertiary.

Some joints of the vertebra of the Mesosaurus, from the lime rock excavated from the cisterns spoken of, are plated or embossed with pyrites, and plates of the shells of Chelonia are found associated with them in a similar condition.

Following up these organic remains in the order of succession, those of the Eocene period next present themselves, and at no point yet explored more conspicuously than at Vicksburg.

Mr. Conrad, who has perhaps bestowed more attention upon the tertiary fossils of the United States than most of our geologists, visited that locality some years since, and devoted several weeks to researches among these remains, and published a descriptive catalogue of them in 1848, in the first volume of the second series of the *Journal of the Academy of Natural Sciences*, Philadelphia.

He enumerates about one hundred and fifty species, many of which he found to be new and undescribed, and most of which he has accurately figured.

Since his visit, these beds have been traced along the base of the bluff range above Vicksburg, as high as St. Peter's, or Hayne's Bluff, on the Yazoo, which has resulted in the discovery of a few others, not included in his catalogue.

A table of all the species found in the scope indicated will be found annexed; and for a more particular acquaintance with the most characteristic the reader is referred to the *Journal of the Academy of Natural Sciences*, vol. i. Plates, 11, 12, 13, and 14, and vol. ii. Plate 1.

The fossils of this locality are not confined to the testacea, but with them are associated the spines and rays of fishes, together with their dental plates, otolites, and scales, as well as the teeth of several species of the shark family—among them the Carcharodon agustidens and Galeocerdo latidens of Agassiz. The Saurocephalus lanciformis of Harlan is also found.

The branched coral, *Madrepora Mississippiensis* of Conrad, is abundant, and one small specimen of a species which seems nearly allied, if not identical, with that of the rock used in the walls of the Castle of San Juan d'Ulloa, Vera Cruz, has been obtained.

Similar beds are represented as occurring in the bluffs on Big Black River, and on Baker's Creek, in Hinds County. Whether these are identical with the Vicksburg fossils, or assimilate more nearly to those found in the tertiary green-sand marl of Jackson, remains to be determined.

This latter deposit is seen most advantageously in the bed of the creek emptying into Pearl River immediately below the crossing of the Jackson and Brandon Railroad. The bed lies about fifteen feet below the level of the adjacent plain, and about four feet of its thickness are exposed in the banks of the creek. Its entire depth has not been ascertained.

The marl is of a bluish-green color in its moist state, and in the bed is of considerable toughness and tenacity. Upon exposure, and becoming thoroughly dried, it parts with much of its color, crumbles to a granular sand-like substance, and assumes a grayish appearance, owing to the large proportion of finely comminuted shell contained in it.

The quantity of entire shells imbedded in it is very great, lying almost in contact with each other, and forming perhaps one-sixth of the volume of the deposit.

When first exposed, these shells present a lively yellow tint, but become somewhat bleached and changed to a dull white by exposure.

Of more than forty species that have been found, very few are identical with those of Vicksburg, and many of them belong to distinct genera. Generally, they exceed the Vicksburg shells considerably in size.

Among them the Rostellaria velata of Conrad is by far the most abundant, amounting perhaps to twenty-five per cent. of the whole number.

An unusually large Mytra is also found here; for which, it proving to be new, I propose the specific name Millingtonii, in respect to my friend, Doctor Millington, first principal geologist of the State.

A Cypræa (fenestrela) having the exterior surface covered with a double series of fine, but very distinct stria, intersecting and crossing each other, seems to be peculiar to this bed, but its greatest novelty is a large depressed patelliform shell, belonging to the genus Umbrella of Swainson, and for which *planulata* is proposed by Mr. Conrad as the specific name.

The foregoing, together with the phorus reclusus may be considered the characteristic shells of the deposit.

Two species of turbinoba, a large flabellum, and two species of the oyster, one of which, of large size and to some extent silicified, is also of common occurrence on the surface in the vicinity, and abundantly in the small prairie half a mile northeast of the State House, are also included in this remarkable group of fossils.

For the subjoined catalogue, I am indebted to Timothy A. Conrad, Esq., whose extensive investigations among the fossils of the cretaceous and tertiary formations, renders him the most competent authority we have in this department of our Natural history. These fossils have been determined and named by him, and prove for the chief part, new and undescribed species.

In the lime-rock exposed by the cut in the railroad near Brandon, PLATE XII., Fig. 1, the Scutella Rogersi of Morton is abundant, but so firmly imbedded as to be detached with difficulty, and very rarely entire.

Imbedded in the lime-rock at Marshall's quarry, are found the Spatangus, Madrepora Mississippiensis, crustacea, and shells, together with numerous casts of panopea.

Fish finely preserved, and exhibiting the fins and scales very distinctly, have also been obtained in this rock, as well as a fossil which has somewhat the appearance which collolites present, but which result, perhaps, from the ravages of teredinæ.

Fossils of the same character are to be had at Steward's quarry, but have been less observed.

In the crabs found in these quarries, the carapace and other plates, as well as the claws, are well defined, the latter, however, being often absent or detached, wholly or in part.

At Long's Quarry, eight miles south of Jackson, when it was formerly worked, many similar fossils of an interesting description were brought to light, and sharks' teeth of small size, were common there.

A fine specimen of Carcharodon megalodon, of Agassiz, of good size, was found in the gypseous marl of Ball Prairie, a few miles southeast of Clinton, Hinds County.

The Carcharodon agustidens, of Agassiz, has also been found in the same county. These species occur in the marls of Virginia, and are there referred to the Miocene period.

In 1843, I obtained from the neighborhood of Long's Quarry, a considerable portion of the remains of the Basilosaurus found in the bank of Pearl River.

Joints of the vertebra, of which examples may be seen in the State cabinet, sometimes measure more than a foot in length, and about eight inches in diameter, giving to one having the slightest knowledge of comparative anatomy, a tolerable conception of the proportions of this gigantic animal—the largest, perhaps, of all animals whose remains have ever been discovered, being from eighty to one hundred feet in length.

Remains of this animal appear first to have been noticed in Louisiana, having been first described by Dr. Harlan in 1835, from specimens sent him by Judge Bry, from the Washitta, in Louisiana.

Similar remains were subsequently discovered in Arkansas, and much more abundantly in Clark County, Alabama, than elsewhere.

A skeleton, made up from portions obtained in different localities in Alabama, was taken to Europe for exhibition under the name of "Hydrarchos Sillimani"—a representation of which, after being reconstructed on anatomical principles, may be seen in the *Iconographic Encyclopædia*, being the central figure on Plate 39. The peculiar and characteristic teeth are also shown on the same Plate, figures 60 and 61.

Subsequently, when it was ascertained to be more nearly allied to the cetacean than to the reptilian order of animals, Dr. Owen, the distinguished comparative anatomist of Great Britain, proposed the name of

Zeuglodon Harlani, from the yoke-like form of the teeth, and in honor of Dr. Harlan, who first described and introduced it to the notice of the scientific world.

The original name is, however, retained by many in respect to the rule established among naturalists which regards the rights of priority of discovery.

It has also been named the Squalodon, Phocodon, and the Dorudon, and for a further description of which the reader is referred to the Monograph of Dr. Robert W. Gibbes, published with figures in the first volume of the second series of the *Journal of the Academy of Natural Sciences*, Philadelphia.

In Mississippi, these remains occur in other localities than those mentioned. The detached vertebra have been found in the City of Jackson, and the immediate vicinity, at Ball Prairie, about six miles to the west; and in Jones's Prairie, Section 15, Township 9, Range 4 E., in Madison County.

In Scott and Smith Counties they are frequently seen, and are said to abound in Clark.

The vertebra and ribs are obtained in nearly a perfect state; the head, being composed of many separate bones or plates held together only by the muscular integument, is rarely found united, and but few perfect teeth have been obtained.

In reference to their variety, their unquestionable foreign origin, and the changed condition from an originally calcareous material to the diversified forms of silification in which they now exist, the fossils of the drift compose a group highly interesting, if not unique.

Of this metamorphosis, or conversion of lime into silex, Dr. Troost, the Geologist of Tennessee, whose loss to the State has been greatly deplored, remarks: "This change in the chemical nature of these remains is certainly unaccountable. The *Polyperfers*, for instance, are, when in their live state, of a calcareous nature, yet we find them now in the strata of our limestones changed into silex." And in this, he further observes, "They differ from the organic substances of other countries."

Many of these organic remains, supposed to have been derived from the silurian rocks, consist of the stony axis or skeletons of polypi, comprising the petrified corals, which, as a class, have been generally designated as madrepores, by the misapplication of a term belonging properly to a single genus, and include the favosites astreas, cyathophylla catenepora, &c. of many species, and of great variety in the size, structure, and arrangement or grouping of the cells. Some of the favosites, from the size and form of the cells, by a very popular fallacy have been regarded as petrified honeycomb.

These, however numerous, are not all the organic remains which enter into this group.

The trilobite, which, in its native lime rock, is generally found of rather delicate or fragile texture, is here met with occasionally, either detached, or its form impressed or wholly incorporated in the chert or jaspery pebble, more durable than granite.

Specimens belonging to the genera calymene and asaphus have been recognized.

Gorgonia, fenestrella, stems of crinoidea or encrenites, as well as orthocera and cyathophyllum, are found in similar condition, all, but most especially the corals, partaking more or less of the mineral character of the associated agates and chalcedony, which, as has before been stated, abound in the drift.

Some of these, when cut and polished by the lapidary, form gems of much beauty, and have been greatly admired.

Petrified wood, although found in most parts of the State, seems to occur most abundantly in the vicinity of the Big Sand and Bayou Pierre, in a limited district, including parts of the Counties of Claiborne, Hinds, and Copiah; and the petrifactions of the family of endogenous plants or palms seem in a great measure peculiar to it.

Many species of the palms, in various conditions of silicification, and apparently lapidified by different mineralizing agents, have been obtained here. These, as well as the woods seemingly allied to or identical with species of the present age and climate, occur in forms and in characters exceedingly diversified, and of high interest in connection with the commonly received theories of petrifaction, the fibre texture and the color of the wood being often preserved or most wonderfully simulated in the process of replacement by mineral atoms; suggesting, in some instances, the idea of an *instant* conversion of the former into the present material.

Agatized specimens are common. Wood opal is also met with; and other specimens bear a striking similitude to jasper, jet, or obsidian, and to chalcedony.

Woods are seen transmuted into a fine translucent carnelian, revealing the minutest details of structure and fibre.

Sometimes an asbestiform appearance is presented, or a resemblance of fibrous gypsum, with minute, splintery, acicular crystals; and a fine white porcelain is counterfeited most successfully.

Although I have scarcely met with an example of the palms beyond this locality, the exogenous plants are of more general distribution, and having succinctly stated some of the aspects which the fossil woods here present,

I will detail some of the localities and conditions in which the latter class have been noticed.

The asbestiform petrifactions have been observed in places near which the gypseous marls occur, as in the vicinity of the Mississippi Springs, in Hinds, and near Pearl River, in Leake County. Trunks of trees of this description, of considerable size, are seen on elevated grounds, and generally of a chalk-like whiteness.

A portion of the trunk of a tree, some two feet in diameter, originally, is to be seen imbedded in the road, about seventeen miles north of Bolochitto Bridge, in the northern part of Hancock County, on a high, sandy ridge. It is of a white porcelain character, of very close, compact texture, the ends, however, of a splintery asbestiform appearance.

On Section 45, Township 7, Range 1 W., in Adams County, several sections of six or eight feet in length, and two feet in diameter, split through the middle in equal parts, present themselves in a sandy cove, which indents the high land bordering the bottom of a branch of Cole's Creek.

Some very large trunks lie also, at the foot of the White Cliffs, on the Mississippi, but are only to be seen at extreme low water.

At Dr. Grant's, in Copiah County, some large trunks lie partially exposed on the declivity of the high lands, on the western side of the Bayou Pierre, about eighty feet above the water-level of the stream; and at Mr. Lloyd's, about two miles distant, on a site of similar elevation, in sinking a well at eighty feet below the surface, a similar tree was encountered. These were very solid, but rather coarse-grained petrifactions.

In the bed of the Bayou Pierre, within a mile of Mr. Lloyd's, there are many blocks of the Grand Gulf sandstone. In one of these, of considerable size, of a bluish color, and of extreme hardness, is imbedded a petrified trunk with projecting branches. The character and appearance of this rock, have before been described, and it may be mentioned that, with the exception of some *impressions* or casts of leaves, and of small seed-vessels noticed at Grand Gulf, this is the only fossil seen imbedded in it.

For more than twenty years past, the existence of a *standing* petrified tree, in the Scutchaloe Hills, a ridge dividing the waters of the Bayou Pierre and Big Sand, in Claiborne County, had been repeatedly asserted and generally believed.

A petrified forest, in a sandy desert near Cairo, in Egypt, has been often described, in which the stumps of trees yet stand erect above the surface, and has been accounted for satisfactorily, by the shifting sands in which it had formerly been involved. And indications of a similar character have been reported in connection with the district known as the Cross Timbers, in Texas.

I need not, therefore, remark upon the interest that would attach to an isolated specimen of a single tree of this character, or speak of my desire to examine it. My search, however, at different times, although guided by persons who were familiar with the region, was fruitless.

But I found, at several places, large trunks of silicified trees, lying on the *surface* of some of the most elevated ridges.

At one place, the trunks of two trees, about three feet in diameter, lie in close proximity. Along one of these, broken into several sections, I measured sixty-five feet to its first or principal bifurcation, beyond which, fragments of less diameter, doubtless portions of the principal branches, were seen extending some distance further, rather out of the direct line of the trunk. It might be rash to assert that these trees lie where they grew; yet they present strong indications that such is the fact.

The but-end, or larger extremity of the principal one, although exhibiting no distinct roots above the ground, presents that curvature or enlargement of outline, that is seen at the base of a standing tree, formed by the expansion of the roots in the earth. It had also the appearance of a tree, which, being considerably advanced in a state of decay, had been broken by falling across a rather sharp ridge before silicification took place. It now lies only slightly imbedded, in a fine white sandy soil.

In the lake marl, which occupies the lacustrine beds of the drift period, we find a few fossil testacea, such as the lymnæa, succinea, cyclas, two species of planorbis, and a very small paludina.

One species of the planorbis, a very minute one, and the paludina mentioned, are not now found living in our waters; the others belong to existing species.

The testacea of the loëss, or loam, referred to the same period, are, on the contrary, all terrestrial, embracing several species of helices or snails, all of which, it is believed, are yet found living in different parts of the Continent, although some of them seem to have disappeared, or to have now no living representative in the fauna of this region.

Among the species most numerous, may be enumerated the Helix albolabris, alternata, concava, elevata, fraterna, perspectiva, profunda, thyroides, tridentata, &c.

The great bone bed of the Mississippi, or the depository

of the extinct mammalia, is also found in the loëss, the limits of which have already been defined. Throughout its extent the remains of the mastodon have been discovered.

Fossil remains of the elephant, although occurring in Kentucky and Texas, are not known to have been found in this State.

The mastodon differs from the mammoth, or fossil elephant, with which it is confounded, chiefly in the structure of the molars, those of the mastodon being invested with an exterior coating of enamel, the grinding surfaces presenting a series of mammillary protuberances; whereas, in those of the mammoth the enamel is disposed in vertical transverse plates. The former also surpasses the latter in dimensions.

Mastodon bones have been obtained in Bayou Sara, near Pinckneyville, in Wilkinson County, in various localities in Adams County, in Jefferson County, near the former town of Greenville, and in Warren County; in the deep cut of the railroad at Vicksburg; and in the vicinity of the Big Black River, near the eastern line of the county.

In a few localities, such as the accompanying testacea would indicate to have been the beds of fresh-water ponds or marshes, considerable portions of the skeleton have been found together, as if the animal may have perished there, and in such cases the bones are frequently in contact with considerable masses of a black, fatty earth entirely dissimilar from the surrounding marl, and which may reasonably be supposed to have resulted from the decomposition of the viscera, and the other perishable animal matter; but most usually the bones appear detached, as if drifted into their present position; and consequently, it is not unusual to find a tusk, or a molar, a bone of the leg, or a joint of the vertebra, where no other vestiges are seen.

The most prolific locality of these remains is in Adams County, on Pine Ridge, in Townships 7 and 8, Range 3 W., about six miles north of Natchez, where a large and deep ravine has extended its ramifications over an area of several miles, and which, in its undermining progress of denudation, has been constantly exposing these remains for more than forty years, or from a period coeval with the first cultivation of the country through which it has its course.

The bones generally lie from ten to twenty feet below the general surface, and in the ravine on Pine Ridge, the remains of other animals have been found associated with them.

Among these, may be enumerated those of the megalonyx, an animal provided with claws of great magnitude and strength, the bony axis of the nail itself being about four inches in length; and the Tapir (*Tapirus Americana*), now extinct here, but still living in South America; a lower maxillary bone containing the molars, and some detached teeth, being the only portions of the latter known to have been procured. These, together with the femur and claws of the megalonyx, have been submitted to the examination of Dr. Leidy, who is preparing a monograph descriptive of them.

Besides these, the teeth of the fossil horse and ox are frequently found. Those of the bos are referred by Dr. Leidy, in his account of them published in the fifth volume of the *Smithsonian Contributions to Knowledge*, to the Bison latifrons.

It would seem, by the discovery of these remains, that the horse, although not found on this Continent when first discovered, once had a place here among the animals now extinct.

I am indebted to Dr. Leidy for the following list of fossil mammalia found in the State:—

Felis atrox, *Leidy*.
Ursus Americanus, fossilis.
Ursus amplidens, *Leidy*.
Equus Americanus, *Leidy*.
Cervus Virginianus, fossilis.
Bison latifrons, *Leidy*.
Bootherium cavifrons, *Leidy*.
Elephus primigenius.
Tapirus Americanus, fossilis.
Tapirus Haysii, *Leidy*.
Megalonyx Jeffersonii, *Harlan*.
Megalonyx dissimilis, *Leidy*.
Mylodon Harlanii, *Owen*.
Ereptedon priscus, *Leidy*,
and the
Mastodon giganteus.

The following tables furnish a catalogue of a considerable portion of the Tertiary testacea of the State. Many rich fields of these not being yet explored, the newly discovered and undescribed species will hereafter be given.

Fossils of the Vicksburg Eocene Beds. Described by T. A. CONRAD, Esq.

(See Journ. of Acad. Nat. Sciences of Philad., Vol. I. Pl. 11, 12, 13, 14, and Vol. II. p. 1.)

Acteon Andersoni.
Avicula argentea.
Amphidesma Mississippiensis.
Arca Miss.
Bulla crassiplica.
Buccinum Miss.
Bisoarca Miss.
——— lima.
——— protracta.
Catopygus ——— ?
Cypræa sphæroides.
——— lintea.
Chenopus liratus.
Cancellaria Miss.
——— funerata.
Cassidaria lintea.
Cassis cælatura.
——— Miss.
Caricella demisa.
Cardium Vicksburgensis.
——— eversum.
——— diversum.
Corbula engongata.
——— intastriata.
——— alta.
Crasatella Miss.
——— ——?
Cytherea Miss.
——— astartiformis.
——— imitabilis.
——— sobrina.
——— perbrevis.
——— semipunctata.
——— pyga.
——— lenis.
——— liciata.
——— eversa.
——— subimpressa.
Cerithium siliceum.
——— solitarium.
——— nassuta.
——— Claibornensis.
Corbis staminea.
Chama Miss.
Clavelithes Vicks.
——— pachyleurus.
Cardita bilineata.
——— subquadrata.
——— subrotunda.
——— vigintinaria.
——— densata.
Catopygus Conradi.
Dentalium Miss.
Discoidea Haldermani.
Fulgoraria Miss.
Fulgar nodulatum.
Fissurella Miss.
Fusus Miss.
——— spinger.
——— Vicks.
Infundibulum trochiformis.
Loripes eburnea.
——— turgida.
Lucina perlevis.
Lima staminea.
Lithophaga Carolinaensis.
——— Claib.
Murex Miss.
Melongena crassicornuta.
Mitra conquesta.
——— Miss.
——— cellulifera.
——— staminea.
——— terebræformis.
——— Georgiana.
Mactra funerata.
——— Miss.
Modiola Miss.
Narica Miss.
Natica Miss.
——— Vicks.
Nucula Vicks.
——— serica.
——— improcera.
——— parilis.
——— Claib.
Nucleolites Mortoni.
——— Lyelli.
Oniscia harpula.
Ostrea Vicks.
——— Georgiana.
Plurotoma Miss.
——— porcellana.
——— servata.
——— congesta.
——— cristata.
——— tantula.
——— tenella.
——— cochlearis.
——— eboroides.
——— abundans.
——— rotædens.
——— decliva.
Phorus humilis.
Psammobia papyria.
——— Missi.
Plolas triquetra.
Panopæa oblongata.
Pecten elixatus.
Pectunculus Miss.
——— arctatus.
Pinna argentea.
Ringicula Miss.
Sagaretus Miss.
Solarium triliratum.
Scalaria trigintanaria.
Turritella Miss.
Terebra diversum.
——— tantula.
Turbinellus Wilsoni.
——— protracta.
Triton Miss.
——— subalveatum.
——— crassidens.
——— abbreviatus.
Tellina lintea.
——— pectorosa.
——— serica.
——— perovata.
——— Vicks.

Since the publication of the preceding list of the Vicksburg fossils, it has been found that some of these fossils should be referred to different genera; priority of description rendering it proper, Mr. Conrad proposes to restore the original names. The following, therefore, must give way to the terms first applied by earlier naturalists.

Bisoarca	to	Navicula.
Chenopus	to	Aporrhais.
Cassidaria	to	Morio.
Citherea	to	Meretrix.
Corbis	to	Fimbria.
Fulgur	to	Busycon.
Infundibulum	to	Trochita.
Loripa	to	Diplidonta.
Melongena	to	Cassidula.
Nucula	to	Leda.
Pectimculus	to	Axinæa.
Sigaretus	to	Stomatia.
Solarium	to	Architectonica.
Terebra	to	Acus.

BIVALVES

Plate XIV

JACKSON TERTIARY SHELLS

PLATE XIV.—SHELLS.

BIVALVES.

1 *a*. Umbrella planulata (*top*).
1 *b*. " " (*bottom*).
2. Astarte paralis.
3. Corbuld bicarinata.
4. Leda multilineata.
5. Navicula aspersa.
6. Cardium nicolleti.
7. Crassatella flexura.
8. Glossus fillosus.
9. Corbula densata.
10. Ostrea trigonalis.
11. Pecten nuperum.

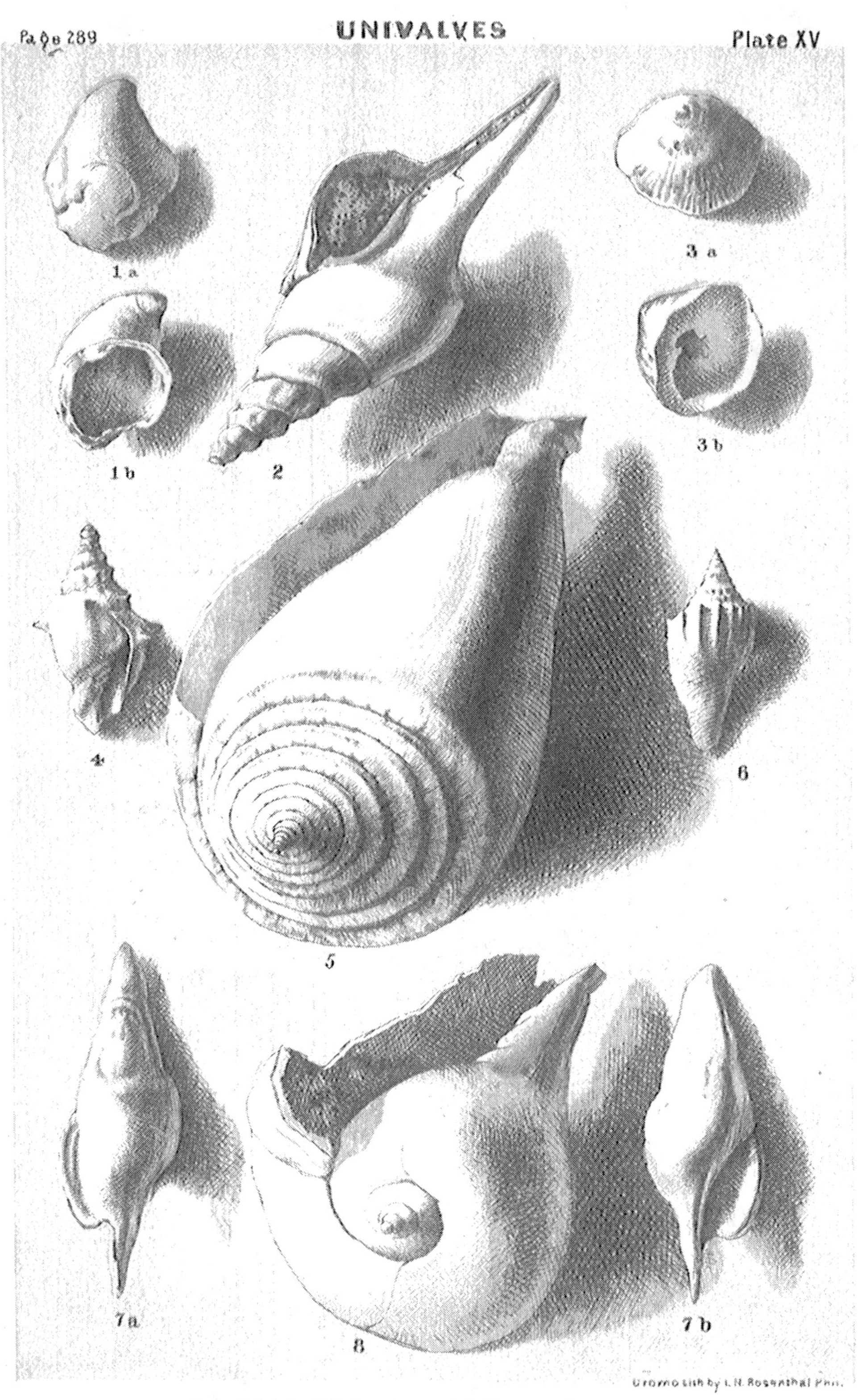

JACKSON TERTIARY SHELLS

PLATE XV.—SHELLS.

UNIVALVES.

1. Capulus Americanus.
2. Clavelithes humerosus.
3. Trochita alta.
4. Mitra dumosa.
5. Conus tortilus.
6. Volutalithes symmetrica.

7 *a*. *b*. Rostellaria vellata.

8. Caricella subangulata.

UNIVALVES

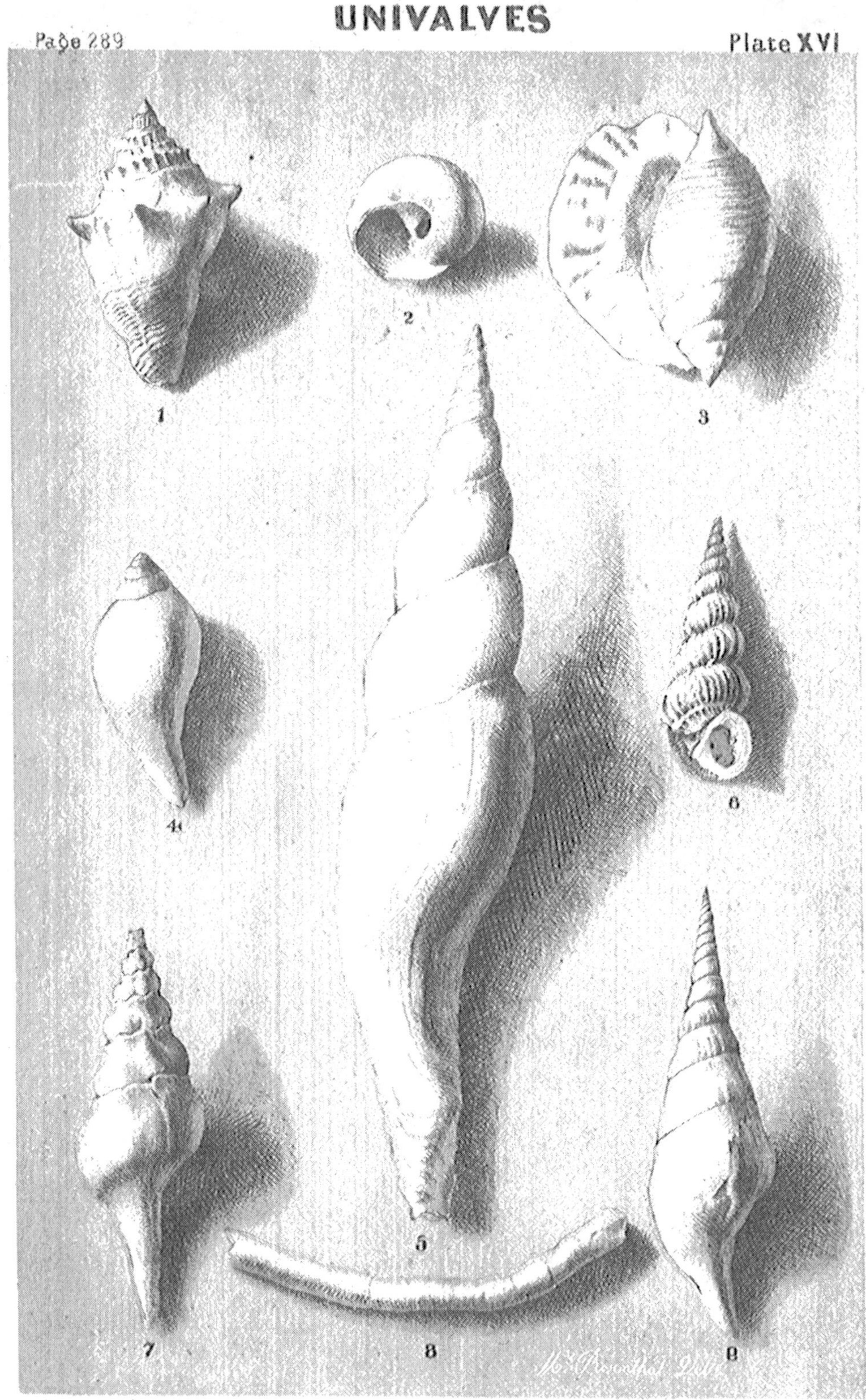

Cromo Lith by L.N. Rosenthal Phil.

JACKSON TERTIARY SHELLS

PLATE XVI.—SHELLS.

UNIVALVES.

1. Architectonica acuta.
2. Architectonica bellastriata.
3. *a. b.* Cypræa pinguis.
4. Gastridium vetustum.
5. Cypræa fenestratis.
6. *a. b.* Phorus reclusus.
7. Turritella alveata.
8. Clavelithes Mississippiensis.
9. Morio Petersoni. (Galeodia, of *Link.*)
10. Strepsidura dumosa.

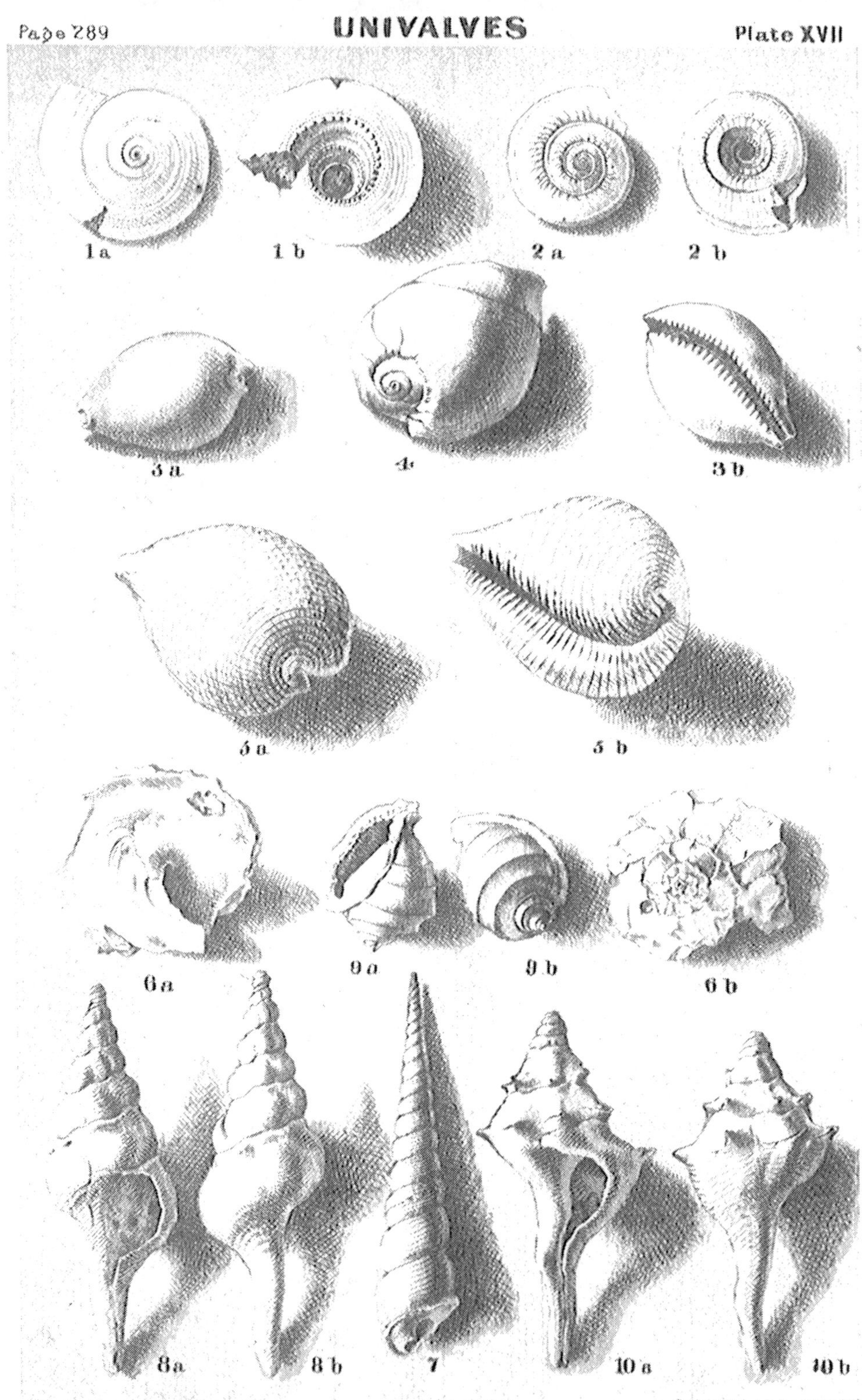

JACKSON TERTIARY SHELLS

PLATE XVII.—SHELLS.

UNIVALVES.

1. Volutalithes dumosa.
2. Natica permunda.
3. Rostellaria extenta.
4. Caricella polita.
5. Mitra Millingtoni.
6. Scalaria nassuta.
7. Clavelithes varicosa.
8. Teredo Mississippiensis.
9. Rostellaria (*young*).

Fossil Testacea of the Tertiary Green-sand Marl-bed of Jackson, Miss.
Determined and named by T. A. CONRAD, Esq.

BIVALVES.

Astarte. *Lamark.*
Astarte parilis. *Con.*

Cardita. *Brug.*
Cardita planicosta. *Lam.*
Cardita tetrica. *Con.*

Cardium. *Lin.*
Cardium Nicolleti. *Con.*

Corbula. *Brug.*
Corbula densata. *Con.*
Corbula bicarinata. *Con.*

Crassatella. *Lam.*
Crassatella flexura. *Con.*

Glossus. *Poli.*
Glossus filosus. *Con.*

Leda. *Schum.*
Leda multilineata. *Con.*

Meretrix. *Lam.*
Meretrix profunda. *Con.*

Navicula. *Blain.*
Navicula aspersa. *Con.*

Ostrea. *Lin.*
Ostrea trigonalis. *Con.*

Pecten. *Lin.*
Pecten nuperum. *Con.*

MULTIVALVE.

Teredo. *Lin.*
Teredo Mississippiensis. *Con.*

UNIVALVES.

Architectonica. *Bolton.*
Architectonica bellastriata. *Con.*
Architectonica acuta. *Con.*

Capulus. *Mont.*
Capulus Americanus. *Con.*

Cypræa. *Lin.*
Cypræa fenestratis. *Con.*
Cypræa penguis. *Con.*

Conus. *Lin.*
Conus tortilus. *Con.*

Caricella. *Con.*
Caricella polita. *Con.*
Caricella subangulata. *Con.*

Clavalithes. *Swain.*
Clavelithes humerosus. *Con.*
Clavelithes varicosus. *Con.*
Clavelithes Mississippiensis. *Con.*

Gastridium. *Sow.*
Gastridium vetustum. *Con.*

Natica. *Adan.*
Natica permunda. *Con.*

Mitra. *Hump.*
Mitra Millingtoni. *Con.*
Mitra dumosa. *Con.*

Morio.
Morio Petersoni. *Con.*

Phorus. *Mont.*
Phorus reclusus. *Con.*

Rostellaria. *Lam.*
Rostellaria vellata. *Con.*
Rostellaria extenta. *Con.*

Scalaria. *Lam.*
Scalaria nassuta. *Con.*

Strepsidura. *Swain.*
Strepsidura dumosa. *Con.*

Trochita. *Schum.*
Trochita alta. *Con.*

Umbrella. *Lam.*
Umbrella planulata. *Con.*

Volutalithes. *Swain.*
Volutalithes dumosa. *Con.*
Volutalithes symmetrica. *Con.*

ANALYSIS.

It is well known that some soils are, by nature, unsuited to the production of particular plants, even where climate and other conditions would favor their cultivation, and that from other soils, originally prolific, the productive elements are continually abstracted in the course of tillage until, in the end, they become exhausted and sterile. It is the province of Agricultural Chemistry, therefore, to determine the elements of plants derived from the earth in which they grow, and the presence or deficiency of those elements in the soils in which they are cultivated, in such manner as to make this knowledge available to the husbandman, and to instruct him also in the chemical composition of the manures, animal or mineral, proper to be applied to supply the exhaustion, or to fit the otherwise unfruitful soil for his purpose. As to the practical value of analysis of soils as usually conducted, or the ability, in the present state of chemical knowledge, of determining those minute constituents in a soil—such as alkali or potash and phosphoric acid—generally regarded as the greatest cause of fertility, eminent chemists are at issue, and, in our own country, many distinguished for high scientific attainments are found to agree with Boussingault, that we are much less interested in the chemical composition of the soil than in its mechanical mixture.

But, whatever may be the differences of opinion as to the value of analysis of soils, and whether the benefits would justify the expense attending the minute and *multiplied* chemical examinations required to impart a useful knowledge of their properties, there can be none as to those of the marls or mineral fertilizers employed, as no one would be willing to apply an ingredient to his land which a simple test might prove to be not only unsuitable, but absolutely pernicious. In view of the general use into which they must come eventually, when their existence and value shall be better known, adequate analyses of all the varieties of marls which abound in the State are highly desirable.

As yet, few have been made, and we are in a great degree left to conjecture their probable value and importance from the general aspect which they present, and from the character of the attendant fossils, as well as from the effects which similar substances have produced in other States where they have been extensively used.

Such analyses as I have been able to procure of our marls, as well as those of the cotton plant and our mineral waters are here subjoined.

Analysis of Lake Marl, Washington, Adams County.

Insoluble silica	17.44
Peroxide of iron	7.10
Carbonate of lime	70.44
Potash	3.64
Soda	.36
Magnesia	.64
Soluble silica	a trace
	99.62

"This will be found a valuable fertilizer; it contains almost half the amount of potash which the green-sands of New Jersey do."—January, 1847: Dr. Emmons.

Indurated Marl, or the Rotten Limestone of the Prairies, according to Dr. Troost.

Carbonate of lime	51.00
Earthy matter, insoluble in water, composed of green-sand and particles of white silvery mica . . .	34.00
Carbonaceous matter	2.00
Alumina, water, and loss	13 00
	100.00

"The particles of green-sand are very minute, and are only perceptible with the aid of the microscope."

Composition of the Green-sand Marl of New Jersey.
By Prof. H. D. Rogers.

Silex	51.00
Protoxide of iron	25.10
Alumina	7.50
Potash	9.30
Water	6.50
Lime	a trace
	99.40

"In a few instances, the deposits are a pure green-sand. The composition of the marl in a great number of instances is green-sand, clay, and quartzose sand; the green-sand varying from 35 to 95 per cent."

Analyses of Green-sand of Tennessee. By Dr. Troost.

Silica	48.00	45.30	51.70
Protoxide of iron . .	20.70	18.00	21.20
Alumina	7.00	6.20	6.50
Potash	10.10	10.40	11.30
Carbonate of lime . .	5.70	10.80	2.00
Water	8.00	8.50	7.30
Loss	.50	.80	0.00
	100.00	100.00	100.00

The foregoing analyses of the green-sand of Tennessee will probably be found to assimilate more nearly to the lower green-sands of Mississippi.

Analysis of Cotton from the Santee in South Carolina. Made by Prof. SHEPARD.

COTTON WOOL.

Carbonate of potassa	44.19
Phosphate of lime, with traces of magnesia	25.44
Carbonate of lime	8.87
Carbonate of magnesia	6.85
Silica	4.12
Alumina, probably accidental	1.40
Sulphate of potassa	2.70
Chlorite of potassium Chloride of magnesia Sulphate of lime Phosphate of potassa Oxalic lime in minute traces } and loss	6.43
	100.00

COTTON SEED.

Phosphate of lime, with traces of magnesia	61.64
Phosphate of potassa, with traces of soda	31.51
Sulphate of potassa	2.55
Silica	1.74
Carbonate of lime	.41
Carbonate of magnesia	.26
Chloride of potassium	.25
Carbonate of potassa Sulphate of lime Sulphate of magnesia Alumina and oxides of iron Manganese in traces } and loss	1.64
	100.00

Analysis of the Fibre of Sea Island Cotton. By Dr. URE.

Carbonate of potash	44.08
Muriate of potash	9.09
Sulphate of potash	9.03
Phosphate of lime	9.00
Carbonate of lime	10.06
Phosphate of magnesia	8.04
Peroxide of iron	3.00
Alumina a trace, and loss	5.00
	100.00

Analysis of Cotton Stalk. By Dr. J. Lawrence Smith.

Lime	303.00
Potash	243.00
Phosphoric acid	91.00
Magnesia	58.00
Oxide of iron	4.00
Sulphuric acid	13.00
Chlorine	8.00
Carbonic acid	270.00
Sand	5.00
	995.00

Analysis of the Ash of a Cotton Stalk, of the Mexican Variety, grown on the Mississippi near Bruinsburg. Made, at the Yale Analytical Laboratory, by Orange Judd.

Potash	29.58
Lime	24.34
Magnesia	3.73
Chlorine	.65
Phosphoric acid	34.92
Sulphuric acid	3.54
Silica	3.24
	100.00

Analysis of the Water of Cooper's Well, Hinds County, Mississippi. By David Stewart, M. D.

REACTION ACIDS.

Specific gravity, 1004.3.
Solid contents of one gallon, 150.2 grains.

COMPOSED OF IODINE, AS—

Hydriodate of potash.	Hydrochlorate of lime.
" of soda.	" of magnesia.
" of lime.	Sulphate of soda.
" of magnesia.	" of potash.
Hydrochlorate of iron.	" of magnesia.

GASEOUS CONTENTS.

Sulphuretted hydrogen. Carbonic acid. Nitrogen.

Chemical Examination of Cooper's Well Water, Hinds County.
By Dr. J. LAWRENCE SMITH. Made December, 1851.

Temperature, 64° Fahr., the air being at 50°.
Taste, not unpleasant.
Odor, little or none.
Color, transparent, with small yellow flakes floating on it.
Specific gravity, 1.00147.

Gas contained in one wine gallon, in cubic inches:—

Oxygen	1.05
Nitrogen	4.05
Carbonic acid	4.00

Solid contents of one gallon, 105 grains, composed as follows:—

Sulphate of soda	11.705
Sulphate of magnesia	23.280
Sulphate of lime	42.122
Sulphate of potash	.608
Sulphate of alumina	6.120
Chloride of sodium	8.360
Chloride of calcium	4.322
Chloride of magnesium	3.480
Peroxide of iron	3.352
Crenate of lime	.311
Silica	1.801
	105.471

The deposit which collects in concentrating the water contains, in 100 grains—

Water	38.00
Crenate of lime	2.00
Sulphate of lime	25.00
Peroxide of iron	35.00
	100.00

Analysis of the Water of Ocean Springs, near Baluxi, in Jackson County, Miss. By J. LAWRENCE SMITH, M. D.

The water colorless, even when kept in bottles for a length of time, provided the bottles be well corked; as soon as opened, the water begins to blacken, from a deposit of sulphur of iron; the odor of the water is that of sulphuretted hydrogen, which the water contains in considerable quantity; the taste, that known to belong to this class of waters.

Specific gravity, 1.00082.

Gaseous contents in one gallon in grains:—

Carbonic acid	4.632
Sulphuretted hydrogen	.481

Solid contents of one gallon in grains:—

Chloride of sodium	47.770
Chloride of calcium	3.882
Chloride of magnesia	4.989
Protoxide of iron	4.712

Iodine, a strong trace.
Chloride of potassium, a trace.
Organic matter, a trace.
Alumina, a trace.

The iron doubtless in combination with both the sulphuretted and carbonic acid gases, the excess of the carbonic acid holding both these combinations in solution.

V. METEOROLOGY.

As introductory to the subjoined meteorological tables, it may be remarked that here, as in other and older States, few are found who have made such observations, or have persevered in them for a long period.

The tables of the late Dr. Henry Tooley, of Natchez, are perhaps the fullest, most continuous, and uninterrupted, and extend through a greater period of time, than those of any other similar observations known to have been made in the State.

Those given in this report were compiled, chiefly from the notes of Dr. Tooley, by Mr. G. L. C. Davis, for the *Southern Rural Almanac*, published by Mr. Affleck, in 1852, who is entitled to credit for thus preserving them.

I am indebted to Dr. Coleman, of Jefferson County, and to Alexander H. Pegues, Esq., of Lafayette, for their observations made for several years past on the fall of rain, and to Mr. Oakley, of Jackson, for the use of his Meteorological Register, kept for the Smithsonian Institution; all of these will be found in the following pages, and will form interesting matter for reference. Other materials have been collected in relation to meteorology generally; but these, not being as full and complete as is desired, or as they can hereafter be made, will be reserved for a future report.

I will only add, in answer to inquiries from abroad, that I have no authenticated instance of the fall of meteoric iron or stone in the State.

The past year (1853) has been a remarkable one for its atmospheric variations. An unusually late spring, of excessive drought, succeeded by profuse rains in the summer, occasioned an injury to the crops, for which the long-continued mild and favorable season for cotton picking could not make amends. In Adams County, so mild and genial was the latter part of the year, that the cotton continued to grow and blossom until the night of the 8th of December, when the first killing frost occurred.

Meteorological Register, showing the lowest and highest points the Thermometer attained during each month of the year, from 1825 *to* 1850 *inclusive.* From the Southern Rural Almanac.

JANUARY.

YEAR.	TEMPERATURE.				MEAN TEMPERATURE.			NO. DAYS.		Quantity rain.
	Lowest.	Date.	Highest.	Date.	5 A. M.	Noon.	4 P. M.	Dry.	Rain.	
1825	31°	23	69°	15	44°		54°	10	13	
1826	23	25	75	11	46		57	10	9	
1827	25	19	79	30	42		55	13	9	
1828	36	21	77	7	56		61	6	12	
1829	25	11	74	1	48		62	6	13	
1830	32	11	75	9	48		60	9	8	
1831	25	16	72	26	39		51	7	12	
1832	13	26	76	18	41		56	8	6	
1833	31	11	74	4	53		61	11	9	
1834	14	5	74	20	44		49	15	21	
1835	30	31	71	26	46		57	5	8	
1836	28	28	74	16	46		56	5	15	
1837	30	3	69	19	42	48°	51	1	10	
1838	28	13	73	17	47	52	55	9	10	
1839	32	20	71	11	43	52	58	9	10	
1840	28	1	69	29	46	50	53	7	8	3.52
1841	19	18	67	28	44	47	49	4	15	13.80
1842	34	21	74	9	49	56	58	8	12	3.52
1843	28	12	71	26	48	56	57	18	5	7.20
1844	33	17	70	23	49	54	57	8	15	8.37
1845	38	18	77	15	49	55	59	9	8	3.10
1846	31	11	70	30	46	52	53	10	7	6.01
1847	21	7	71	25	43	47	52	7	8	4.90
1848	26	10	79	16	52	56	62	15	6	4.49
1849										
1850	32	1	78	24	52	55	63	8	15	10.21

FEBRUARY.

YEAR.	TEMPERATURE.				MEAN TEMPERATURE.			NO. DAYS.		Quantity rain.
	Lowest.	Date.	Highest.	Date.	5 A. M.	Noon.	4 P. M.	Dry.	Rain.	
1825	30°	3	82°	27	46°		62°	9	7	
1826	33	15	79	27	51		65	8	10	
1827	44	11	81	24	56		68	5	11	
1828	42	28	78	9	56		64	4	12	
1829	26	14	74	27	41		54	6	10	
1830	28	6	78	4	48		62	8	9	
1831	24	7	72	27	37		56	9	8	
1832	30	24	81	9	55		64	21	9	
1833	38	25	74	28	46		60	10	14	
1834	32	1	78	22	43		65	4	8	
1835	10	8	71	21	36		49	8	8	
1836	29	1	76	22	50		56	9	11	
1837	33	18	68	6	49	53°	57	5	10	
1838	18	3	65	28	37	42	47	12	10	
1839	31	3	68	14	45	52	55	14	10	
1840	26	2	72	28	50	58	62	7	12	3.04
1841	28	11	74	26	48	55	61	14	3	1.34
1842	31	9	71	28	50	56	56	15	9	7.31
1843	24	15	75	22	45	51	55	10	4	3.70
1844	35	9	78	29	52	49	65	21	1	0.05
1845	35	5	73	20	51	54	64	11	6	4.65
1846	33	26	66	12	41	52	58	5	9	3.65
1847	27	3	75	20	50	53	60	11	7	10.58
1848	34	7	77	20	54	59	64	19	4	1.61
1849										
1850	27	5	80	28	47	52	61	7	9	5.46

MARCH.

YEAR.	TEMPERATURE.				MEAN TEMPERATURE.			NO. DAYS.		Quantity rain.
	Lowest.	Date.	Highest.	Date.	5 A. M.	Noon.	4 P. M.	Dry.	Rain.	
1825	45°	9	83°	28	56°		72°	8	12	
1826	46	24	83	4	63		74	6	13	
1827	44	28	80	9	61		70	9	8	
1828	37	4	79	29	55		69	8	10	
1829	32	22	76	27	49		64	8	10	
1830	44	9	82	21	59		69	9	11	
1831	36	17	81	31	48		68	8	10	
1832	30	18	84	25	52		71	9	2	
1833	25	2	72	19	51		66	4	20	
1834	39	3	81	30	56		67	6	13	
1835	32	1	82	31	46		65	6	15	
1836	32	2	83	15	50		62	8	12	
1837	40	15	78	28	54	60°	64	10	12	
1838	38	8	79	26	55	60	66	23	6	
1839	27	4	74	21	53	59	64	11	8	
1840	42	26	79	18	58	59	67	8	12	3.50
1841	38	11	77	25	53	62	68	13	10	4.73
1842	48	15	84	25	66	69	73	16	9	3.93
1843	23	16	69	31	41	48	51	6	8	6.06
1844	38	31	83	27	53	61	65	12	9	4.18
1845	39	21	78	8	57	61	68	9	13	6.43
1846	43	2	79	18	56	63	67	8	10	4.81
1847	35	14	80	9	52	59	63	14	10	4.17
1848	35	4	81	20	56	64	66	10	6	5.34
1849										
1850	32	28	84	14	54	60	67	6	9	3.25

Meteorological Register, from 1825 *to* 1850 *inclusive*—Continued.

APRIL.

Year.	Temperature. Lowest.	Date.	Highest.	Date.	Mean Temperature. 5 A. M.	Noon.	4 P. M.	No. Days. Dry.	Rain.	Quantity rain.
1825	50°	2	80°	23	60°		67°	6	15	
1826	43	11	83	24	63		75	7	9	
1827	50	25	82	9	67		74	14	7	
1828	36	6	82	29	59		69	10	6	
1829	45	26	85	15	55		72	6	11	
1830	45	2	83	14	60		73	8	5	
1831	45	9	82	19	66		72	12	10	
1832	51	11	86	3	61		76	11	11	
1833	55	14	88	26	63		76	9	9	
1834	49	7	88	30	61		76	6	8	
1835	46	16	82	23	57		65	7	12	
1836	53	11	86	26	63		77	7	13	
1837	41	8	80	22	57	65°	71	11	6	
1838	48	12	85	26	61	71	74	11	5	
1839	49	1	84	24	69	74	82	9	5	
1840	54	2	86	30	66	72	75	7	11	8.73
1841	51	13	87	25	63	73	77	12	9	2.16
1842	53	27	84	30	65	71	76	9	8	5.07
1843	44	1	85	26	63	71	77	17	4	5.16
1844	47	1	87	23	65	73	75	12	4	0.72
1845	48	8	87	30	62	69	77	8	8	4.10
1846	43	14	81	26	61	68	71	5	12	9.04
1847	48	15	84	7	64	72	80	11	4	2.11
1848	51	20	85	28	60	67	63	17	5	2.43
1849	41	16	85	29				10	5	2.43
1850	40	7	85	18	58	64	71	12	9	9.84

MAY.

Year.	Temperature. Lowest.	Date.	Highest.	Date.	Mean Temperature. 5 A. M.	Noon.	4 P. M.	No. Days. Dry.	Rain.	Quantity rain.
1825	59°	1	90°	30	70°		83°	18	8	
1826	58	6	88	22	73		82	13	8	
1827	52	8	86	29	64		73	11	12	
1828	62	13	87	29	70		78	10	18	
1829	55	10	87	28	68		78	6	13	
1830	56	25	87	31	67		79	6	13	
1831	57	25	86	30	66		70	10	6	
1832	56	14	93	29	68		83	10	6	
1833	66	4	89	19	70		82	11	15	
1834	53	8	93	29	66		89	18	12	
1835	58	10	89	29	69		77	10	4	
1836	58	11	88	5	67		80	10	14	
1837	54	16	87	29	65	75°	79	18	5	
1838	48	8	84	14	62	70	73	5	13	
1839	53	14	92	25	68	80	81	10	7	
1840	52	10	89	19	65	74	78	16	5	2.25
1841	54	1	88	31	67	78	81	11	7	11.66
1842	54	5	90	29	69	78	84	25	3	0.45
1843	58	31	91	27	69	76	81	18	6	2.16
1844	66	31	90	11	71	79	83	13	12	4.36
1845	56	16	89	28	68	75	79	9	7	8.19
1846	59	1	90	26	68	78	84	10	7	6.96
1847	54	5	88	16	67	72	80	18	5	8.42
1848	57	12	91	28	71	78	83	11	7	3.45
1849	59	11	87	24				6	14	4.73
1850	46	6	88	26	62	70	76	14	8	6.12

JUNE.

Year.	Temperature. Lowest.	Date.	Highest.	Date.	Mean Temperature. 5 A. M.	Noon.	4 P. M.	No. Days. Dry.	Rain.	Quantity rain.
1825	65°	4	91°	18	74°		82°	3	12	
1826	72	6	88	20	75		83	12	18	
1827	70	8	93	19	74		85	12	3	
1828	70	20	91	25	76		86	12	6	
1829	64	9	90	19	71		84	18	12	
1830	63	9	92	30	76		84	14	7	
1831	64	5	90	10	73		84	14	7	
1832	64	8	95	19	71		87	12	5	
1833	65	25	93	30	75		87	15	6	
1834	71	22	94	26	76		87	6	5	
1835	71	15	92	19	75		83	7	15	
1836	65	5	90	27	73		83	14	11	
1837	60	22	94	9	74	82°	86	12	8	
1838	62	7	94	25	72	85	88	28	2	
1839	65	5	95	24	74	84	88	16	3	
1840	64	8	94	30	74	82	87	12	9	4.19
1841	65	25	93	18	73	84	86	7	10	2.12
1842	71	14	93	1	75	83	87	15	9	6.40
1843	63	1	91	30	72	80	84	4	14	10.68
1844	64	1	91	20	73	83	86	10	7	2.54
1845	69	2	93	28	74	83	87	12	9	3.47
1846	64	11	93	29	72	80	87	13	8	5.56
1847	68	22	93	15	74	83	85	11	10	3.45
1848										
1849	68	22	93	15				9	12	3.82
1850	56	1	90	23	69	77	82	10	10	10.92

Meteorological Register, from 1825 *to* 1850 *inclusive*—Continued.

YEAR.	JULY. Temperature. Lowest.	Date.	Highest.	Date.	Mean temperature. 5 A. M.	Noon.	4 P. M.	No. days. Dry.	Rain.	Quantity rain.
1825	72°	4	94°	31	76°		86°	8	12	
1826	72	25	92	16	78		88	7	7	
1827	75	4	94	11	78		87	9	12	
1828	70	16	94	27	77		88	9	6	
1829	66	2	90	21	75		86	6	13	
1830	72	13	93	17	77		87	3	15	
1831	70	1	92	9	77		88	14	11	
1832	71	27	97	5	73		90	15	8	
1833	69	5	96	12	63		89	5	12	
1834	74	25	96	10	77		89	6	13	
1835	63	2	92	27	75		82	4	22	
1836	73	28	94	22	77		86	10	11	
1837	73	12	93	26	76	84°	88	6	12	
1838	73	13	94	6	76	82	85	9	14	
1839	69	15	94	24	75	86	89	8	8	
1840	68	4	91	9	76	85	86	5	14	7.70
1841	73	6	95	15	78	85	91	22	5	1.44
1842	67	3	94	20	75	82	83	11	7	1.74
1843	69	4	92	16	75	83	85	9	10	6.75
1844	73	25	95	6	78	85	89	11	8	2.34
1845	70	31	97	23	76	84	88	9	12	3.98
1846	67	19	93	29	75	86	87	8	10	2.85
1847	71	10	91	16	75	82	84	13	16	16.42
1848										
1849	71	27	91	4				4	21	18.01
1850	68	21	90	11	73	82	86	7	11	6.30

YEAR.	AUGUST. Temperature. Lowest.	Date.	Highest.	Date.	Mean temperature. 5 A. M.	Noon.	4 P. M.	No. days. Dry.	Rain.	Quantity rain.
1825	72°	22	97°	10	76°		91°	7	11	
1826	68	29	91	25	75		89	6	11	
1827	72	29	90	17	76		86	19	8	
1828	73	9	91	3	77		86	15	17	
1829	72	19	91	6	76		88	7	19	
1830	71	19	95	27	77		89	18	7	
1831	63	9	86	2	69		78	10	12	
1832	70	30	94	12	75		88	13	8	
1833	69	17	95	14	74		89	20	6	
1834	73	30	98	20	77		90	6	12	
1835	68	27	96	17	75		88	6	18	
1836	68	31	93	12	76		86	9	9	
1837	68	15	93	3	75	84°	87	15	6	
1838	71	23	92	14	74	83	84	10	12	
1839	68	31	95	6	74	84	86	11	6	
1840	69	9	93	7	75	85	87	25	3	0.75
1841	70	2	93	6	75	85	86	10	9	3.05
1842	65	3	89	30	72	81	84	10	10	1.94
1843	67	2	92	31	74	81	84	13	9	2.70
1844	67	29	93	9	75	81	86	18	12	4.79
1845	68	1	96	21	75	84	86	11	9	2.68
1846	71	26	91	6	76	81	80	6	10	8.40
1847	69	8	92	5	76	81	86	11	6	1.88
1848										
1849	70	5	92	5				12	9	4.90
1850	72	28	94	9	75	82	89	8	10	2.10

YEAR.	SEPTEMBER. Temperature. Lowest.	Date.	Highest.	Date.	Mean temperature. 5 A. M.	Noon.	4 P. M.	No. days. Dry.	Rain.	Quantity rain.
1825	57°	28	93°	2	71°		83°	18	4	
1826	52	28	92	3	74		81	17	12	
1827	62	28	92	19	73		86	16	4	
1828	57	4	88	1	68		79	8	6	
1829	62	17	89	27	70		82	12	7	
1830	55	30	94	1	71		81	14	8	
1831	59	29	91	14	70		81	8	8	
1832	57	30	94	4	71		80	5	12	
1833	62	23	94	10	74		86	10	9	
1834	59	29	91	1	69		70	7	14	
1835	55	27	87	15	67		77	14	4	
1836	61	30	88	3	73		82	10	15	
1837	55	19	90	10	71	73°	81	5	13	
1838	51	24	88	8	66	76	78	15	6	
1839	62	14	90	8	68	79	82	18	4	
1840	58	19	90	8	69	77	81	5	6	3.90
1841	55	23	90	9	67	77	78	11	9	4.32
1842	63	18	90	9	72	79	81	16	12	4.64
1843	70	27	91	13	75	81	83	9	12	4.93
1844	47	29	92	3	69	79	82	13	4	3.94
1845	56	22	89	13	70	79	81	13	9	9.35
1846	60	29	95	17	73	81	84	20	9	5.23
1847	60	10	87	2	68	77	81	15	4	5.19
1848										
1849	61	8	90	20				9	6	3.41
1850	59	30	92	15	68	79	86	22	1	0.19

Meteorological Register, from 1825 *to* 1850 *inclusive*—Continued.

YEAR.	OCTOBER.									
	TEMPERATURE.				MEAN TEMPERATURE.			NO. DAYS.		Quantity rain.
	Lowest.	Date.	Highest.	Date.	5 A. M.	Noon.	4 P. M.	Dry.	Rain.	
1825	40°	29	91°	14	61°		80°	12	3	
1826	46	23	85	4	62		75	7	7	
1827	43	31	88	5	60		74	12	5	
1828	48	16	82	25	64		76	19	4	
1829	51	30	88	7	63		75	19	5	
1830	44	20	86	23	61		77	15	4	
1831	40	28	84	15	52		74	13	9	
1832	49	2	83	9	69		73	16	8	
1833	37	22	83	14	58		69	18	6	
1834	41	20	87	8	60		75	14	8	
1835	45	8	82	1	58		72	11	10	
1836	41	21	79	25	56		67	10	5	
1837	39	28	86	1	61	68°	72	17	5	
1838	40	30	83	1	56	65	65	8	6	
1839	53	30	84	5	64	74	77	22	3	
1840	42	25	85	13	62	70	72	14	6	4.60
1841	38	23	81	8	59	68	73	18	5	8.62
1842	43	26	85	6	58	69	74	14	4	1.73
1843	37	27	83	6	58	65	68	15	7	4.04
1844	41	19	83	16	59	69	71	19	4	5.34
1845	44	12	78	31	57	66	70	10	4	1.24
1846	44	19	84	8	58	68	74	13	2	1.40
1847	46	27	83	6	61	67	74	14	4	1.75
1848										
1849	45	8	87	4				13	4	11.79
1850	35	27	84	4	57	67	77	23	1	0.77

YEAR.	NOVEMBER.									
	TEMPERATURE.				MEAN TEMPERATURE.			NO. DAYS.		Quantity rain.
	Lowest.	Date.	Highest.	Date.	5 A. M.	Noon.	4 P. M.	Dry.	Rain.	
1825	38°	18	82°	5	52°		61°	9	7	
1826	34	26	86	3	57		70	14	3	
1827	38	30	81	6	55		66	17	4	
1828	35	23	77	7	55		67	10	7	
1829	28	23	77	21	51		63	13	9	
1830	39	8	79	1	58		68	5	11	
1831	35	28	78	2	48		63	10	9	
1832	31	19	76	2	49		60	12	6	
1833	30	25	78	7	49		63	14	7	
1834	31	26	81	3	55		63	12	8	
1835	30	24	79	19	54		60	12	14	
1836	33	29	71	17	46		58	10	4	
1837	36	23	78	12	55	64°	72	7	8	
1838	31	19	70	3	46	56	55	14	8	
1839	22	26	73	13	48	54	55	10	9	
1840	25	26	74	7	47	55	57	9	4	1.88
1841	28	29	77	19	53	63	63	12	4	2.53
1842	27	18	75	1	50	55	57	7	9	5.42
1843	38	8	76	28	57	62	64	7	13	11.24
1844	33	14	78	11	54	60	63	14	5	4.38
1845	27	28	76	5	51	57	60	15	4	0.87
1846	32	26	78	11	55	62	66	12	6	5.13
1847	26	27	80	7	54	60	64	9	7	4.85
1848										
1849	40	26	77	4				6	8	6.85
1850	24	17	83	5	48	56	61	15	6	2.20

YEAR.	DECEMBER.									
	TEMPERATURE.				MEAN TEMPERATURE.			NO. DAYS.		Quantity rain.
	Lowest.	Date.	Highest.	Date.	5 A. M.	Noon.	4 P. M.	Dry.	Rain.	
1825	27°	3	70°	8	36°		52°	8	7	
1826	24	27	73	1	46		60	10	7	
1827	36	30	77	16	54		64	10	7	
1828	39	23	78	3	52		60	10	13	
1829	34	13	78	1	53		62	5	12	
1830	22	22	76	1	46		58	5	11	
1831	23	16	60	1	36		44	6	10	
1832	39	21	75	1	53		62	9	9	
1833	36	26	68	6	48		56	6	12	
1834	35	27	72	1	47		55	13	13	
1835	34	23	72	19	47		59	8	7	
1836	21	21	67	12	40		52	8	8	
1837	30	24	73	16	46	55°	59	7	11	
1838	21	24	59	13	38	46	50	11	9	
1839	32	9	59	20	44	47	49	7	9	
1840	32	28	70	15	46	52	53	10	6	4.68
1841	31	24	74	10	47	61	55	7	10	4.01
1842	28	23	75	7	45	51	55	20	2	1.37
1843	35	13	64	31	48	52	55	7	15	14.03
1844	29	17	68	30	45	52	53	13	6	4.90
1845	21	21	62	6	39	44	50	8	10	4.94
1846	34	20	77	7	54	58	62	7	9	2.80
1847	27	21	74	8	45	51	56	12	9	11.00
1848										
1849	26	11	77	16				10	6	3.98
1850	18	7	77	2	44	47	52	8	12	13.91

Table showing the Coldest and Hottest Day in the Year, from 1825 to 1850 inclusive, with the Average Temperature, Fall of Rain, &c.

YEAR.	COLDEST DAY IN THE YEAR.					HOTTEST DAY IN THE YEAR.					Average temperature of the year.	WEATHER.						Inches rain in the year.
	Date.	TEMPERATURE.				Date.	TEMPERATURE.											
		5 A. M.	Noon.	4 P. M.	Mean.		5 A. M.	Noon.	4 P. M.	Mean.		Clear.	Cloudy.	Rain.	Thunder.	Sleet.	Snow.	
1825	Dec. 3	27°		42°	35°	Aug. 10	80°		97°	88°	66.5°	178	83	88	9			
1826	Jan. 25	23		41	32	July 16	82		92	87	69.2	134	117	112	40		1	
1827	" 19	25		37	31	" 11	80		94	87	68.8	143	118	97	15			
1828	Nov. 23	35		59	47	" 27	80		94	87	69.5	133	118	106	29	1		
1829	Jan. 11	25		47	36	Aug. 6	79		92	85	66.2	108	97	149	36	2	1	
1830	Dec. 22	22		36	29	" 27	80		96	88	68.1	161	113	84	50	2	2	
1831	" 16	23		34	28	Sept. 14	71		91	86	62.9	161	159	43	41	3	5*	
1832	Jan. 26	13		29	21	July 5	79		97	88	68.8	195	137	61	20	2	2	
1833	Mar. 2	25		37	31	" 12	75		96	85	67.0	177	138	84	34		1	
1834	Jan. 5	14		27	20	Aug. 20	82		98	90	67.0	104	250	94	46	3	3	
1835	Feb. 8	10		28	19	" 17	79		96	87	64.0	104	251	135	50	3	4	
1836	Dec. 21	21		32	26	July 22	80		94	87	65.3	77	274	128	61	1		
1837	Jan. 15	28	36°	42	35	Aug. 3	80	89°	93	87	66.9	95	166	93	32	2	2	
1838	Feb. 3	18	19	29	22	July 6	77	91	94	87	64.1	43	193	92	38	2	3	
1839	Nov. 26	22	30	36	29	Aug. 6	79	88	95	87	67.8	26	236	82	28	1	1	
1840	" 26	26	33	43	34	June 30	78	88	94	87	67.1	37	234	95	34			48.48
1841	Jan. 18	19	27	30	25	July 15	81	93	95	89	68.0	42	214	98	44	1		59.78
1842	Nov. 18	27	31	40	32	" 20	76	88	94	86	67.4	37	233	95	26	2		43.52
1843	Mar. 16	23	29	40	30	" 16	75	86	92	84	66.1	38	221	104	37		2	78.73
1844	Dec. 17	29	42	50	40	" 6	81	90	95	88	68.2	35	243	78	32			45.91
1845	" 20	21	23	31	25	" 23	82	91	97	90	67.1	51	215	99	36	2	1	53.10
1846	Jan. 10	31	43	44	39	Sept. 17	78	88	95	87	67.7	51	214	100	27			61.84
1847	" 7	21	24	32	26	June 15	78	85	93	85	66.7	63	215	87	37	1	2	74.72
1848	" 10	26	33	42	34													17.32†
1849	Dec. 11	26		37	30	Aug. 16	75		94	84								59.92‡
1850	" 7	18		26	21	" 9	76		95	84	65.6							71.27

* Snow began to fall on 5th February, six inches deep, and lay till 15th; and again on the 14th December, and lay till 23d.

† From January to May inclusive.

‡ From April to December inclusive.

Table showing the Day in the Year at which Frost Appeared and Disappeared, from 1825 *to* 1850 *inclusive, with the Time of Blooming of the Cotton Plant, and when killed by Frost, &c.*

YEAR.	WHITE FROSTS.				ITEMS OF COTTON CROP.				Sugar crop of United States.
	LATEST IN SPRING.		EARLIEST IN FALL.		Date of first blooms.	When killed by frost.	Crop of United States.	Consumption of United States.	
	Date.	Temp. at sunrise.	Date.	Temp. at sunrise.					
1825	February 15	42°	October 19	44°			Bales.	Bales.	Hhds.
1826	April 11	43	November 18	41			937,000	104,483	(1818, 25,000
1827	March 19	44	" 30	38			712,000	120,593	1822, 30,000)
1828	" 17	42	" 12	44			857,744	118,853	88,000
1829	" 22	32	" 1	43			976,845	126,512	48,000
1830	February 14	41	October 20	44			1,038,848	182,142	70,000
1831	March 21	41	" 28	40			987,477	173,800	75,000
1832	" 18	30	November 9	36			1,070,438	194,412	70,000
1833	" 30	44	October 20	44			1,205,394	196,413	75,000
1834	" 30	39	" 20	41			1,254,328	216,888	100,000
1835	" 23	42	" 10	46			1,360,725	236,733	30,000
1836	" 25	43	" 22	44			1,422,930	222,540	70,000
1837	April 9	44	" 26	42			1,801,497	246,063	65,000
1838	March 18	43	" 22	44			1,360,532	276,018	70,000
1839	" 6	37	November 7	42			2,177,835	295,193	115,000
1840	" 31	41	October 25	42	June 6	October 26	1,634,945	297,288	87,000
1841	" 18	45	" 23	38	" 10	" 23	1,683,574	267,850	90,000
1842	February 22	42	" 26	43	May 17	November 1	2,378,875	325,714	140,000
1843	April 1	44	" 28	39	June 9	October 28	2,030,409	346,744	100,346
1844	March 31	38	" 19	41	May 25	" 29	2,394,503	389,000	200,090
1845	" 21	42	" 12	44	" 30	November 3	2,100,537	422,597	186,650
1846	April 14	43	" 19	44	June 10	October 19	1,778,651	427,627	140,000
1847	March 27	40	November 19	42	May 30	November 26	2,347,634	531,772	240,000
1848	" 14	43			June 1	None	2,728,596	518,039	220,000
1849	April 16	41	November 8	41	" 6	December 3	2,096,706	487,769	247,923
1850	" 7	40	October 26	36	" 24	October 26	2,300,000*	400,000*	211,203

* Estimated.

Statement of the Amount of Rain (in inches) that fell at Church Hill, Jefferson County, Mississippi, during the years 1850, '51, '52, *and* '53. By Dr. COLEMAN.

MONTH.	1850.	1851.	1852.	1853.
January	7.37	2.25	1.57	.75
February	4.95	9.85	4.57	7.92
March	2.41	2.85	3.08	5.23
April	6.87	1.61	3.89	2.08
May	5.49	.96	1.31	4.75
June	9.09	1.03	.24	1.97
July	3.55	1.91	3.38	7.92
August	3.78	5.16	.81	9.13
September	.70	.46	2.27	1.37
October	.20	3.27	1.89	4.19
November	2.47	8.09	5.10	2.58
December	11.52	6.64	8.81	4.83
Total	57.40	44.16	37.00	52.72

The instrument by which the above facts were ascertained, is one of Pike's Conical Raingauges, with a scale attached graduated so as to determine the fall of $\frac{1}{200}$ part of an inch.

It was placed in an open and exposed situation, elevated several feet above the surface of the ground, and at a distance from any building, trees, or shubbery.

Register of the Fall of Rain kept by A. H. Pegues, Esq., at his Residence, near Oxford, Lafayette County, Miss.

MONTH.	1849.	1850.	1851.	1852.	1853.
January	$9\frac{1}{8}$	$9\frac{7}{8}$	$1\frac{4}{16}$	$2\frac{15}{16}$	.80
February	5	$6\frac{6}{8}$	$14\frac{15}{16}$	$6\frac{15}{16}$	8.90
March	$4\frac{3}{8}$	$10\frac{1}{8}$	$4\frac{3}{16}$	$4\frac{4}{16}$	8.30
April	$1\frac{1}{8}$	$8\frac{7}{8}$	$4\frac{3}{16}$	$4\frac{1}{16}$	6.40
May	$4\frac{5}{8}$	5	$4\frac{6}{16}$	$2\frac{8}{16}$	3.00
June	$5\frac{2}{8}$	$3\frac{1}{8}$	$1\frac{4}{16}$	$1\frac{4}{16}$	1.40
July	$7\frac{4}{8}$	$2\frac{5}{8}$	$0\frac{11}{16}$	$2\frac{6}{16}$	4.20
August	$3\frac{5}{8}$	$6\frac{7}{8}$	5	$4\frac{2}{16}$	3.90
September	$2\frac{1}{8}$	$0\frac{1}{8}$	$0\frac{4}{16}$	5	6.00
October	$6\frac{7}{8}$	1	$2\frac{1}{16}$	1	1.30
November	$2\frac{3}{8}$	$2\frac{3}{8}$	$5\frac{1}{16}$	$4\frac{2}{16}$	1.30
December	$11\frac{2}{8}$	8	$5\frac{4}{16}$	$7\frac{1}{16}$	1.40
Total	$63\frac{2}{8}$	$62\frac{6}{8}$	$48\frac{3}{16}$	$45\frac{10}{16}$	46.90

Meteorological Register of the Oakland Institute, Jackson, Miss., for 1850 *and* 1851.*

MONTH.	TEMPERATURE.		DAILY VARIATION.		Mean temperature.	Fall of rain.
	Highest.	Lowest.	Greatest.	Least.		
1850						Inches.
January . . .	27°	38°	25°	4°	54.53°	14
February . . .	83	20	33	5	51.49	5.38
March	85	30	32	5	59.06	3.06
April	86	38	29	4	63.41	9.70
May	90	47	27	1	68.52	9.17
June	91	53	32	3	76.21	3.40
July	90	68	20	2	80.09	3.71
August	93	68	20	1	81.54	3.80
September . . .	91	56	27	8	76.15	0.43
October . . .	90	29	43	10	65.70	0.39
November . . .	84	23	30	7	53.99	1.25
December . . .	81	17	34	1	47.50	8.91
1851						
January . . .	76	23	33	3	50.16	5.30
February . . .	78	29	28	1	54.21	9.50
March	76	32	31	4	58.17	1.82
April	80	42	9	34	63.14	2.74
May	90	42	30	2	74.41	2.30
June	92	62	20	6	77.88	5.92
July	98	62	28	7	81.72	0.98
August	100	65	22	4	81.38	3.16
September . . .	95	41	31	7	76.75	
October . . .	90	32	44	7	63.52	2.22
November . . .	82	25	19	2	53.24	9.23
December . . .	76	20	39	1	53.24	8.11

* Kept by the young ladies of the institution, under the supervision of Mr. and Mrs. Oakley.

Meteorological Register of the Oakland Institute, Jackson, Miss., for 1852 *and* 1853. (Continued.)

MONTH.	TEMPERATURE.		DAILY VARIATION.		Mean temperature.	Fall of rain.
	Highest.	Lowest.	Greatest.	Least.		
1852						Inches.
January . . .	76°	11°	34°	7	38.79°	2.02
February . . .	79	32	31	2	53.47	3.34
March	86	31	31	6	63.58	2.30
April	85	37	33	5	62.05	3.68
May	88	56	26	4	72.07	4.73
June	92	34	31	7	75·61	4.09
July	94	66	21	4	79.30	7.95
August	92	64	24	11	78.17	2.30
September . . .	89	52	28	3	72.51	2.89
October . . .	88	43	36	6	67.87	0.76
November . . .	85	27	31	2	53.03	5.50
December . . .	78	29	37	1	54.84	7.00
1853						
January . . .	69	23	34	4	44.80	1.03
February . . .	71	25	37	2	48.81	7.64
March	77	32	28	2	54.36	9.21
April	85	42	29	6	65.71	2.57
May	87	48	28	7	69.00	2.19
June	92	62	27	6	77.56	3.73
July*	90	61	20	4	77.68	7.73

* These observations were here interrupted by the occurrence of the epidemic.

VI. FAUNA.

THE animal kingdom comprehended under the term Zoology, is divided by naturalists into Vertebrate and Invertebrate animals.

The Vertebrate, or those provided with a spinal column, or backbone, are subdivided into the following classes, namely: I. Mammalia, or beasts. II. Avis, or birds. III. Reptilia, or reptiles, and IV. Pisces, or fish.

The Invertebrate comprises the following classes: I. Mollusca, or shell-fish. II. Articulata, or insects, and III. Radiata, which include star-fish, &c.

The whole are arranged in their relative stations, according to their structure, characters, peculiarities, and habits; and the different species are grouped into genera, families, and orders, in conformity with systems proposed by naturalists, but in which perfect uniformity has not been attained. It is unnecessary, however, here to detail the principles of classification.

The fauna of Mississippi will perhaps be found to afford few species not already described by naturalists, and which are not common to the adjacent States, and of these the limits of this report will not admit of a full *descriptive list.* A bare catalogue must for the present suffice, accompanied by such general remarks as may seem pertinent and necessary.

VERTEBRATA.

Class I.—MAMMALIA.

ANIMALS WHICH SUCKLE THEIR YOUNG BY TEATS.

MARSUPITA.

Didelphidæ.

Didelphus Virginiana.	American opossum.

CARNIVORA.

Vespertilionidæ.

Vespertilio noveboracensis.	Leather-wing bat.

Soracidæ.

Scalops aquaticus.	Shrew mole.

Ursidæ.

Ursus Americanus.	Black bear.
Procyon lotor.	Raccoon.

Mustelidæ.

Mephitis Americana.	Polecat.
Mustela vulgaris.	Weasel.
Mustela vison.	Mink.

Lutridæ.

Lutra canadensis.	Otter.

Canidæ.

Lupus occidentalis.	American wolf.
Canis lupus.	Black wolf.
Vulpes Virginianus.	Gray fox.

Felidæ.

Felis concolor.	Northern panther.
Lyncus rufus.	Wild-cat.

RODENTIA.

Sciuridæ.

Sciurus lucatis.	Common gray squirrel.
S. capistratus.	Red fox squirrel.
" "	Black fox squirrel.
Sciurus niger.	Small black squirrel.
S. striatus.	Ground squirrel.
Pteramys volucella.	Flying squirrel.

Castoridæ.

Castor fiber.	Beaver.
Fiber zibethicus.	Musk-rat.

Muridæ.

Mus decumanus.	Common rat.
Mus ——— ?	Large wood rat.
Sigmodon hispidum.	Cotton rat.
Mus musculus.	Common mouse.
Arvicola ——— ?	Wood mouse.

Leporidæ.

Lepus nanus.	Common gray rabbit.
" Americanus.	American gray rabbit.
" sylvaticus.	Cane or wood rabbit.
" aquaticus.	Swamp hare.

UNGULATA.

Cervidæ.

Cervus Virginianus.	American deer.

REMARKS.—In the arrangement of the preceding list, reference has been had to the quadrupeds of North America, by Audubon and Bachman, Dekay, in his *Report on the Natural History of New York*, and other writers. The list is believed to embrace *nearly all* of the mammals of the State, and none are claimed not found in it.

Our domestic animals, such as horses, cattle, sheep, swine, &c., not found indigenous to the country at the time of its discovery, but being since introduced from Europe, will not be further noticed; nor will the extinct species that formerly had an existence in our limits, of which we have now only the fossil remains.

The latter, such as the mastodon, megalonyx, zeuglodon, mososaurus, tapir, &c., those colossal and antique forms of animal existence, will find a more appropriate place; constituting a prominent feature of the palæontology of the State, they will under that head occupy their proper position in this report.

Of the Opossum, it may be said that it continues to be quite abundant even in the older settled and most densely populated parts of the State, notwithstanding that it is the favorite game of the negroes, by whom it is much hunted and highly esteemed. The flesh is regarded by many as truly an epicurian dish, in despite of popular prejudice, and the fat is said to possess a mildness that never cloys.

The abdominal pouch with which it is provided, for rearing and sheltering its young, has ever excited the curiosity and stimulated the inquiries of the naturalist; and its office, connected with the gestation and parturition of the animal, has been much discussed.

The speculations on the subject, and the problem whether the young is originally produced in the exterior sack, or pouch, in connection with the mammæ, as has been supposed by some, or receives its early development in the uterus, has only been recently solved satisfactorily by the patient and minute investigations of Audubon and Bachman.

How curious is the structure of our miniature pterodactyle, the bat, the connecting link between the denizens of the air, and those of earth? Its large crape-like leather wing is a study of itself.

Of more grovelling instinct is our Mole, of which it is not known that we have more than one species, and he rarely "blunders into light."

Although the traces of his burrowing are common enough in our gardens, it is not complained of for much damage, and this is doubtless compensated for by the destruction of the larvæ of insects more mischievous. How striking are the form and flesh-like resemblance of its fore feet, with the palms turned outward, to the human hand.

Bruin, once so numerous that, sixty years since, one hundred were killed in a single winter's hunt, between Natchez and the Homochitto, has now withdrawn to gloomy recesses and almost impenetrable canebrakes, from which he makes an occasional foray, and levies contributions upon the hogpens of the frontier settlers, or revels in the milky sweets of the maturing maize of convenient plantations, breaking down the stalks and gathering them in a bed around him to feast at leisure. The lean flesh is dark and coarse, but is highly esteemed by many, and the oil is much valued for the *cuisine* and the toilet.

The sides or *middlings* of a fat bear, cured as bacon, none can condemn, resembling the rich brisket of the beef, and vying with the vaunted buffalo hump in texture and flavor.

Nearly as abundant as the possum is the Raccoon, although equally hunted, not so much for his flesh as his hide, which commands from the dealers in peltry a price sufficiently remunerating to make his capture an object. His depredations on young corn in the field forms an additional motive for his destruction. He is taken ordinarily at night with the common cur dog, or under baited logs set as dead falls. When overtaken in the day, he has been known to *play possum*, and simulate death.

When Iberville made his first settlement at Baluxi, Raccoons were very numerous upon the islands on the coast, and were mistaken by the French for the cat; hence the name which one of those islands yet bears.

The Polecat! Faugh! *Mephitic*, indeed! Strange it is that from an animal so beautiful should proceed a fetor so abominable. Surely, its "offence was rank and smelt to———," when Father Charlevoix named this little animal "l'enfant du diable."

Since the Indians have left the State, the Otter has become more abundant, and is evidently on the increase. The skin is less in demand for the felt than for dressing with the fur on, and is chiefly used when so prepared for hunting-pouches and caps. The otter is often shot with the rifle about mill-ponds.

The Wolf, like the Bear, has been driven into retirement, and is now rarely seen in the older settled parts of the country. Wolves are still numerous, however, in the sparsely settled districts of the State, and emerge in packs occasionally from their fastnesses, on marauding excursions to the neighboring sheepfolds, and, with a wasteful prodigality of blood, destroy and mangle ten times as much as they can devour.

They are taken in pens or traps made of poles, and baited with fresh meat, which is previously dragged over the ground for miles through the woods near their haunts, to lure them on the trail. Pits are also constructed with a slight covering of twigs and leaves, into which they fall in attempting to reach the bait suspended over them.

The Gray Fox only is known with us, and, although less hunted than in other States, is not very numerous.

The destruction which would be occasioned to the cotton crop, forbids a too free indulgence in the exciting chase.

Occasionally, the tribute of a bale of cotton may be paid for a *brush;* less could not well be destroyed in an ordinary run of a full pack. This is, therefore, too expensive an amusement to be made a practice of.

The Panther is now rarely met with, except in dense and extensive swamps and canebrakes.

Our Wild-cat, however, is rather inconveniently numerous, even in the settled and cultivated districts. He is not the cowardly and timid animal that our naturalists describe, but has often been known to attack man.

Several instances of this have occurred in Adams County, the oldest settled part of the State. They have entered negro cabins, and seized the children, and one was known to attack a gang of field-hands in open day, when hoeing cotton, severely lacerating some of them and the overseer, before he was overcome.

Of Squirrels, the most numerous are the Gray and Red Fox Squirrel.

In the thickly settled portions of the State, where the timber has become scarce, they have been much diminished. The Gray Squirrel, especially, is greatly exposed from a habit which it seems difficult for him to overcome. His inclination, when running up a tree, to pause and take a peep at his enemy, seems irresistible, and is generally fatal.

The Fox Squirrel is more artful, concealing himself very adroitly by stretching himself out, and lying flat upon the upper part of a projecting limb, in such a manner as to be protected from the shot.

The little striped Ground Squirrel, and the Flying Squirrel, are now not often met with. The distance which the latter will *sail* (rather than fly), from tree to tree, by extending his limbs, and expanding the membrane or skin connecting his fore and hind legs along his sides, is truly surprising; the direction is always obliquely downward.

The small Black Squirrel confines himself chiefly to the low-lands or swamps that are annually inundated.

Our naturalists have been strangely in error as to the geographical distribution of the Beaver. DeKay assigns New York as his *southern* limit, and Audubon and Bachman state that they have never seen a Beaver in Louisiana, although they have been informed that it *formerly* existed there.

The same cause which has occasioned the preservation of the Otter (the departure of the Indians from the country), has tended to the increase of the Beaver, which may now be said to be *abundant* in the State. They are found in nearly all of our principal streams, and have become rather troublesome in some situations in flooding plantations by means of their dams.

A few winters since, a party from Ohio spent the season in taking Beaver on the Homochitto, and in many quarters some of our old hunters habitually trap for them.

Our space does not admit of giving details of the habits and character of this interesting animal, and I must refer those curious in the matter to the *Quadrupeds of North America*, and DeKay's *Natural History Report of New York.*

The Weasel, Mink, and Muskrat, exist in the State; the latter in the salt-water creeks near the sea-shore, and the former in the northern counties of the State.

Our large *domestic* rat is in some situations very numerous and troublesome, and the terrier and house-cat are called in requisition frequently, to suppress them.

The cotton rat I include in our catalogue, on the authority of Audubon and Bachman, although I do not identify it from the figures they have given, with any species I have seen.

Our Gray Rabbit is abundant, and, comparatively tame, and is frequently seen in the evening about twilight, skipping playfully across lanes, and along the roadsides.

The Swamp Hare is much larger and more shy.

The Deer is much diminished, and, like the Buffalo and Elk, is perhaps, destined to become extinct in our limits. At seasons of general inundation of the Mississippi Bottoms, numbers of them perish. At such times, many of them retreat to the highlands, and are for the time numerous in the timbered lands in the settlements.

The mode of hunting them chiefly pursued, is by *driving* with a pack of hounds; the hunters posting themselves at *stands* where the deer are known habitually to cross the roads or ridges, or to ford the small streams.

Class II.—AVES, OR BIRDS.

Most ornithologists differ in their systems of classification. The division into five orders, proposed by Swainson, seems the most natural and best suited to the arrangement of this abridged catalogue :—

Order I.—Insessores, or Perching Birds; comprising all those whose organization enables them to live habitually among trees.

ORDER II.—Raptores, or Rapacious Birds; those that live exclusively on animal substances, being analogous to the Tigers, Hyenas, and other carnivorous quadrupeds.

ORDER III.—Natatores, or Swimming Birds; web-footed, and fitted to live habitually in the water.

ORDER IV.—Grallatores, or Wading Birds; with long legs and necks, fitted for the pursuit of fish and animals inhabiting shallow water and marshes.

ORDER V.—Rasores, or Walking Birds; rearing their young and living chiefly on the ground.

I. INSESSORES.

Hirundinidæ.

Hirundo purpurea.	Purple, or house martin.
H. rufa.	Barn swallow.
Acanthylis pelasgia.	Chimney swallow.

Caprimulginæ.

Caprimulgus vociferus.	Whippoorwill.
" "	Chuckwills widow.

Alcedinidæ.

Alcedo alcyon.	Kingfisher.

Trochilidæ.

Trochilus colubris.	Humming-bird.

Troglodytinæ.

Troglodytes ædon.	House wren.

Merulidæ.

Merula migratoria.	American robin.

Ampelidæ.

Bombycilla Carolinaensis.	Cedar bird.

Sylviadæ.

Sialia Wilsonia.	Bluebird.

Merulidæ.

Orpheus polyglottus.	Mocking-bird.
Orpheus rufus.	Brown thrush.

Sylvicolidæ.

Tyrannus intrepidus.	King bird, or Bee martin.

Corvidæ.

Garrulus cristatus.	Blue jay.
Corvus Americanus.	Common crow.

Quiscalidæ.

Quiscalus versicolor.	Crow blackbird.
Sturnella ludoviciana.	Meadow lark.
Icterus Baltimore.	Golden oriole.
Icterus phœniceus.	Red-winged oriole.
Sturnus prædatorius.	Red-winged starling.

Fringillidæ.

Pitytus cardinalis.	Crested red-bird.
Pyranga æstiva.	Red-bird.

Picidæ.

Picus pileatus.	Crested woodpecker.
—— erythrocephalus,	Redheaded woodpecker.
—— varius.	Yellow-bellied woodpecker.
—— pubescens.	Downy woodpecker.
—— aurantus.	Golden-winged woodpecker.
—— principalis.	Ivory-bill woodpecker.

Cuculidæ.

Coccyzus Americanus.	American cuckoo. (Rain crow.)

Psittacidæ.

Psittacus Carolinensis.	Paroquet, Carolina parrot.

Columbidæ.

Columba migratoria.	Wild pigeon.
Ectopistes Carolinensis.	Turtle dove.

II. RAPTORES.

Vulturidæ.

Cathartes aura.	Turkey buzzard.
——— atratus.	Carrion crow.

Falconidæ.

Haliætus leucocephalus.	Bald, or Brown eagle.
Butes borealis.	Red-tailed hawk.
Falco anatum.	Chicken hawk.
Nauclerus furcatus.	Swallow-tailed hawk.
Falco sparverius.	Sparrow hawk.

Stringidæ.

Bubo Virginianus.	Great-horned owl.
—— Asio.	Screech-owl.
Otus palustris.	Short-eared owl.
Ulula nebulosa.	The barred owl.

III. NATATORES.

Podicipidæ.

Podiceps cristatus.	Water-witch, or dipper.

Colymbus.

Colymbus glacialis.	Great loon, or diver.

Procellaridæ.

Puffinus obscurus.	Shearwater.
Thalassidroma Wilsonii.	Petrel. (Mother Carey's chicken.)

Pelecanidæ.

Phælacracorax Brazilensis.	Cormorant.
Pelicanus trachyrhynchus.	White pelican.
Tachypetes aquilus.	Gannet, or frigate bird.

Laridæ.

Rhynchops nigra.	Cutwater.
Sterna anglica.	Marsh tern.
Larus zonorhynchus.	Common gull.

Anatidæ.

Fuligula erythrocephala.	Redhead duck.
Anas boschas.	The mallard.
—— sponsa.	Wood duck.
—— acuta.	Sprigtail duck.
—— strepera.	Gray duck.
—— discors.	Blue-wing teal.
—— Carolinensis.	Greenwing teal.
—— clypeata.	Spoonbill duck.
Fuligula albeola.	Diedipper duck.
Anser Canadensis.	Wild goose.
—— bernicla.	Brant.

IV. GRALLATORES.

Charadridæ.

Charadrius semipalmatus.	American ring plover.
C. melodus.	Piping plover.
C. Wilsonius.	Wilson's plover.
C. vociferus.	Killdeer plover.
Squatarola helvetica.	Whistling plover.

Gruidæ.

Grus Americana.	Whooping crane.
Ardea herodias.	Great blue heron.
—— leuce.	Great white heron.
—— candidissima.	White-crested heron.
—— cerulea.	Blue heron.
—— virescens.	Green heron.
—— exilis.	Bittern.
—— minor.	Indian hen.

Rostridæ.

Platalea ajaja.	Roseate spoonbill.

Tantalidæ.

Ibis alba.	White ibis.
—— Mexicanus.	Glossy ibis.

Scolopacidæ.

Numenius longirostris.	Spanish curlew.
Totanus Bartramius.	Gray plover.
Scolopax Wilsoni.	American snipe.
Rusticolar minor.	Woodcock.

Railidæ.

Ortygometra Carolinensis.	Rail.

Podicapidæ.

Fulica Americana.	Coot, or mud hen.

V. RASORES.

Phasianidæ.

Meleagris galliparvo.	Wild turkey.

Tetraonidæ.

Ortyx Virginiana.	Partridge, or quail.

REMARKS.—The foregoing is a very defective list of our birds—of the aquatic tribes especially. Many of the Incisores, or perchers, are also omitted, and some very familiar ones have doubtless escaped notice.

Of a few of the birds embraced in the catalogue, some casual observations will be offered in the order in which they occur.

Of the nighthawk, or whippoorwill, we have two *varieties*, distinguishable perhaps, only by the difference of note. In size, plumage, and habits, I believe they are alike.

The *variety* found in the southern part of the State (south of about 32° 30′ north latitude), is known familiarly as the *Spanish* whippoorwill, or Chuckwill's widow. The other, restricted to the upper counties, is the common whippoorwill of the Northern States.

Of our single species of the Humming-bird, the plumage of the male is exceedingly rich and beautiful.

The color of the head and back is of a vivid green and gold, and the throat a brilliant ruby. In the season of flowers, they are seen by the dozen humming over our shrubberies, darting with the speed of light from flower to flower, and sipping the honeyed sweets, sustained on wings vibrating with a velocity so great as almost to elude the eye.

The Cedar-bird appears in flocks early in the fall, and lingers late in the spring. It seems to delight in the pearl-like berries of the mistletoe, and is also very fond of those of the lauria mundi.

The Robin arrives in considerable numbers late in winter. In our coldest weather it appears suddenly, and is then quite fat. It feeds ravenously whilst with us, on the China berry, with which the trees are then loaded, which occasions it frequently to fall from the trees apparently stupefied, when it is easily caught. Whether this is owing to a narcotic or intoxicating property of the berry, or is the effect of temporary strangulation, is not known.

In form, attitude, and motion, nothing exceeds the grace of our matchless "Orpheus," the Mocking-bird. In music and mimicry unrivalled, proud of his gift of song, he is not content with its daily exhibition, but for hours in the "stilly night" pours forth a flood of melody.

The delicate Blue-bird, the noisy *garrulous* Jay, the Cardinal, Red-bird, and the resplendent Oriole, or Baltimore-bird, are conspicuous among the less brilliant denizens of the air that hover about our houses, and animate our groves.

Chief of his tribe, the majestic ivory-bill Woodpecker cleaves his way through the air, in a series of peculiar and singularly graceful *undulations,* produced by the regularly intermitting strokes of his muscular wings.

"Disdaining the grovelling haunts of the *common herd* of woodpeckers," he seeks his favorite resorts in the loftiest trees in the most secluded forests, and from the blasted arms of the lordly cypress or the mast-like trunk of the towering pine, sends forth his clear and clarion notes, and startles the ear with the resounding strokes of his powerful beak. The Downy Woodpecker, best known to us as the *sap sucker*, is the most social and perhaps the most *mischievous* of the tribe.

It doubtless subsists in part on insects; but, unlike others of the family, prefers living trees to those which are decayed.

It perforates the bark of those with a succession of lines or small holes penetrating only to the woody fibre, and sometimes extending entirely around the trunk or branch, by which it is materially injured or destroyed.

The trees preferred are the maple, the apple, and others which yield a rich and abundant sap, upon which, according to the popular belief, it feeds. In opposition to the opinion of most of our other naturalists, Dr. Kirkland adopts this opinion, in which my own observations for many years lead me to concur.

The Paroquet or Carolina Parrot, with his plumage of vivid green and golden crest, was formerly very numerous, and often resorted in large flocks to inhabited districts, and made himself familiar with the apple orchards.

Now the Paroquet has become quite scarce and shy, and is seldom seen in flocks of more than half a dozen together, retiring habitually to the swamp or tall timber. Its favorite food is the cocklebur, *Zanthium strumarium*. They have a shrill, piercing note, which they always utter together or alternately when on the wing.

The Wild Pigeon visits us occasionally in large numbers, and sometimes establishes roosts and rears young.

They appear occasionally in such incredible flocks as to obscure the sun and darken the air in their flight, which has been known to continue, scarcely diminished, for several days.

These migrations are occasioned by the breaking up of large roosts, where they have remained until the timber has been stripped of the branches by the large numbers roosting upon them, and killed by the heating effects of the large accumulations of the ordure about the roots. In most of the large flights observed in a period of forty years, their direction has been to the northeast through the State.

In the winter of 1851 and 1852, large numbers entered the State and remained several months, establishing temporary roosts in different quarters, from which they ranged daily in every direction in search of food, which consisted chiefly of beechnuts and acorns. They were killed in large numbers, and were taken in common bird traps.

Sixty years since an extensive roost existed on Pigeon-Roost Creek, in Choctaw County, where the timber was all killed, and the roost necessarily abandoned.

The prince of birds, the Eagle, shuns the abode of man, and is met with chiefly on the borders of our principal streams, and is perhaps most numerous in the vicinity of the sea-shore. Besides the Hawks enumerated, we have doubtless several others, but with which I am not sufficiently familiar to distinguish from foreign species.

Like the cry of the Nighthawk, or Whippoorwill, the startling *Bob White* of the Partridge, or the notes of other imitative birds which are *imagined* to articulate words or sentences, the hooting of our great owl suggests similar resemblances, and ludicrous associations of sound. A hunting party, encamped for the first night in the woods, were grouped around the camp-fire, making arrangements for the preparation of the evening repast, when an owl perched over head, and, seemingly much interested in their proceedings, startled the party with this inquiry: "Who cooks, who cooks, who cooks, for y–o–u a–l–l?"—At least, *so they understood him.*

The large White Pelican has been killed in the Mississippi River, near Natchez, in the month of June, and is by no means rare in our waters.

The Cormorant flocks to our secluded lakes in immense numbers.

In brilliancy of plumage, none of its tribe can match our wood or summer duck. It remains with us throughout the year, and builds its nest in hollow trees, from which the downy unfledged ducklings, light as balls of puff, are said to fall unharmed to the ground.

Most of our ducks are migratory, and visit us only during the winter months. They frequent the lakes and bayous chiefly of the Mississippi bottoms, and those of our other rivers, and resort in myriads to the marshes and creeks of the sea-coast.

The same may be said of the Goose and Brant.

The Woodcock, *Rusticolar minor*, is occasionally found in considerable numbers. Some years since, they were so abundant in Jefferson County, during the winter months, that they were killed at night by fire hunting between the cotton rows in flat, wet situations. Blinded by the torchlight, they suffered themselves to be stricken down with small rods.

Even in the most populous neighborhoods, the Wild Turkey continues yet to rear its young. Within a few miles of Natchez, young broods are yearly produced.

The wary and watchful character of this bird prevents the entire destruction of the race.

In more secluded neighborhoods and in other parts of the State, the wild turkey is as numerous as ever.

The Partridge, or Quail as it is termed in other States, seems to be more abundant in northern and middle counties than in those bordering on the Mississippi. This may in part be attributed to the circumstance that very little small grain is produced on the large cotton estates.

CLASS III.—REPTILIA, OR REPTILES.

TESTUDINATI.

Chelonidæ.

Trionyx ferox.	Soft-shell turtle.
Chelonura Temmincki.	Loggerhead turtle.
——— serpentina.	Snapping turtle.
Emys terrapin.	Couta.
——— serrata.	"
——— picta.	"
——— ———?	"
Chelonura mydas.	Green turtle.
——— caretta.	Hawk-bill turtle.
Kinosternon Pennsylvanium.	Mud turtle.
Cistuda Carolina.	Terrapin.
——— Blandingi.	"
——— ———?	"
——— ———?	"
——— ———?	"
——— ———?	"
Testudo polyphæmus.	Gopher.

SAURIA.

Emysauridæ.

Alligator Mississippiensis.	Alligator.

Iguanidæ.

Anolis Carolinensis.	Chamelion. (Green lizard.)
Tropidolepis undulatus.	Gray lizard.

Lacertidæ.

Cnemidophorus sexlineatus.	Striped lizard.

Schincidæ.

Ligosoma quinquelineatus.	Redheaded lizard.

BATRACHIA.

Salamandridæ.

Salamandra salmonea.	Ground puppy.
S. faciata.	" "
S. bilineata.	" "
S. fusca.	" "
S. porphyritica.	" "
S. ——— ?	" "
S. ——— ?	" "
Triton niger.	Spring lizard.

Sirenidæ.

Menobranchus lateralis.	Water lizard.
Siren lacertina.	" "

Ranidæ.

Rana pipiens.	Bull-frog.
R. fontanalis.	Spring-frog.
R. sylvatica.	Wood-frog.
Hyla halecina.	Leopard-frog.
—— viridis.	Tree-toad.
Buffo Americanus.	Common toad.

The following catalogue of our Serpents has been obligingly revised by Prof. Spencer F. Baird, who has done me the favor of identifying the species with specimens preserved in the Smithsonian Institution, and described in his work on the *Serpents of North America.*

OPHIDIA.

Crotalidæ.

Crotalus durissus.	Banded rattlesnake.
Crotalophorus milarius.	Ground rattlesnake.
Agkistrodon contortrix.	Copper-head
Toxicophis piscivorus.	Water mocassin.
Toxicophis atrofuscus.	Upland mocassin. Highland mocassin. Cotton-mouth.

Elapsoidea.

Elaps fulvius.	Harlequin snake. Bead snake.
Elaps tristis.	" "

Coluberidæ.

Eutænia saurita ?	Swift garter-snake.
Eutænia sirtalis.	Striped snake.
Nerodia Holbrooki ?	Water snake.
Heterodon platyrhinos.	Blowing viper. Hog-nose snake.
Heterodon niger.	Spreading adder.
Heterodon simus.	Hog-nose viper.
Scotophis guttatus.	Black pilot snake.
Ophibolus clericus.	Chicken snake. Milk snake. Cow snake.
Ophibolus Sayi.	Egg snake. King snake.
Bascanion constrictor.	Common black snake.
Masticophis flagelliformis.	Coach-whip snake.
Leptophis æstivus.	Green snake.
Chlorosoma vernalis.	" "
Diadophis punctatus.	Ring-necked snake.
Rhinostoma coccinea.	Scarlet snake.
Haldea striatula.	Brown snake.
Celuta amœna.	Worm snake.
Tantilla coronata.	" "
Osceola elapsoidea.	Ring snake.

Remarks.—The Alligator, chief of our reptiles, attains a great size. Some have been taken measuring twelve or fifteen feet in length. All intermediate sizes, from the newly-hatched young, not exceeding six inches in length, are met with in the lakes and bayous, chiefly of the Mississippi bottoms and those of our other principal streams. The introduction of steamboats seems to have driven them in a great degree from our navigable streams, and they have evidently been greatly diminished in the last half century.

Formerly, they were killed in large numbers by the French, or Creole boatmen (*couriers de bois*), for the oil, which was much used in our tanneries for dressing leather. The skins were often tanned, and formed a unique and ornamental seat for saddles, having the appearance of quilted or embossed work. They were also sometimes manufactured into shoes and boots.

The Alligator lays quite a number of eggs of an oval form, of equal size at both ends, and three to four inches in length. These they deposit in nests constructed of branches of decayed wood and leaves, intermixed with mud, to be hatched by atmospheric heat.

We have in the State Cabinet, a young alligator about a foot in length, which was hatched on the mantle-piece in the parlor of a gentleman in Vicksburg, from an egg which had lain there several days. It lived several months.

The shell of the largest of our turtles, the *Chelonura Temmincki*, sometimes measures three feet in its greatest diameter. When fully grown, this species is rarely less than two feet in length of the carapace, and has been known to measure four or five inches between the eyes.

The couter, or *Emys terrapin*, the second in size, is found to measure twelve or fourteen inches along the back, and the average size may be given at about eight to ten inches. The *Emys serrata* is rather smaller.

The Snapping-turtle, or *Chelonura serpentina,* has the thinnest shell of the family; and I have never met with one quite as large as the full grown Emys terrapin.

The Soft Shell, *Trionyx ferox,* is very flat, has a long pointed nose, no external shell proper, the skeleton being invested with a thick, gelatinous cartilage. It measures frequently twelve or fourteen inches across the back, and of all our turtles is esteemed the greatest delicacy.

The Emys terrapin is also much in demand, and both are extensively used, and find a ready sale to steamboats and restaurants.

The Gopher, *Testudo polyphœmus,* is an inhabitant of our pine flats, near the sea-shore, and is rarely seen much north of the thirty-first degree of north latitude. It attains considerable size, and possesses sufficient strength when full grown, it is said, to walk off with a man standing upon his back. The largest I have seen, however, did not measure more than a foot in diameter. He was invested in a thick elastic carapace, the sutures of which separating the plates, or bosses much depressed.

The gopher is said to burrow ten or twelve feet in the sandy soil, and is, therefore, not easily taken, except when found roaming abroad.

An ingenious mode of capturing him, which is practised, was related to me. A common box terrapin is used for the purpose, being sent into the gopher's hole, from which he is speedily driven out; but, in the eagerness of pursuit, the gopher frequently follows him so far above ground as to be cut off from his retreat and captured by the waiting hunter.

Numbers of them are taken to the fashionable watering-places on the sea-shore, and find a ready sale, being in much demand by epicures.

Our small green lizard is not a chamelion, although popularly so called. Nuttall terms it the chamelion lizard.

The tail of the small striped and large redheaded lizard is extremely brittle, and in consequence, is frequently broken off, but is soon restored by a new growth.

A specimen of the *Tropidolepis undulatus*, in our collection, has a branched or *double* tail, for two-thirds of its length, as if, mindful of the adage "two strings to a bow," he had made provision in advance against a possible repetition of a catastrophe which had deprived him of the original member.

We have several species of the Salamander, a slimy, offensive looking reptile, locally called the *Ground puppy*, some of which I have not seen figured or described.

Our frogs are believed to be common to the Southern States.

Class IV.—PISCES, OR FISH.

CATALOGUE OF THE FISHES OF MISSISSIPPI, PREPARED AND REVISED BY PROF. LOUIS AGASSIZ.

PLACOIDS.

Rajæ.

1. Trygon Sabina. *Les.*	Sting ray.
2. Pristis pectinatus. *Lath.*	Saw-fish.

GANOIDS.

Sturiones.

3. Scaphirhynchus platirhynchus.	Shovelnose sturgeon.
4. Polyodon folium. *Lac.*	Spoonbill sturgeon.

Sauroids.

5.	Lepidosteus spatula. *Lac.*	Alligator gar.
6.	Lepidosteus ———*	Pike gar.
7.	Lepidosteus Chasei. *Wailes.*	Black gar.

Cælacanths.

8.	Amia calva.	Mud-fish.

Ostraciontes.

9.	Ostracion ———*	Cow-fish.

Gymnodontes.

10.	Diodon maculato-striatus. *Mitch.*	

Siluroids.

11.	Galeichthys marinus. *Cuv.*	Cat-fish, salt water.
12.	Arius Milberti. *Cuv.*	Cat-fish, salt water.
13.	Pimelodus cœrulescens. *Raf.*	Cat-fish, fresh water.
14.	Pimelodus limosus. *Raf.*	Cat-fish, fresh water.

CTENOIDS.

Pleuronectidæ.

15.	Achirus mollis. *Mitch.*	

Chætodonts.

16.	Ephippus faber. *Blo.*	Angel-fish.
17.	Chætodon striatus. *Lin.*	

Sparoids.

18.	Sargus Ovis. *Mitch.*	Sheepshead.
19.	Sargus rhomboides. *Cuv.*	Pine perch.

Sciænoids.

20.	Otolithus Carolinensis. *Cuv.*	Trout.
21.	Otolithus Drummondi. *Rich.*	Trout.
22.	Corvina ocellata. *Cuv.*	Red-fish.
23.	Umbrina alburnus. *Cuv.*	Whiting.
24.	Pogonias Chromis. *Lac.*	Big drum.
25.	Pogonias fasciatus. *Lac.*	Young drum.
26.	Amblodon ———*	White perch.
27.	Micropogon undulatus. *Cuv.*	Croaker, or grunt.

* Species not yet identified.

Percoids.

28.	Labrax ———*	Striped bass.
29.	Labrax lineatus. *Cuv.*	Rockfish.
30.	Serranus erythrogaster. *De K.*	Red snapper.
31.	Serranus ———*	Snapper.
32.	Diploprion fascicularis. *Hol.*	
33.	Mesoprion uninotatus. *Cuv.*	
34.	Mesoprion chrysurus. *Cuv.*	Yellow-tail.
35.	Centropristis trifurca. *Cuv.*	
36.	Calliurus gulosus. *Ag.*	Goggle-eye.
37.	Pomotis incisor. *Val.*	
38.	Pomotis hæmatodes. *Ag.*	
39.	Pomotis atrorubens. *Ag.*	

Mugiloids.

40.	Mugil Plumieri. *Cuv.*	Jumping mullet.

CYCLOIDS.

Sphyrænoids.

41.	Sphyræna Barracuda. *Cuv.*	

Scomberoids.

42.	Cybium maculatum. *Cuv.*	Spotted mackerel.
43.	Naucrates ductor. *Cuv.*	Pilot-fish.
44.	Lichia Carolina.	Pompeno.
45.	Caranx ———*	
46.	Argyrius Vomer. *Lac.*	
47.	Vomer Brownii. *Cuv.*	Silver-fish.
48.	Elacate atlantica. *Cuv.*	

Scomberesoces.

49.	Belone caribæa. *Let.*	Bill-fish.

Esoces.

50.	Esox ———*	Pike.

Lophioids.

51.	Malthea vespertilio. *Cuv.*	Toad-fish.

* Species not yet identified.

Labroids.

52. Lachnolæmus aigula. *Cuv.*

Cyprinoids.

53. Ichthyobus ———*	Gaspærgoo.
54. Carpiodes ———*	Buffalo.
55. Catostomus ———*	Sucker.

Cyprinodonts.

56. Zygonectes olivaceus. *Ag.*	Top water.
57. Cyprinodon ovinus. *Val.*	
58. Fundulus spilotus. *Hol.*	Minnow.
59. Heterandria Holbrookii. *Ag.*	

Scopelini.

60. Saurus mexicanus. *Cuv.*

Clupeoids.

61. Clupea ———*	
62. Megalops cyprinoides. *Lam.*	Tarpon, or Big-scale.

Anguillidæ.

63. Anguilla ———*	Eel.

REMARKS.—The foregoing catalogue of our fishes, although far from complete, is, perhaps, the most perfect and reliable list of the fish of the southwest yet published.

Prof. Agassiz, who has done me the favor to prepare and revise it for the press, observes "that, when upon the southern coast of Mississippi, he paid little attention to the sharks and skates, and cannot, therefore, furnish a list of the species of those families found in the waters of the Gulf of Mexico washing the shores of the State of Mississippi." The only species of Sting Ray, the Tragon sabina, he obtained in great abundance upon the sand-flats.

* Species not yet identified.

"The *Pristis pectinatus*, or Saw-fish, is occasionally found, and is known sometimes, it is said, to ascend the Mississippi River. That the *Pristis antiquorum* ascends the Senegal River for several hundred miles above its mouth has long been known. Our saw-fish is by no means the Pristis antiquorum, which is only found in the Old World, and the statements of the occurrence of the P. pectinatus in the Old World are incorrect."

"Much," he remarks, "remains to be done, to ascertain all the species of this order found in the waters of the Mississippi."

The Spoon-bill Sturgeon, *Polyodon folium*, more familiarly known in Mississippi as the *Spoon-bill Cat*, is abundant in our bayous and lakes, and attains nearly as great a size as the alligator gar, being often taken several feet in length.

Prof. Agassiz states that he has not seen any genuine sturgeon from our waters.

Of the family of Cottoids, he obtained one species of Priontus, and one of the Scorpæna, but has not yet identified them.

Where the specific name is omitted in the list, it is not to be understood that the species are doubtful, but that Prof. Agassiz has not yet duly compared them with others of the genus.

Three species of small fish found in the clear creeks of our State, and familiarly known as *horny-heads*, or *Stone-toters*, were obtained during the past summer, and forwarded to Prof. Agassiz for examination; but being unaccountably delayed in the transmission, it remains yet to be determined whether either of them is identical with the Chologaster cornutus, found by him in South Carolina, or with those discovered by Prof. Safford, in Tennessee.

Most probably some will be found to correspond with the Tennessee fish, as ours were chiefly obtained in North Mississippi, near Oxford, and not remote from the Tennessee line.

One species of the Chologaster, at least, has been taken in Adams and other southern counties of the State.

An undescribed species of the Lepidosteus, or Alligator Gar, not yet seen by Prof. Agassiz, has been obtained, and a specimen about three feet in length is preserved in the collection of the Rev. Benjamin Chase, of Natchez. The Taxidermist, who procured and preserved it for Mr. Chase, named it the *black gar*, in contradistinction to the other species which are not so dark.

In general form and appearance of the head and body, it resembles the L. spatula nearly. The distinctive characteristic of the species is found in the biordinate disposition of the rows of scales, which range in opposite directions from the extremities, those from the posterior end taking a direction contrary to that in other species; and the rows from the head and tail meeting about midway of the body, gives the line of junction a zigzag, or serrated appearance.

For this species I propose the name of the accomplished and zealous cultivator of Natural History, who possesses it. It is, therefore, added to our catalogue, and will be known as the Lepidosteus Chaseii, of *Wailes*.

Doubtless our catalogue of the fishes of the southwest will hereafter be much enlarged.

INVERTEBRATA.

Class I.—MOLLUSCA, OR SHELL-FISH.

Of this class my observations enable me to give but little more than a catalogue of the family Unionidæ, or fresh-water mussle, and this is as yet imperfect. Our collections embrace the following species:—

Uniones.

Unio anadontoides.
— asperimus.
— cylindricus.
— circulus.
— globosa.
— glans.
— hydranus.
— heros.
— inflata.
— lens.
— Mississippiensis.
— multiplicatus.
— nodiferus.
— nobilis.
— nasutus.

Unio nodulatus.
— obesus.
— plicatus.
— perplicatus.
— porrectus.
— purpuratus.
— pustulosus.
— pustulatus.
— quadrulus.
— rectus.
— silliquoides.
— subovatus.
— trapezoides.
— trigonius.
— tuberculatus.

Anadontoides.

Anadonta grandis.
——— plana.
——— suborbiculata.

Anadonta decora.
——— Stewartiana.

Remarks.—Of our list of Uniones, the Mississippiensis and Porrectus are newly determined species, and have been figured and described by Conrad, in the *Journal of the Academy of Natural Sciences.*

The trapezoides is the most common and widely dispersed species. The purpuratus (Ater, or lugubris), Anadontoides (or teres), and the Silliquoides are abundant.

Of the Univalves, we have the

Paludina,	Lymnæa,
Planorbis,	and
Melania,	Succinea.

The paludina only is found in any abundance. The melanias appear to be very rare. The lymnæa and succinea occur in the fossil state, associated with the helices in the mastodon bone-beds.

Helices, or Snails.

Among those now found living, I enumerate the following:—	Those found fossil, are—
Helix alternata.	Helix albolabris.
—— auriculata.	—— concava.
—— fraterna.	—— elevata.
—— hirsuta.	—— profunda.
—— interna.	—— perspectiva.
—— pulchella.	—— palliata.
—— tridentata.	—— Sayi.
	—— thyroides.
	—— helicina.

CRUSTACEANS.

Our collection in this department is yet very limited. I enumerate at present only the following:—

SCIENTIFIC NAME.	POPULAR NAME.
Loligo punctata.	Cuttle fish.
Polyphemus occidentales.	Horse-foot crab.
Lupa dicantha.	Common edible crab.
Gelasimus vocans.	Fiddler crab.
Ocypode arenaria.	Small sand-crab.

SCIENTIFIC NAME.	POPULAR NAME.
Pagurus longicarpus.	Hermit crab.
Pseudocarcinus mercenaria.	Stone crab.
Cambarus leprosus, ? *Agaz.*	Large crawfish.
" fluviatilis.	Smaller crawfish.
" fossor.	" "
Peneus setiferus.	Sea prawn, or shrimp.
Hippolyte Carolinana.	Mississippi shrimp.

Class II.—ARTICULATA, OR INSECTS.

Class III.—RADIATA—STAR-FISH, ETC.

These classes of the Invertebrata must, for the present, be wholly omitted.

VII. FLORA.

A systematic and comprehensive catalogue of the Botany of the State cannot, with propriety, be undertaken until the close of the survey. At present, only a popular and familiar synopsis of some of the most useful and ornamental of our trees and plants will be attempted, without regard to classification or arrangement in a scientific form.

I. FOREST-TREES.

POPULAR NAME.	SCIENTIFIC NAME.
Apple, crab	Pyrus coronaria.
Ash, blue	Fraxinus quadrangulata.
" white	" accuminata.
Beech,	Fagus Americana.
Barberry,	Barberis vulgaris.
Birch,	Betula populifolia.
Bay, sweet,	Magnolia glauca.
Bay berry,	Myrica cerifera.
Box elder,	Acer negundo.
Buck-eye dwarf,	Aesculus pavia.
" "	" spicta.
Candleberry,	Myrica cerifera.
Cherry,	Cerasus Virginiana.
Cucumber-tree,	Magnolia auriculata.
Chestnut,	Castanea vesca.
Chinquepin,	" pumila.
Cottonwood,	Populus deltoides.

POPULAR NAME.	SCIENTIFIC NAME.
Cypress,	Cupressus disticha.
Cedar,	Juniperus Virginiana.
Dogwood,	Cornus florida.
Dogwood, swamp	" sericea.
" "	Cephalanthus occidentalis.
Elm, red	Ulmus Americana.
Elm, slippery	" fulva.
Elm, cork-bark	" racemosa.
Elder,	Sambucus Canadensis.
Gum, sweet	Liquidambar styraciflua.
Gum, black	Nyssa multiflora.
Haw, black	Viburnum prunifolium.
" possum	" nudum.
Hackberry,	Celtis occidentalis.
Hickory,	Carya tomentosa.
Hazel,	Corylus Americana.
Hazel, witch	Hamamelas Virginicus.
Holly,	Ilex opaca.
Hawthorn,	Cratægus crusgalli.
"	" punctata.
" parsley-leaved,	" apiifolia.
Hornbeam,	Carpinus Americana.
Honeysuckle,	Azalea rubra.
" white	" viscosa.
Huckleberry,	Vaccinum corymbosum.
" swamp	" vascillans.
Hyderangea,	Hyderangea arborescens.
Hercules club,	Aralia spinosa.
Ironwood,	Ostrya Virginica.
Lauria mundi,	Cerasus Carolinensis.
Laurel,	Lauro cerasus.
Laurel, swamp	Kalmia glauca.
Linn,	Tilia Americana.
Leatherwood,	Dirca palustris.
Locust,	Robina pseuda-acacia.
Locust, honey	Gleditschia triacanthos.
" "	" brachyloba.
Magnolia,	Magnolia grandiflora.
"	" auriculata.
Maple, sugar	Acer saccharinum.

POPULAR NAME.	SCIENTIFIC NAME.
Maple, red	Acer rubrum.
" silver-leaved	" dasycarpum.
" swamp	" negundo.
Mulberry,	Morus rubra.
Myrtle,	Myrica inodorata.
Myrtlewax,	" cerifera.
Oak, live	Quercus virens.
" red	" rubra.
" black	" tinctoria.
" blackjack,	" niger.
" white	" alba.
" Spanish	" falcata.
" post	" obtusiloba.
" chestnut	" castanea.
" chinquepin	" prinoides.
" overcup	" macrocarpa.
" swamp	" aquatica.
" willow	" phellos.
" pin	" palustris.
Osage orange,	Maclura aurantica.
Pride of Barbadoes,	Amorpha fructicosa.
Pacon,	Carya olivæfermis.
Pacon, bitter	Hicorea texana.
Pig-nut,	Carya amara.
Plum,	Prunus Americana.
"	" chickasaw.
" blue	" ——?
" red	" ——?
" "	" ——?
Prickly ash,	Zanthoxylum tricarpum.
Paupau,	Uvaria triloba.
Pine, long leaf	Pinus palustris.
" short leaf	" rigida.
" swamp	" mitis.
" pitch	" tæda.
Poplar,	Liriodendron tulipifera.
Persimmon,	Diospycus Virginiana.
Redbud, *Judas-tree*,	Cercis Canadensis.
Sycamore,	Platanus occidentalis.
Sumac,	Rhus glabra.

POPULAR NAME.	SCIENTIFIC NAME.
Sumac dwarf,	Rhus typhina.
Strawberry-tree,	Euonymus Americanus.
Swamp spice,	Ilex prinoides.
" snow-ball,	Hydrangea quercifolia.
Sassafras,	Laurus sassafras.
Shellbark,	Carya-alba.
Starry annis,	Kalmia glauca.
Spanish mulberry,	Calicaspa Americana.
Service-tree,	Aronia arbutifolia.
Stewartia,	Stewartia malacodendron.
Spice wood	Laurus benzoin.
Tupelo,	Nyssa villosa.
" large fruited	" tomentosa.
Toothache-tree,	Zanthoxylum clavaherculis.
Umbrella-tree,	Magnolia tripetala.
Walnut,	Juglans nigra.
Willow,	Salix nigra.

II. PARASITES, RUNNERS, AND CLIMBERS.

POPULAR NAME.	SCIENTIFIC NAME.
Blackberry,	Rubus villosa.
" swamp	Rubus hispidus.
Creeper,	Bignonia radicans.
Cross vine,	" crucigera.
Cornucopia,	Glycene fructescens ?
Coral vine,	Lycium europeum ?
Dewberry,	Rubus Canadensis.
Green moss,	Tillandsia ?
Jasmine, yellow,	Gelceminum nitidum.
Mistletoe,	Viscum verticillatum.
Poison oak,	Rhus toxicodendron.
Passion flower,	Passiflora incarnata.
Spanish moss,	Tillandsia usneoides.
Suplejack,	Ziziphus volubilis.
Strawberry,	Fragaria Virginiana.
Sensitive brier,	Mimosa instia.
Tie vine, *Morning glory*	Convolvulus arvensis.
Wild potatoe vine,	" panduratus.

POPULAR NAME.	SCIENTIFIC NAME.
Sarsaparilla vine,	Schisandra coccinea.
Woodbine, red,	Lonicera sempervirens.
" yellow,	" flava.

III. UNDERGROWTH PERENNIALS.

POPULAR NAME.	SCIENTIFIC NAME.
Bear grass,	Yucca filamentosa.
Cane,	Arundo gigantea.
China brier,	Smilax China.
Fern,	Polypodium ——— ?
Fern,	" ——— ?
Green brier,	Smilax rotundifolia.
" "	" spinulosa.
Palmetto, fan	Sabal minor.
Prickly pear,	Opuntia vulgaris.
Reed,	Arundo tecta.

IV. NOXIOUS WEEDS, HURTFUL TO PLANTATIONS.

POPULAR NAME.	SCIENTIFIC NAME.
Burdock,	Lappa major.
Beggarsticks,	Bidens connata.
Cocklebur,	Zanthium strumarium.
Dock,	Rumex obtusifolia.
Dogfennel,	Anthemis cotula.
Jamestown weed,	Datura stramonium.
Sneeze weed,	Helenium autumnale.
Stinging nettle,	Urtica urens.
Spanish needles,	Bidens bipinnata.
Smart weed,	Polygonum articulatum.
Thistle,	Circum lanceolatus.
"	" pumilus.
Wild coffee weed,	Cassia occidentalis.
" chamomile,	Anthemis arvensis.

V. VITUS, OR GRAPE.

POPULAR NAME.	SCIENTIFIC NAME.
Muscadine,	Vitis rotundifolia.
Choke grape,	" cordifolia.
Small sour grape,	" ——— ?

VI. PLANTS, USEFUL, MEDICINAL, AND ORNAMENTAL.

POPULAR NAME.	SCIENTIFIC NAME.
Aster,	Aster radula.
Boneset,	Eupatorium perfoliatum.
Columbo,	Frasera walteri.
Chickweed,	Stellaria medea.
Cotton rose,	Hibiscus grandiflorus.
Calamus,	Acorus calamus.
Cats-tail,	Typha latifolia.
Centaury plant,	Sabbatia angularis.
False foxglove,	Gerardia flava.
Ginger, wild	Asarium Canadensis.
Green dragon,	Arisæma dracontium.
Gall of the earth,	Nabulus fraseri.
Ground Ivy,	Ipegæa repens.
Horsemint,	Monarda fistulosa.
Horehound,	Marrubium vulgare.
Heartsease,	Viola tricolor.
Indian turnip,	Arisema triphyllum.
Jerusalem oak,	Ambrina anthelmintica.
" cherry,	Physalis viscosa.
Lucern,	Medicago sativa.
Lambsquarter,	Chenopodium album.
Lobelia,	Lobelia cardinalis.
Milk weed,	Acerates viridiflora.
May apple,	Podophyllum peltatum.
Monoca nut,	Nelumbium speciosum.
Mallow,	Hibiscus militaris.
Mullein,	Verbascum thapsus.
Pleurisy root,	Asclepias tuberosa.

POPULAR NAME.	SCIENTIFIC NAME.
Pink-root,	Spigelia marylandica.
Pocoon,	Sanguinaria Canadensis.
Purslane,	Portulacca oleracea.
Poke-weed,	Phytolacca decandra.
Pine-sap,	Monotropa hypopithys.
Pickerel weed,	Pontederia cordata.
Pansey,	Viola tricolor.
Peppermint,	Mentha piperita.
Partridge pea,	Lathyous variosa.
Rattlesnake master.	Hieracium venosum.
Rush,	Eques hyemale.
Silk-weed,	Asclepias purpurescens.
" "	Asclepias variegata.
Sorrel,	Oxalis stricta.
Senna, wild	Cassia Marylandica.
Pepper-grass,	Lepidium campistre.
Specularia,	Specularia perfoliata.
Violet,	Viola rotundifolia.
White-water lily,	Nymphia odorata.
White clover,	Trifolium repens.
Wild indigo,	Baptisia tinctoria.
" sensitive plant,	Cassia nictitans.
" parsnip,	Pastinaca saliva.
Water plantain,	Alisma plantago.
Wild senna,	Cassia Marylandica.
Vinnella,	Cacalia sauveolus.
Virburnum,	Virbena spuria.
Yellow pond-lily,	Nuphar advena.
Vervain,	Verbena spuria.
Trailing arbutus,	Epigæa ripens.
Bears-foot,	Fetid hellebore.

REMARKS.—Of our timber and timber-trees much of interest might be said, did our space admit of it.

The Cypress, for many purposes of building, stands unrivalled. I have no means of estimating the value of the trade in this timber, but it is immense.

There is scarcely a town or village on the Mississippi,

or its tributaries, within the limits of the State, in which there is not one or more steam-mills busily employed in sawing this timber. Add to these the numerous mills similarly employed on plantations, and take into view the logs rafted to New Orleans, and along the river coast below our borders, and it will be perceived that the annual consumption of this valuable timber, the growth of our swamps, is enormous.

No inconsiderable quantity of this timber is floated into the Yazoo River in *cribs*, or single logs, from the *Cypress brakes*, or swamps, at periods when the low grounds are sufficiently inundated, and the *slues and bayous* are filled with water. The cribs and logs are then united by pinning poles across them, forming rafts sometimes two hundred feet or more in length.

It is a curious and imposing spectacle in passing up the Yazoo River, at the period of high water, to observe the vast accumulations of logs, covering in the aggregate, miles of the surface of the stream, awaiting the subsidence of the flood for a *current* in the river, to be floated out. Much of this timber comes from the sources of the Yazoo, and from the Bayous and Lakes connecting with them in time of high water.

The Big Black, the Pearl, and the Homochitto Rivers also contribute large supplies.

Much of the Cypress was formerly cut from the public lands, but some restraint has of late been imposed upon these depredations.

A large class of raftsmen are habitually engaged in this pursuit, to an extent that has greatly reduced, if not exhausted, the supply in many of the most accessible localities.

The general extension of the levies or embankments on the Mississippi, of late years, by restraining the overflow of water into the swamps, has, to a considerable extent, impeded the operations of these timber-men, who are, in consequence, unable sometimes for years to get out the logs which they have cut and prepared for floating.

The Red Cypress, the most valuable variety, not floating, in consequence of its greater specific gravity, can only be brought out by pinning or securing the log between others of a more buoyant kind.

Next in value to the Cypress, and perhaps more inexhaustible, is the Long Leaf Pine, which is taken to the mills along the seaboard, or shipped in logs to Europe or the West Indies.

Suitable sticks for masts or spars in ship-building, are greatly in demand at very lucrative prices, and a great quantity of this description of timber is purchased for the French navy.

Logs are cut at proper seasons, hauled by means of large timber-wheels to convenient places, and rolled into the hollows or dry channels of the *wet-weather* streams, out of which they are floated when the rainy season sets in.

Where the country is very flat, and destitute of streams or natural channels, the simple expedient is adopted of cutting small ditches, sometimes miles in length, barely large enough to receive the logs which are rolled into them, end to end, and along which they are pushed by hand, so soon as the rains have filled the ditches.

In the counties bordering on the sea-shore, the Pine is made to afford a considerable supply of tar and charcoal, much of which is taken across the lake to New Orleans.

The tar-kilns are formed from the heart and *knots*, or

the fatty portions of the fallen pine timber, from which the sap has completely decayed away, or been burned off in the periodical firing of the woods.

Ample supplies can always be obtained in a limited space, for the construction of the kiln, which is frequently made upon public lands, there being no hindrance to the use of the dead or fallen timber, by the government timber agents.

The kilns are rarely conical, but of a rectangular shape, eight or ten feet high, made by arranging the *lightwood,* finely split, and disposed in a suitable manner, for running off the melted tar over an inclined plane into a pit or receptacle sunk at the lower end.

The kilns sometimes contain a hundred cords, each cord yielding about two barrels of tar, worth one and a half to two dollars per barrel, at the kiln.

The residuum forms the charcoal, which is put up in coarse sacks for convenience of transportation to the city.

A distillery for spirits of turpentine and camphene, was established a few years since, at Napoleon, in the County of Hancock, on Pearl River, and some *pineries* of considerable extent, were formed in the neighborhood for collecting the rosin.

This is done by *boxing*, or cutting a receptacle in the side of the tree two or three feet above the ground, to receive the exuding turpentine, the flow or running of which is promoted by paring away the bark for some extent above it.

The trees are said to yield well, and to afford one more *dipping* than in North Carolina, owing to the greater length of the season for the running of the sap. The barked surface requires to be extended and scraped periodically, with an instrument, suited to the purpose, to remove the hardened rosin that accumulates.

Much watchfulness is required to keep the fire out of the pineries during the period of burning off the undergrowth and straw of the neighboring pine forests, as the burning over and charring the decorticated surface effectually prevents any further flow of the turpentine, if the tree itself is not wholly consumed.

When effectually protected from these firings, the trees last for three or four years, before they cease to be productive.

The hands employed in these pineries being withdrawn by the proprietors, who were planters engaged in the culture of cotton, in a distant part of the State, the supply of the raw turpentine failed, and the distillery was broken up and removed.

The stores of valuable oak timber we possess, have been little used, except for plantation purposes, the rails for fencing being chiefly made of it.

Beyond the small local demand for wagon-making and for cotton-baskets, the white-oak, scarcely less valuable than the live-oak, has given little employment to the industry of the country.

In remote sections, however, where the cultivation of cotton does not absorb the whole attention, the getting out of staves or puncheons has been found profitable.

Staves and hoop-poles have been brought down from the head of keel-boat navigation, on the Tallahatchie, in Pontotoc County.

The live-oak is highly prized as an ornamental shade-tree, but does not now exist on our coast in such abundance as to furnish any considerable supply of timber for ship-building.

An intelligent observer, residing in Marion County,

informs me that, although the live-oak timber approaches quite near to the thirty-first degree of north latitude, in a state of nature it has never been noticed by him *north* of that parallel. He has made the same observation with respect to the chestnut, which has its *southern* limit about the same line.

The geographical distribution of some of our forest-trees, seems to be well defined. For example, the Magnolia tripetala (Umbrella-tree), as a prevailing growth, seems to be confined to a narrow belt extending northwardly from our southern boundary, in a direction parallel with the general course of the Mississippi River, and twelve or fifteen miles to the east of it.

I have not met with it north of the thirty-third degree of north latitude, which seems also to be about the northern limit of the Spanish moss, *tillandsia usneoides.*

Over extensive districts of country, a single species of timber sometimes is found to prevail almost exclusively, with the exception of the inferior shrubs and plants that constitute the undergrowth. This is the case, mainly, with the long and short-leaf pine, which, though sometimes blended, occupy generally, distinct tracts; and also with the post-oak and black-jack. The same may be said, but to less extent, of the hickory and the chestnut.

Other tracts exhibit a remarkable variety of the forest-trees in close association, which generally affect distinct soils and situations. This was noticed as forming a remarkable feature of the forests in the eastern part of Wilkinson County, and in part of Amite.

The evergreens and deciduous trees are seen intermingled, and forming varied and pleasing contrasts. Indeed, it was often difficult to detect on quite limited areas the absence of any of our forest-trees. The grouping of these, together with the presence of the azalias, woodbines, jasmine, and other flowering shrubs and vines, gives to the scenery a truly park-like character, as if art had co-operated with nature to display, at a single view, all the riches of our flora.

A few years since, Lieut. W. D. Porter, of the United States Navy, called the attention of the people of the United States, to the cultivation of the Sumac (*Rhus Coriaria*), as practised in Sicily, and which he represented as a highly profitable pursuit, and suggested the introduction of the plant and some of the operatives accustomed to its management. It is understood that the Sumac is extensively used in Jersey and the neighboring States for tanning, and that considerable quantities of the cured leaves are exported from that quarter.

The occurrence, in this State, of extensive natural plantations of the dwarf species, *Rhus Typhina*, as an undergrowth on some of our pine lands, suggests their availability for this purpose without the labor of cultivation.

The sweet-gum was formerly regarded as a useless cumberer of the earth, and from its great size on the rich alluvial lands, difficult to be got rid of except by the slow process of deadening, by *belting* or cutting around the tree through the sap. Of late years, it has come into considerable use as a fuel on steamboats, and, when seasoned, little difficulty is experienced in burning it.

The Sassafras, a valuable timber-tree, and formerly abundant, and in great demand in past years for shingles, where the Cypress was less convenient, has in consequence been greatly diminished, and large trees of it are now rarely seen.

The Lynn has also become scarce in many situations where it was formerly very abundant. In early times, the bark was very useful in manufacturing ropes and for other purposes, and was one of the early causes of its destruction. It is a soft-grained wood, of even texture, free from knots and other imperfections, and not liable to shrink or warp when seasoned, and therefore very suitable for ceilings and other interior parts in buildings.

Bees are very fond of the flowers, and the honey made from them is reputed to possess a peculiarly delicate flavor. That from the flowers of the Chinquepin, on the contrary, is said to be poisonous.

The Lynn appears to be most abundant at this time, in the western part of Jefferson County.

The Cottonwood, *Populus Deltoides*, now the chief resource for steamboat fuel, on the lower Mississippi—the ash timber having become nearly exhausted at all accessible points—is of a very quick growth, and the rapidity with which it is reproduced, is consequently a very favorable circumstance. Every new deposit made by the inundations of the river, is speedily covered with a spontaneous growth of young Cottonwood, standing as thickly as a crop of small grain. This arrests the sediment subsequently brought by the river, and new islands and bars are formed, upon which the growth, by a natural process, becoming sufficiently thinned out, attains a considerable size in a very few years, thus renewing the supply of fuel, which otherwise would speedily become exhausted.

The Chestnut is only found in the interior, and most abundantly in the northern counties. The tree seems to have become diseased in latter years, and is rapidly dying out.

The small species or Chinquepin, *Castanea pumilla*, flourishes best on the rich bluff lands bordering on the Mississippi.

Among the several species of our wild plums, none of which are fit for use until preserved in the form of sweetmeats or jellies, I notice a small blue species, resembling in color the damson. It was observed in greatest abundance, on Pearl River, in Marion County, and is sometimes called "the Sloe." The fruit is of small size, but pulpy, with a very small pit. The trees seem more vigorous, healthy, and prolific than the other species of the wild plum, producing the fruit abundantly in clusters. It is doubtless worthy of cultivation and introduction into our orchards.

The service-tree, *Aronia Arbutifolia*, found in Amite and Wilkinson Counties, is rather a novelty, very few trees having been met with.

Although our fan palm or Palmetto, *Sabal pumilla* (the *Sabal adansoni*, of Loudon, and *Sabal minor*, of Nuttall), grows with the greatest luxuriance, in the low swamp lands; yet it is met with sometimes, in more arid and elevated situations, and is abundant on our seaboard, growing on the sandy pine lands, sometimes on the very verge of the ocean.

Some of our noxious plants are not exclusively the pests of the South. The Jamestown weed, *daturia stramonium*, and the Cocklebur, *Zanthium strumarium*, have a very wide geographical range. They have been observed, growing with the greatest luxuriance, in the New England States, and, on the rocky shores of Nahant, are moistened by the spray from the surf of the ocean dashing over the rocks on which they thrive.

The space allotted to this branch of the report will admit of no further extension of these remarks.

The additional observations which have been made, and the information acquired in reference to our Flora, must consequently be deferred to another occasion.

APPENDIX.

A.

THE PRESIDENT OF THE BOARD OF TRUSTEES OF THE STATE UNIVERSITY TO THE GOVERNOR OF THE STATE.

JACKSON, MISS., *January* 12, 1854.

His Excellency JOHN J. MCRAE,

Governor of Mississippi.

SIR—In pursuance of an order of the Board of Trustees of the University of Mississippi, I herewith lay before you the Report of Prof. B. L. C. Wailes, on the Agriculture, Geology, and Natural History of Mississippi; and in doing so, I embrace the occasion to express the entire satisfaction of the Board with the able manner in which the professor has discharged the duty which had been assigned him.

With due respect, your obedient servant,

J. THOMPSON,

Prest. Board of Trustees.

B.

MESSAGE OF GOVERNOR MCRAE TO THE LEGISLATURE.

EXECUTIVE OFFICE, *January* 17, 1854.

TO THE SENATE AND HOUSE OF REPRESENTATIVES.

I invite the attention of the two houses to the Report of Prof. B. L. C. Wailes, Geological Department of Mississippi University, on the Agriculture, Geology, and Natural History of Mississippi, which, in pursuance of an order of the Board of Trustees of the University has been presented as required by law to the Governor, and which I have the honor to submit for the consideration of the Legislature.

The Board of Trustees express their entire satisfaction with the able manner in which Prof. Wailes has discharged his duties, and as an individual member of the Board, I concur in their unanimous opinion in favor of the publication of the report.

It is the first of a series, which will form the Geological History of our State, and is preceded by an interesting historical outline of the discovery and early settlement of the Mississippi Territory, with other valuable statistical information, which will be useful and interesting to the people of the State.

I recommended the printing of the report by the authority of the Legislature in neat and durable style, and in such numbers as will be sufficient for distribution in our own State, and for partial distribution in other States.

Should the printing of the report be ordered as recommended, it is proper to say that I am informed by Prof. Wailes, that the preliminary historical outline is not entirely finished, the period during which the country was subject to the Spanish rule having yet to be supplied to bring it down to the time of the surrender of the country to the United States.

The department of Zoology is also incomplete, and there are blanks in the tables of statistics, to be filled up when the census returns are published, and several plates representing the fossils and geological sections, required properly to illustrate the report, are yet to be added.

These can all be perfected, and the report be revised by the State Geologist, before it is printed.

I accompany the report with the letter of the President of the Board of Trustees, of the University, submitting it to the Governor.

JOHN J. McRAE.

C.

REPORT OF THE COMMITTEE OF THE SENATE.

January 20, 1854.

IN THE SENATE.

Mr. Cobb, from a Select Committee, made the following report:—

MR. PRESIDENT—The Select Committee, to whom was referred the special message of his Excellency, communicated to the Senate on the 17th inst., together with a manuscript copy of a scientific work, by Prof. Wailes, of the Geological Department of the State University, and recommending the publication of the same by the authority of the Legislature, have had the same under consideration, and do earnestly advise that provision be made for carrying into effect his Excellency's recommendations.

The advantages to be derived from the circulation of a work so eminently meritorious as this, under the patronage of the Legislature, cannot be questioned or easily calculated; for it will, in all likelihood, prove to be the initiative step to great attainments in developing the scientific talent and resources of our State.

Science, in many of its branches, as we are taught by history, can never be successfully prosecuted or made to subserve extended useful purposes without adequate patronage; and in the absence of any incorporated scientific societies, or institutions possessed of the requisite means and influence to extend material aid in this respect, your Committee are of opinion that such patronage should, as a matter of justice as well as policy, be cheerfully and seasonably extended by the Legislature.

The end for which this department of the State University was established, can never be attained, if assistance of this character shall be refused or grudgingly extended; and that benefit which is to be derived from the experience and labors of learned professors, will be entirely cut off.

The branch of science embraced and illustrated in this work, has been too long neglected to admit of further delay in rendering the aid necessary to its proper development, if the Legislature design to promote beneficial and practical results.

With this view, and in conformity with the recommendations of his Excellency, your Committee beg leave to report the following bill, and recommend that it be passed.

D.

AN ACT TO AUTHORIZE THE PRINTING OF THE FIRST ANNUAL REPORT OF THE AGRICULTURAL AND GEOLOGICAL SURVEY OF THE STATE.

SECTION 1. *Be it enacted by the Legislature of the State of Mississippi*, That two thousand copies of the report of Professor B. L. C. Wailes, State Geologist, be printed, under his supervision, in quarto form, and in such manner, and with such illustrations and plates, therein given, as his Excellency, the Governor, shall deem appropriate and necessary for its illustration.

SECTION 2. *Be it further enacted*, That, when printed and bound, the said report shall be deposited in the office of the Secretary of State, to be by him distributed as follows: Fifty copies to be deposited in the State Library; twenty-five copies to be deposited in the State University; one copy to each State in the Union; one copy to be given to each incorporated college and academy in the State; one copy each to the Governor, Secretary of State, Auditor of Public Accounts, State Treasurer, Adjutant-General, the Chancellor and Vice-Chancellors, the Judges of the High Court of Errors and Appeals, the Attorney-General, the Judge and District Attorney of each District, each member of the present Senate and House of Representatives; and one hundred copies to the said State Geologist, to be by him exchanged for similar reports from other States, and to furnish to scientific societies and public libraries.

SECTION 3. *Be it further enacted*, That one thousand copies of said report shall be deposited in the office of the Secretary of State, to be sold by any agent or agents to be appointed by the Governor, under such regulations, and for such a sum each, as he may deem proper and advisable, for the purpose of reimbursing the State for publishing the same, and the balance to be distributed among the several counties of the State, in proportion to their representation in the Legislature, to be furnished to the people thereof, in such manner as the Boards of Police of the several counties, shall direct.

SECTION 4. *Be it further enacted*, That, previous to the printing of said report, it shall be revised and completed by the said State Geologist; and the portion of it which treats of Zoology, as far as prepared, shall be omitted, and in lieu thereof, a catalogue of the Fauna of the State, as far as ascertained, be substituted.

SECTION 5. *And be it further enacted*, That for the

further and more efficient prosecution of the survey, analyses of the marls, soils, mineral waters, and the chief agricultural productions of the State, shall be made at the University of Mississippi, as the Trustees may designate; and the State Geologist may, from time to time, furnish such marls, soils, and waters as may be required for analyses, and shall receive in return from the chemist, full and precise reports of all analyses which may be made; and specimens of the marls and soils shall be preserved in convenient glass bottles, in the State Cabinet, and in the Cabinet of the University, properly labelled, with the chemical character of the substance, and the locality from which the same was obtained.

SECTION 6. *And be it further enacted,* That the said Geologist shall make collections of specimens to illustrate the mineral character and Palæontology of the State, in addition to the Zoological productions, which by law he is now required to collect, and to cause them to be suitably arranged and preserved in the State Cabinet, and that of the University; and any duplicates that remain, may be distributed by him among such of the incorporated colleges as may apply for them.

SECTION 7. *And be it further enacted,* That the sum, not to exceed two thousand five hundred dollars, be appropriated out of any money in the treasury, to be drawn upon the requisition of the Governor, for the purpose of carrying into effect the provisions of this Act.

SECTION 8. *Be it enacted,* That this Act shall take effect, and be in force, from and after its passage.

Approved March 1, 1854.

E.

EXTRACTS FROM DR. MILLINGTON'S REPORT TO THE GOVERNOR.

About the 1st of February, 1854, Dr. Millington, (late principal professor of Geology in the State University of Mississippi), then connected with the Medical School at Memphis, made a report to Governor McRae, but which was not received until several weeks had elapsed after the Trustees of the University had adjourned and left Jackson. The following extract from the concluding part of that report, exhibits its character and extent:—

"An assistant geologist was provided for, who was to travel over the State, and make examinations and investigations under my directions, and to report all that he could learn, and had done, from time to time, and likewise to make collections of specimens of what he met with, and to transmit the same, from time to time, to the museum of the University at Oxford, where they might be deposited, and examined or analyzed, and be described as most necessary; and fortunately, Mr. B. L. C. Wailes was appointed to that situation, and he has conducted it, as far as the examination has gone, in the most ample and satisfactory manner, as will appear by the abstract of his monthly reports to me before given. All, therefore, that I have been able to do, has been to *transcribe his reports*, with occasional observations, and to take charge of and arrange the specimens which he has sent on, which already form the nucleus of a useful, if not a very full and complete museum; and I hereby tender my warmest thanks for the assistance Mr. Wailes has rendered to me, and to the cause in which we have been engaged.

"But it has always appeared to me that the person who travels, and personally examines the geological and mineralogical formations of a country, ought to be considered as the principal officer; and he who is the curator or examiner, or analyzer, as of less importance; and I have always considered myself as placed in an inferior position in respect to Mr. Wailes. * * * * Being no longer connected with the University, which has my warmest wishes for its prosperity, I beg leave most respectfully to recommend that, in any future appointment, the Professor of Chemistry and Geology should be separate and unconnected persons; the first to remain at the University, and to undertake the examination and analysis of whatever may be sent to him by the Professor of Geology, and to report accordingly."

F.

MR. WILLIAM DUNBAR'S CLASSIFICATION OF LAND CLAIMS.

In May, 1799, when the inhabitants of the District of Natchez were under much anxiety and suspense respecting the titles of their lands, Mr. William Dunbar, an English gentleman by birth, of a liberal and scientific education, who came to this country in 1773, and under the succeeding Spanish administration had superintended much of the surveying in the Natchez District as the deputy of Don Carlos Trudeau, the Surveyor-General of the province of Louisiana, in writing on the subject of the land claims, makes the following classification of them. The shades of distinction between some of them are very slight, and, as far as the essential conditions of validity are concerned, may be comprised in the two grades in which they are treated of in the chapter on Land Titles, page 117:—

"*First.*—Lands granted by the British Government, and not abandoned by the proprietors or their representatives, either by purchase or power of attorney, and have been cultivated. Such titles we repute the best of all.

"*Second.*—Land granted by Mandamus by British Government, without condition of occupancy or improvement, but which has never been occupied by the proprietors or their agents.

"*Third.*—British letters patent of lands from provincial governors, containing a condition of certain improvements within three years, to be forfeited by non-performance, and which lands have never been occupied by their proprietors or agents.

"*Fourth.*—The last description of lands once occupied, but afterwards abandoned for many years to the present time.

"*Fifth.*—Spanish grants by letters patent on Mandamus lands.

"*Sixth.*—Spanish grants, or lands formerly granted by British governors, but never occupied by the British patentees, not residing in the country.

"*Seventh.*—The last description, with this difference, that the patentee, although he never occupied or improved his land, was a resident in another part of the colony, who, upon resisting this new grant of his lands, by petition to the Spanish governor, has been rejected upon the principle of non-occupancy and want of improvement, agreeably to the conditions of his British grant, as well as reiterated Spanish proclamations to the same effect.

"*Eighth.*—Spanish grants upon lands which were always vacant under the British government.

"*Ninth.*—Lands purchased at public sale, of the Spanish government, which lands had been declared forfeited in consequence of an insurrection or species of rebellion in favor of the English, soon after the Natchez had been surrendered by capitulation to the Spaniards.—*Note.* Within the above description are mandamus lands, as well as patents by governors of West Florida.

"*Tenth.*—Lands for which warrants of survey had been obtained prior to the ratification of the Spanish treaty, but which could not be patented until after that period.

"*Eleventh.*—Lands of the above description, but never patented, the proprietor holding the warrant of survey, and plot, and certificate of the district surveyor, prior to the treaty.

"*Twelfth.*—Land for which warrants of survey were obtained before the treaty, surveyed and patented after the ratification of the treaty.

"*Thirteenth.*—Lands for which warrants of survey were obtained prior to the treaty, and surveyed after the treaty, but not patented.

"*Fourteenth.*—Warrant of survey and patent obtained since the treaty, but during the exercise of the Spanish jurisdiction, as agreed to by the then representatives of the government of the United States, Commissioner Ellicott and Lieutenant Pope, as appears by an instrument of writing then made between the Spanish government and the people, ratified by Messrs. Ellicott and Pope.

"*Fifteenth.*—Warrant of survey, with plot and certificate of the District Surveyor, obtained since the treaty, but no patent.

"*Sixteenth.*—Warrant of survey obtained before the treaty, and improvement, but the land not measured.

"*Seventeenth.*—Warrant obtained since the treaty, with improvement, including houses, crop, stock, &c., but land not measured.

"*Eighteenth.*—Warrant before the treaty, without improvement or measurement.

"*Nineteenth.*—Warrant since the treaty, without improvement or measurement.

"*Twentieth.*—Improvement by houses, crops, stock, &c., without authority, by warrant or otherwise.

"*Twenty-first.*—Lesser improvements by raising small crop without residence.

"*Twenty-second.*—Improvement by occupancy, and verbal permission of the Spanish Governor, with the Surveyor's certificate at the time of taking possession."

G.

WHITNEY'S SPECIFICATIONS AND DESCRIPTION OF HIS GIN.

The Schedule referred to in the letters patent to Eli Whitney, granted March 14, 1794.

A short description of the machine invented by the subscriber, for ginning cotton:—

The principal parts of this machine are: 1st, the frame; 2d, the cylinder; 3d, the breastwork; 4th, the clearer; and 5th, the hopper.

1st. The frame, by which the whole work is supported and kept together, is of a square or parallel organic form, and proportionable to the other parts, as may be most convenient.

2d. The cylinder is of wood. Its form is perfectly described by its name, and its dimensions may be from six to nine inches diameter, and from two to five feet in length. The cylinder is placed horizontally across the frame, leaving room for the clearer on one side and the hopper on the other.

In the cylinder is fixed an iron axis, which may pass quite through, or consist only of gudgeons driven into each end.

There are shoulders on this axis to prevent any horizontal variation, and it extends so far without the frame as to admit a winch at one end, by which it is put in motion, and so far at the other end as to receive the whirl by which the clearer is turned.

The surface of the cylinder is filled with teeth, set in annular rows, which are at such a distance from each other as to admit a cotton seed to play freely in the space between them. The space between each tooth, in the same row, is so small as not to admit a seed or half a seed to enter it. These teeth are made of stiff iron wire driven into the wood of the cylinder. The teeth are all inclosed the same way, and in such a manner that the angle included between the tooth and a tangent drawn from the point, into which the tooth is driven, will be about 55 or 60 degrees.

The gudgeons of the cylinder run in brass boxes, each of which is in two parts, one of which is fixed in the wood of the frame, and the other is confined down upon the axis with screws.

3d. The breast-work is fixed above the cylinder, parallel and contiguous to the same. It has transverse grooves, or openings, through which the rows of teeth pass as the cylinder revolves, and its use is to obstruct the seeds while the cotton is carried forward through the grooves by the teeth.

The thickness of the breast-work is two and a half or

three inches, and the under side of it is made of iron or brass.

4th. The clearer is placed horizontally with, and parallel to, the cylinder. Its length is the same as that of the cylinder, and its diameter is proportioned by convenience. There are two, four, or more brushes or rows of bristles fixed in the surface of the clearer, in such manner that the ends of the bristles will sweep the surface of the cylinder.

Its axis and boxes are similar to those of the cylinder. It is turned by means of a band and wheels, moves in a contrary direction from the cylinder, by which it is put in motion, and so far outruns it as to sweep the cotton from the teeth as fast as it is carried through the breast-work.

The periphery of the whorls is spherical, and the band a broad strap of leather.

5th. One side of the hopper is formed by the breast-work, the two ends by the frame, and the other side is movable from and towards the breast-work, so as to make the hopper more or less capacious.

The cotton is put into the hopper, carried through the breast-work by the teeth, brushed off from the teeth by the clearer, and flies off from the clearer with the assistance of the air, by its own centrifugal force.

The machine is turned by water, horses, or in any other way, as is most convenient.

There are several modes of making the various parts of the machine, which, together with their particular shape and formation, are pointed out and explained in a description, with drawing, attested as the act directs.

ELI WHITNEY.

H.

CONVEYANCE OF A RIGHT TO USE A WHITNEY GIN.

STATE OF GEORGIA:

To all to whom these presents shall come, Phineas Miller, of the State aforesaid, and Eli Whitney, of the State of Connecticut, send greeting:

Whereas, The said Eli Whitney, by virtue of a patent under the Great Seal of the United States, dated the fourteenth day of March, in the year one thousand seven hundred and ninety-four, became entitled unto the full and exclusive right and liberty of making, constructing, using, and vending to others, to be used, a certain new and useful improvement in the mode of ginning cotton, for the term of fourteen years, beginning from the sixth of November, one thousand seven hundred and ninety-three; the principle of which improvement consists in the use of teeth, to draw off the cotton, which passes between bars or divisions of a breast-work, too narrow to give passage to the seeds, and of a brush to detach the cotton from the teeth.

And whereas, By deed of transfer, executed on the twenty-first day of June, in the year one thousand seven hundred and ninety-four, the said Eli Whitney conveyed to the said Phineas Miller, the one moiety or half part of all his right, title, claim, and interest to the said improvement in ginning cotton.

And whereas, By articles of copartnership, made and entered into by and between the said Eli Whitney and Phineas Miller, on the twenty-first day of June, in the year last before mentioned, it was mutually agreed by said parties, that all concerns which in any way respected the employment or disposed of the new invented machine or improvement in ginning cotton, should be conducted under the firm of Miller and Whitney.

Now know ye, That for and in consideration of the sum of two hundred dollars, to the said Miller and Whitney, at and before the sealing and delivery of these presents, well and truly paid by Levin Wailes, of the County of Elbert, and State of Georgia, the receipt of which is hereby acknowledged, the said Miller and Whitney, by these presents, have bargained, sold, assigned, transferred, and set over unto the said Levin Wailes, his executors, administrators, and assigns, all right, title, interest, privilege, and emolument whatever, which shall appertain to the construction, repairing, and entire use of one machine, which shall contain forty circles of saws, for the period of eight years, or until the patent right shall expire; to be constructed upon the principles of the new improvement before mentioned, invented and patented by the said Eli Whitney; and to be erected and used in no other place but in the county of Elbert, aforesaid;

To have and to hold, receive and enjoy, the full benefit, immunity, and privilege belonging to the use of the said cotton ginning machine, to him, the said Levin Wailes, his executors, administrators and assigns, for the period of eight years, or until the patent right shall expire.

In witness whereof, the said Miller and Whitney have hereunto set their hand and seal, and caused these presents to be delivered to the said Levin Wailes, for the purposes therein mentioned, on the 6th day of January, in the year 1808.

[L. S.] RUSSELL GOODRICH,
Agent for MILLER & WHITNEY.

Signed and sealed in presence of

C. TAIT,
NATH'L GREEN.

www.ingramcontent.com/pod-product-compliance
Lightning Source LLC
LaVergne TN
LVHW020105110826
845151LV00001B/72